Promises Not Kept

Kumarian Press Library of Management for Development

Selected Titles

Promises Not Kept

The Betrayal of Social Change in the Third World

Second Edition

John Isbister

Kumarian Press

Dedicated to my parents
Ruth and Claude Isbister

Promises Not Kept: The Betrayal of Social Change in the Third World, Second Edition.
Published 1993 in the United States of America by Kumarian Press, Inc.
630 Oakwood Avenue, Suite 119, West Hartford, Connecticut 06110.

Cover design by Laura Augustine
Copyedited by Dorothy Brandt
Typeset by Rosanne Pignone and Jenna Dixon
Proofread by Kevin R. Frazzini
Index by Barbara J. DeGennaro

Printed in the United States of America on recycled acid-free paper by
McNaughton & Gunn. Text printed with soy-based ink.

Library of Congress Cataloging-in-Publication Data
Isbister, John, 1942–
    Promises not kept : the betrayal of social change in the Third World,
second edition / John Isbister. — 2nd ed.
        p.   cm. — (Kumarian Press library of management for
development)
    Includes bibliographical references and index.
    ISBN 1-56549-027-4 (pbk : alk. paper)
    1. Social change. 2. Economic development. 3. Nationalism—
Developing countries. 4. Imperialism. I. Title. II. Series.
HN980.I83   1993
303.4'09172'34—dc20   93-28670

97   96   95   94   93   5   4   3   2   1
First printing, 1993

Grateful acknowledgement is made for permission to reprint previously published and copyrighted material from the following sources:

On page 4, from *The Autobiography of Kwame Nkrumah* by Kwame Nkrumah (London: Thomas Nelson and Sons, 1957). Used with permission of the publisher.

On page 7, from *The Poverty Curtain: Choices for the Third World* by Mahbub ul Haq (New York: Columbia University Press, 1976). Used with permission of the publisher.

On pages 7 and 84–85, from *Arrow of God* by Chinua Achebe (New York: Doubleday and Company, 1969), and on page 137 from *A Man of the People* by Chinua Achebe (New York: Doubleday and Company, 1967). Used with permission of HarperCollins Publishers and Octopus Publishing Group Library.

On pages 7–8, from *Child of the Dark* by Carolina María de Jesús, translated by David St. Clair (New York: E. P. Dutton and Company, 1962). Translation copyright 1962 by E. P. Dutton and Company, Inc., New York, and Souvenir Press, Ltd., London. Used with permission of the publisher, Dutton, an imprint of New American Library, a division of Penguin Books USA, Inc.

On pages 9–11, from *The State of the World's Children, 1982–83* edited by James P. Grant (New York: Oxford University Press, 1982). Used with permission of Oxford University Press.

On pages 11–12, from *Let Me Speak: Testimony of Domitila, a Woman of the Bolivian Mines* by Domitila Barrios de Chungara, edited by Moema Viezzar (New York: Monthly Review Press, 1978; copyright 1978 by Monthly Review Press). Used with permission of Monthly Review Foundation.

On page 16, from *World Development Report 1990* by the World Bank (New York: Oxford University Press, 1990; copyright 1990 by the International Bank for Reconstruction and Development/The World Bank). Used with permission of Oxford University Press, Inc.

On page 18, from *World Military and Social Expenditures 1987–88* by Ruth Leger Sivard (Washington, D.C.: World Priorities, 1988). Used with permission of the publisher.

On page 32, from "The Structure of Dependency" by Theotonio Dos Santos, *American Economic Review* 60 (May 1970): 231–36. Used with permission of the American Economic Association.

On pages 32 and 57, from *The African Bourgeoisie: Capitalist Development in Nigeria, Kenya and the Ivory Coast* edited by Paul M. Lubeck (Boulder, Colo.: Lynne Rienner Publishers, 1987). Used with permission of the Social Science Research Council.

On page 32, from *Development Theory in Transition* by Magnus Blomstrom and Björn Hettne (London: Zed Books, 1984). Used with permission of the publisher.

On page 67, from *Congo: Background of Conflict* by Alan P. Merriam (Evanston, Illinois: Northwestern University Press, 1961). Used with permission of the publisher.

Contents

Preface to the Second Edition

A GREAT DEAL HAS CHANGED in the world in the two years since the first edition of this book appeared. Most importantly, the Soviet Union has disappeared, and with it so has the cold war. For almost half a century, the cold war dominated international relations, including relations between the rich and the poor countries. The cold war set the terms of the competition between east and west in the Third World. It created the context for the end of imperialism, for the nationalist movements of independence and for the struggles of Third World countries for economic development. With its demise come new opportunities, but also new dangers and new uncertainties. It is too early to tell whether Third World people will fare better or worse in a world which has shed its principal conflict. The early signs are ambiguous.

This edition has been revised to take account of the end of the cold war, to bring the various sections on current events up to date. and to use the latest available data. Chapter 7, North-South Relations, has been extensively rewritten, and other changes have been made throughout the book.

The basic message of the book is unchanged. Most of the promises made to the people of the Third World—from their own leaders and from abroad—relating to peace, human dignity, human rights and the prospect for freedom from poverty, have not been kept. One can find pockets of progress, but for most of our fellow human beings the future is not bright.

Preface to the First Edition

OFF AND ON for over 20 years I have been one of a group of people designing and teaching an interdisciplinary "core course" at Merrill College in the University of California at Santa Cruz. The course is entitled "Social Change in the Third World," and it is taught to first-year undergraduate students in the college.

Our small group who founded the college in 1968 wanted to create a new kind of course and a new kind of curriculum focused on the problems of the world's majority, the people living in the Third World countries of Asia, the Middle East, Africa and Latin America. We wanted to reach all of our students, not just those few who were making a major commitment to Third World studies, but also the physics and the art majors, and all the others. We wanted to engage the students' intellect and challenge their minds, and we also wanted to speak to their hearts.

So we designed a course that was to transport students quickly into the center of many Third World people's basic concerns. We revised the readings each year, but we insisted that they all be immediate and compelling. We read, for example, the diary of a poor woman living on the edge of a garbage dump in Brazil, an autobiography of a rural guerrilla, an ethnographer's account of a Pygmy tribe, a revolutionary's manifesto, a novel about Gandhi's impact on an Indian village, a village study conducted just after the Chinese Revolution, a novel of a mother's burdens in Nigeria, an account of a peasant's life in the Nile valley and many similar pieces. Some of these readings are the bases for the case studies in Chapter 2.

The course has been a success; in fact, some of our former students have come back to tell us that it remains the most vivid memory of their undergraduate years. But there was always a problem with it. The students came to college, and the course, with little background in the subject, little understanding of the basic history and problems of Third World peoples. Those of us on the faculty were uncertain how to address this problem. We wanted to retain the immediacy and the power of the readings and not to revert to social science–type texts. But at the same time, we saw that our students were having trouble with the context of the readings, with seeing how they fitted into a broader picture.

For years I looked for a book that we could add to our reading list that would fill the gap. It needed to be brief and attractively presented so that readers could get into it with minimum discomfort. It should deal with the great issues of Third World history, along with the present problems and future prospects. It should present conflicting viewpoints and arguments. Most importantly, I was looking for a book that would help the students make sense of the incredibly challenging and confusing world of which they were becoming citizens.

Perhaps I did not search hard enough, but I failed to find just the right book. So I decided to write it myself, and this is the result. Drafts of the book have been used in the course for several years now, and I have revised the chapters extensively in response to the feedback from the students. I hope that it will now be of use to a wider group of readers. It is intended for undergraduate general education courses that emphasize international perspectives; for supplementary use in disciplinary courses such as economics, politics, sociology, anthropology and history that deal with Third World topics; and also for general readers who want to reflect a little more about their world.

In thinking and writing about the subject I have accumulated many debts. Thanks first to Philip W. Bell, the founding provost of Merrill, who invited me to join the college faculty and started this project. My colleagues Edmund Burke, a historian, and Walter Goldfrank, a sociologist, joined me in planning the first core courses in the late 1960's, and then years later helped me by reading drafts of the text. Others who gave generously of both time and insight were Dilip Basu, Paige Baty, Claude Isbister, Suzanne Jonas, Joseph Lubow, John Marcum, Sherri Paris, Sarah-Hope Parmeter, Daniel Scripture, Walter Smith, Patricia Sullivan and David Sweet. Hundreds of Merrill students have helped to sharpen my arguments by engaging me in seminar discussions. I am particularly grateful to my wife Roz Spafford, who helped me turn what were frequently inchoate musings into something approaching presentable prose. The remaining errors of fact and interpretation, I regret to admit, are mine alone.

CHAPTER ONE

Introduction

MOST PEOPLE ON the planet are poor. They live in the Third World countries of Asia, Africa and Latin America, where the typical standard of living is so far below that of the industrialized countries as to be almost unimaginable to those who have not experienced it. Many lack adequate nutrition, shelter and clothing. They are susceptible to disease and early mortality. They are insecure, since the margin separating them from catastrophe is thin.

One of the myths that is prevalent about Third World people is that they are unchanging, that their societies are static. One often hears the word *traditional* used to describe the network of relationships in which they seem trapped. But the opposite is true. The Third World is undergoing rapid and sometimes chaotic social change: populations are growing and becoming more urbanized. Public health measures are lowering death rates. Within recent memory, the nationalist independence movements created dozens of new sovereignties. Since then, governments have changed often, revolutions and counterrevolutions have been instigated, warfare has ensued. Modern technology has penetrated the Third World and transformed production. Education at all levels is spreading.

The lives of people in the Third World are changing. There is little evidence, however, that they are improving, at least for the great majority. Here and there one finds privileged groups, or even entire countries, where economic conditions have progressed and where human and political rights are respected. But these are the exceptions; most people in the Third World are desperately poor. That is to say, for most people the promises of social change in the Third World have not been kept. The dreams of independence, a more comfortable life, security and human rights have been betrayed. In this respect, the Third World shares the fate of the entire world in the twentieth century, where prospects that seemed all but certain have been distorted and lost.

Throughout the world, twentieth-century people have known moments of intoxicating optimism: in Europe and North America, the century opened in a spirit of almost infinite expectations, as the industrial revolution seemed to bring the promise of comfort and even opulence to ordinary people. In the second decade of the century, the Russian Revolution promised the overthrow of oppression and the creation of a new society in which the human personality would be free to flourish. As the midpoint of the century approached, the people of the Indian subcontinent were the first of the nonwhite world to emerge from colonialism and assume their equal place in the community of free nations, while the Chinese Revolution promised liberation for the most downtrodden of social groups, the peasants. In the 1960's, the young American[1] president John F. Kennedy brought to the western world a sense of limitlessness, while a new generation of young people committed themselves to the remaking of their societies. Science and technology developed exponentially, and with them the hope for prosperity for the entire world. What marked these moments, and others, was the sense of freedom, the collapse of the past's boundaries.

To recall these moments now is to recall, however, how exceptional they were. While they seemed to those in their midst to be universal, they were in fact closely circumscribed, in both time and place. The heady enthusiasm of the first decade of the century was exploded by the guns of August 1914, as Europeans settled into the incredibly destructive First World War. A decade after that conflagration ended, the world was plunged into the economic catastrophe of the Great Depression of 1929–39. The Russian revolutionaries degenerated into tyrants and mass murderers. The Second World War, beginning in 1939, was truly a worldwide war in contrast to the First, which had really been just a European war. The Second World War unleashed not only unbelievable military carnage, but this time genocide, as the Jews of Europe were destroyed in the Holocaust. With the end of the Second World War came an era of relative peace, but it was a peace with dangerous forebodings. Nuclear technology and the cold war brought with them the prospect of global winter. As science advanced, people became aware of the limited capacity of the globe to absorb ecological change. Improvements in world health conditions led to a population explosion that threatened to overrun the world. Regional conflicts produced warfare, terrorism and even further genocide. Political regimes that had seemed to promise liberation in fact delivered despotism. The twentieth century has turned out to be a century of potential dangers and actual disasters, as the power of scientific technology has raced wildly ahead of the wisdom of human beings in harnessing it.

The subject of social change in the Third World shares this grand theme of the twentieth century: the betrayal of the promise of progress.

For almost all of known history, prior to the twentieth century, most ordinary people were poor: that is to say, sick, insecure, poorly clothed and sheltered and vulnerable to an early death. At times the twentieth century, with its extraordinary technology, has seemed to promise an end to the human condition of poverty. And, in fact, some countries have reduced poverty substantially—in Europe and North America, as well as Australia, New Zealand and, more recently, Japan. While pockets of poverty remain in those societies, and shamefully so, still the great majority of the people there enjoy a comfortable life, reasonably secure and healthy, with enough income to cover not only the necessities but at least some of the pleasures and even luxuries of life. The victory over poverty in these prosperous countries has been one of the remarkable achievements of the twentieth century. It has been one of the promises of the twentieth century to extend this material progress to all of the world's people.

Yet, it has not happened, nor does it show signs of happening. The majority of the world's people, most of the people living in the Third World, remain poor. The gap between themselves and the rich is not closing. The number of poor people in the world is increasing, not decreasing. While most people in the Third World are healthier than were their forebears of a century ago, and are living longer lives, the quality of life has for the most part not improved, and has in some respects deteriorated. For hundreds of millions of people, rural poverty, which while hard was imbedded in a rich cultural network, has been replaced by the dislocation and alienation of urban poverty.

The plight of the Third World is not only economic; it is social and political as well. The independence movements and revolutions of the middle part of the century seemed to imply a new age of freedom and self-reliance for Third World peoples but often produced tyranny and terror. Democracy was usually intended but seldom attained. Millions were killed in regional warfare and internal repression: in Indonesia, in Cambodia, in Argentina, in Uganda, in China, in Vietnam and in many other countries.

This book shows how many of the promises of the twentieth century have been transformed and abandoned in the Third World.

The story is not a simple one of good and evil. There is no worldwide conspiracy to deny human rights, representative institutions and material security to Third World people. The Third World in the twentieth century is not enacting a morality play. While there are some villains, both in the Third World and in the rich countries, the plight of the world's poor has not been brought about fundamentally by a few imperialists, a few dictators or a few multinational companies. The history is more complex than that. Social scientists have struggled with the issue of causality in trying to explain conditions in the Third World, and they have come up with a variety of often contradictory theories, some of which are discussed in these pages.

Still it is the case that the promises that once seemed inherent in the twentieth century—the promises of technology, of material comfort, of democracy, of human rights, of fairness, of basic respect and decency

—have not been fulfilled in much of the Third World. Two major promises, in particular, have been violated.

The first was the promise made by the leaders of the nationalist, independence movements and the revolutions in the Third World. In the three decades following the end of the Second World War, the people of the Third World succeeded in dismantling the European empires to which they had been subjugated. A spirit of nationalism swept their countries. A new generation of leaders proclaimed that the poverty of the Third World was due to centuries of colonial exploitation; when the empires were cast off, the emerging autonomous nations would settle into the hard work of bringing prosperity, and not incidentally dignity, to their people. They promised that the people's labor would now be used for their own progress, not for the enrichment of foreigners.

Almost every one of the new nationalist leaders made this commitment. A few months after the independence of India in 1947, Prime Minister Jawaharlal Nehru told his people in a nationwide radio address:

> We talk of freedom, but today political freedom does not take us far unless there is economic freedom. Indeed, there is no such thing as freedom for a man who is starving or for a country which is poor. The poor whether they are nations or individuals have little place in this world. Therefore, we have to produce in order to have sufficient wealth, distributed by proper economic planning so that it may go to the millions, more especially to the common man. Then not only the millions prosper, but the whole country becomes rich and prosperous and strong.[2]

Kwame Nkrumah, the charismatic president of Ghana, wrote in his autobiography in 1957:

> Once freedom is gained, a greater task comes into view. All dependent territories are backward in education, in agriculture and in industry. The economic independence that should follow and maintain political independence demands every effort from the people, a total mobilization of brain and manpower resources. What other countries have taken three hundred years or more to achieve, a once dependent territory must try to accomplish in a generation if it is to survive.[3]

The goal of an end to poverty, which was an explicit part of the independence movements, has been met only intermittently. In most cases it has been waylaid as the new political elites have entrenched their positions of privilege and have neglected the welfare of the majority of the people.

The second promise was made by leaders of the rich countries. As they witnessed the nationalist movements of the Third World gain momentum and win independence for their people, some of them began to see the world through new lenses. At the end of the Second World War, when the victorious allies had sought to reconstruct a world that could sustain peace, they had been concerned about how to get the devastated countries of Europe back on their feet, but they had spared few thoughts for the majority of the world's people living in Asia, Africa and Latin America. By around 1960, with Europe now fully recovered, this blind spot was beginning to disappear. The international institutions that the rich countries had established, especially the World Bank, began to pay serious attention to the plight of the Third World. Foreign aid was increased. The motivations were not disinterested—the new attention paid to the Third World derived mostly from the cold war competition between the western and the Soviet blocs—but nevertheless there was a new spirit of cooperation between the rich countries and the poor, and promises were made that the rich would work together with the poor for economic development.

No one captured, and helped to create, this spirit better than President Kennedy. In his inaugural address on January 20, 1961, he spoke to the people of the Third World:

> To those new states whom we welcome to the ranks of the free, we pledge our word that one form of colonial control shall not have passed away merely to be replaced by a far more iron tyranny. We shall not always expect to find them supporting our view. But we shall always hope to find them strongly supporting their own freedom. . . .
>
> To those peoples in the huts and villages of half the globe struggling to break the bonds of mass misery, we pledge our best efforts to help them help themselves, for whatever period is required—not because the communists may be doing it, not because we seek their votes, but because it is right. If a free society cannot help the many who are poor, it cannot save the few who are rich.
>
> To our sister republics south of our border, we offer a special pledge—to convert our good words into good deeds—in a new alliance for progress—to assist free men and free governments in casting off the chains of poverty.

In the decades since his inaugural, the problems of the Third World to which President Kennedy alluded have not been resolved. The gap that divides the rich countries from the poor is still unconscionably large. About 15 percent of the world's population, living in the north, enjoy a standard of living that is extraordinarily more lavish than that of the world's majority.

Some people in the rich countries try to respond responsibly to this terrible reality. They support church missions and foreign aid; they assist human rights organizations and refugees. They endorse popular movements in Central America, in South Africa and elsewhere. They argue for constructive government policies, and they would like to proclaim that their countries are being helpful to the world's majority.

For the most part, however, the rich countries are not fulfilling the promises that were made. Far outbalancing the helpful policies are the harmful ones they engage in: the geopolitical struggles, the economic policies, the debts and the many other ways in which the countries of the north make the struggles of the world's poor people harder not easier. While many individuals act in good faith, their countries largely reject their responsibilities to the world's poor.

Notes

1. Throughout I use the term *American* to refer to the people of the United States—with apologies to Latin Americans who believe the term should not be appropriated by just one country in the western hemisphere, and who prefer instead the term *North American.* My Canadian origins prevent me, however, from using *North American* to refer to the United States alone. Since *United Statesian* is not in use, and in the absence of another suitable adjective, I am stuck with *American.*

2. Jawaharlal Nehru, *Independence and After* (London: The John Day Company, 1950), 160.

3. Kwame Nkrumah, *The Autobiography of Kwame Nkrumah* (London: Thomas Nelson and Sons, 1957), x.

CHAPTER TWO

A World of Poverty

A poverty curtain has descended right across the face
of our world, dividing it materially and philosophically
into two different worlds, two separate planets, two
unequal humanities—one embarrassingly rich and the
other desperately poor.
—Mahbub ul Haq, *The Poverty Curtain*

"And what about the people of your household?" he
asked Akuebue.

"They were quiet when I left them. There was no sick-
ness only hunger."
—Chinua Achebe, *Arrow of God*

Five Lives

The story of today's Third World is told best not in the statistics, nor in
the treatises of the social scientists and the historians, but in the details
of its people's lives. In the following paragraphs we will meet five real
people whose lives have been documented either by themselves or by
interviewers, five people chosen to convey something of the variety of
human experience in the Third World.

In the urban slum, or *favela*, of Caninde in São Paulo, Brazil, a mid-
dle-aged mother of three, Carolina María de Jesús,[1] rises early in the
morning from the battered mattress in her shack and sets out through
the streets of the city looking for trash. The paper she collects she can
sell for about one U.S. cent for every 4 pounds. The old clothes she
saves for her family or for trading; the scraps of food that are edible
she puts aside for her family. She keeps a diary on scraps of paper. The
following are excerpts from that diary:

> I didn't have one cent to buy bread. So I washed three bottles
> and traded them to Arnoldo. He kept the bottles and gave me bread.
> Then I went to sell my paper. I received 65 cruzeiros. I spent 20
> cruzeiros for meat. I got one kilo of ham and one kilo of sugar, and
> spent six cruzeiros on cheese. And the money was gone.
> I was ill all day. I thought I had a cold. At night my chest pained
> me. I started to cough. I decided not to go out at night to look for
> paper. . . .

I went to Senhor Manuel, carrying some cans to sell. Everything that I find in the garbage I sell. He gave me 13 cruzeiros. I kept thinking that I had to buy bread, soap and milk for Vera Eunice. The 13 cruzeiros wouldn't make it. I returned home, or rather to my shack, nervous and exhausted. I thought of the worrisome life that I led. Carrying paper, washing clothes for the children, staying in the street all day long. . . .

On a later day:

It finally stopped raining. The clouds glided towards the horizon. Only the cold attacked us. Many people in the favela don't have warm clothing. When one has shoes he won't have a coat. I choke up watching the children in the mud. It seems that some new people have arrived in the favela. They are ragged with undernourished faces. They improvised a shack. It hurts me to see so much pain, reserved for the working class. I stared at my new companion in misfortune. She looked at the favela with its mud and sickly children. It was the saddest look I'd ever seen. Perhaps she has no more illusions.

Carolina is a loner, suspicious of her neighbors, sometimes scornful of them. While some of her neighbors in the *favela* join together to form organizations, Carolina stays aloof. She works without stopping and jealously guards what she has for herself and her children. When a local journalist discovered her diaries and published them under the apt title *Child of the Dark,* she had a moment of respite from her hard life—but her fortune lasted only a couple of years, and soon she was back in the Caninde *favela* again.

Shahhat is a young Egyptian *fellah,* or peasant, living in the village of Berat on the banks of the Nile River, 450 miles south of Cairo. His father recently died, and he lives with his mother, Ommohamed, in a two-story house made of unbaked mud bricks with a roof of palm branches and palm leaves. Along with about half of the villagers, his family owns land, in his case 2 acres; the other villagers work for wages, or as sharecroppers, or in the local stores. The details of Shahhat's life have been recorded by Richard Critchfield, a British journalist who has written extensively about Third World peasants, and who lived with him for a year.

As Critchfield explains it, an extraordinary change has come over Berat village during Shahhat's short lifetime. For millennia, the annual flood of the Nile River determined the rhythms of agricultural life. The river flooded each September to November, then receded, leaving a fertile layer of silt. Crops of wheat, barley and lentils were then planted, to be harvested in April. There was just one crop a year, and summer was a time of rest.

But in the region of Berat, the Nile flooded for the last time in 1966;

thenceforth the flow of the great river was controlled by the towering Aswan Dam. The dam and its works provide continuous, planned irrigation of fields in place of the annual flood, and continuous cultivation is now possible, with up to three crops a year.

Shahhat and most of the *fellahin* were unprepared for this immense change in their lives. It was not simply that they now needed to work 12 months a year, without the summer rest; the whole technology of agriculture changed. Chemical fertilizers were required, to supplement the soil's fertility. Motorized pumps were installed. New high-yielding varieties of grain were introduced. A government inspector instructed the *fellahin* which crops to plant. Railway networks were expanded to gather the crops. Shahhat's people had been peasants for generations; overnight they were expected to become farmers, knowledgeable of the latest methods and the fluctuations of markets.

In a sense, all of this represented progress. It led to sharply increased crop yields per acre of land, needed by Egypt's rapidly growing population. More income was generated in the village.

Yet the process of technical change has not been smooth. Salinity levels in the soil have risen and threatened the fertility of the land. The government officials sometimes make crop choices that are unwise, in terms of the productivity of the crops or of the market for them. The railway boxcars are sometimes unavailable, and the crop has to be abandoned. In the old days the *fellahin* were dependent, as peasants always are, upon the vagaries of the weather. Now they are still dependent upon the weather and upon much more besides—chemical processes, international market forces and organizational structures that are far beyond their control, even comprehension.

So Shahhat has experienced wrenching changes in his culture, and in return for enduring these changes he has gained little, if anything. He is no more prosperous, although he works more continually than he once did. Distressed by the disruption of his life, he has left his village several times to seek his fortune in Cairo, but he has always returned. He has no savings, no protection from the uncertainties of his life. While some of his fellow villagers have taken advantage of the new technology to amass some wealth, Critchfield demonstrates that Shahhat has not. He is confused and passive. He and his mother both trust in the providence of Allah and do not plan actively for the future. Perhaps his children, who will grow up in the new world of scientific agriculture, will be able to cope with it more creatively, but Shahhat is at a loss.

Bernard Ledea Ouedraogo[2] is a Mossi tribesman from the Yatenga Province of Burkina Faso, formerly Upper Volta. Burkina Faso, one of the world's five poorest countries, is a landlocked, desert country of West Africa. It suffers from some of the poorest health conditions in the world, and consequently an average baby has a very low life expectancy of only about 45 years. Ouedraogo was born in a small village, herded goats as soon as he was able and tilled the land with his father. One day a group of French colonial administrators visited his village and, without warning, enrolled eighty-one children in a primary school. Eighty of the children stayed in school only a couple of years, not long enough to stay literate. By a mysterious combination of determination and chance, Ouedraogo persisted at school, becoming literate and much more. He moved on from level to level and eventually earned a doctorate in agronomy from the Sorbonne in Paris.

He dedicated his education and good fortune to his people, the Mossi. Returning to Yatenga, he founded the modern *Naam* movement for social and economic development. The *Naam*, a traditional form of social organization of the Mossi, is a small group formed in the village for collective work. Under Ouedraogo's leadership, *Naams* have been formed to dig wells, build dams, install mills and in other ways improve the desperately poor economy. There are 2,000 *Naam* associations now in 1,000 villages throughout Burkina Faso, Mali and Senegal. Ouedraogo works with international organizations such as the United Nations Children's Fund (UNICEF) to get resources for his people. Peter Adamson describes him sitting on his haunches, explaining foreign aid to the elders at a meeting: "If the load you have to carry is too heavy to lift onto your head, then it is right to be glad of the hand that helps you. But a Mossi must always use two hands of his own."

The load that the Mossi have to carry is frighteningly heavy. They are still living with the legacy of the colonial administration that uprooted their society by forcing the men to travel year after year to the coffee plantations of the Ivory Coast. After the colonialists were replaced, the same migration patterns persisted, as the most able-bodied young men left to seek wages, returning only sporadically. For long periods of time, wives have lived without their husbands, and children without their fathers. Meanwhile, as the population has grown, the land has had to be tilled more intensively, and consequently the pace of soil erosion has increased. Periodic droughts have hastened the erosion. Throughout the 1970's and 1980's, the devastation in the Sahel region of Africa was massive. As colonialism sapped the cultural strength and self-confidence of the Mossi, overcultivation and drought sapped the soil's fertility. The pictures of starving African tribespeople have become familiar sights to television viewers around the world.

Even when the rains come, there is seldom enough grain stored in the villages to last until the next harvest. The infant mortality rate in Burkina Faso is tragically high: 15 percent of the babies die before their first birthday. The village children who survive typically decline in health once they are weaned. Many have the swollen bellies characteristic of the undernourished, and they suffer fever, pains and rashes from parasitic infections and worms. They are underweight and have unhealed sores. They are frequently listless. The nutritional deficiencies they suffer from in early childhood leave permanent disabilities that typically cannot be reversed at older ages even if their diets improve.

Ouedraogo moves back and forth between this village world of Yatenga, the national capital of Ougadougou and the capitals of Europe—seeking help abroad while trying to inspire his people to work together at home. His method is to respect and build upon the existent social structure of the Mossi, not to uproot it. He addresses the elders in a responsive mode:

> Did the young respect the elders in the old days? What about today? Were the taboos observed in our young days? But what about today?. . . . If you are my friend is our relationship not holy? But what about today? Would a man who was a Mossi ever tell a lie even if tortured to death? But what about today?. . . . If in the old days you were having a siesta and a man came and knocked at your door would you ever say to him "go away, I am sleeping"? But what about today?

When the rains come and the harvest is ample, he makes a little progress.

Domitila Barrios de Chungara[3] is the wife of a miner in Siglo XX, a tin-mining camp in the central highlands of Bolivia. She, her husband and seven children live in a one-room house measuring about 12 by 20 feet. The house is owned by the mining company, and if her husband retires, dies or is laid off she will have to leave the house within a few days. The house has no running water or sanitation facilities; these are provided centrally in facilities that quickly become filthy. Her husband works a backbreaking and dangerous 8-hour shift in the mines. What he earns is not enough to live on, and Domitila sells *saltenas*, small meat and potato pies, on the street to make ends meet.

The mine workers are members of several militant labor unions that have periodically gone on strike for higher wages and improvements in living conditions. As Domitila describes it, the strikes have generally been met by strong resistance from the army, with mass arrests frequent. On at least two occasions, there were armed confrontations, resulting in the shooting of dozens of miners and their family members. Leaders of the union are sometimes jailed for long periods of time or deported to Argentina or Chile.

During one strike in Siglo XX, when the union leaders were arrested, the women in the camp went on a hunger strike to protest the arrests and secure the freedom of the men. From this hunger strike a permanent organization was born, "The Housewives Committee of Siglo XX," of which Domitila is a leader. Year after year, she says, she has worked with her comrades, both men and women, to secure a better life in the mining camp. In 1975, she was sent to the International Women's Year Tribunal organized by the United Nations and held in Mexico City, and it was there that she spoke and got her story out.

Her life has been unbelievably hard. Once during a strike, the army invaded Siglo XX, killing workers, women and children. Although pregnant, Domitila was arrested, then released, arrested again and tortured. She was accused of being an agent for revolutionary communist guerrillas. She denied the charges and was beaten brutally. In anger she struck back against her torturer, biting his hand; in turn she was beaten into submission, and six of her teeth were broken. She was in her eighth month of pregnancy.

It turned out that her torturer, with the bitten hand, was the son of the commanding colonel. The next day the colonel took over the proceedings. He beat her relentlessly and said, "All right, luckily you're expecting a baby. We'll take our revenge on your baby," and then he began to sharpen a knife in front of her. She shortly gave birth to a boy, alone, in a filthy prison cell, and passed out. When she awoke her baby was dead; she does not know whether he was born dead or died after birth. The colonel was summoned. Furious at being denied his revenge, he grabbed the dead baby and threw him at Domitila.

Eventually Domitila was given medical care, and she survived. She was exiled for a time to a farming area in the lowlands, but she eventually returned to Siglo XX with her husband. He begged her to give up her organizing activities so that the family could have some peace. She consented for a while but eventually went back to her Housewives' Committee. The strikes and armed confrontations continued.

Domitila is a socialist; she thinks progress can come to her coworkers only when a workers' party is in control of Bolivia. Although she has been recognized by feminists, she says she is not a feminist: "Our position is not like the feminists' position. We think our liberation consists primarily in our country being freed forever from the yoke of imperialism and we want a worker like us to be in power and that the laws, education, everything, be controlled by this person. Then, yes, we'll have better conditions for reaching a complete liberation, including our liberation as women."

Rigoberta Menchu is a young Quiche Indian woman from the village of Chimel in the mountains of northwestern Guatemala. She was extensively interviewed by the anthropologist Elisabeth Burgos-Debray, and the interviews were edited together into an autobiography entitled *I, Rigoberta Menchu.*

Rigoberta describes how the Indians from Chimel travel back and forth several times a year between their homes and the cotton and coffee plantations on the coast where they work as laborers. In the springtime in the village they plant maize (corn), which is their staple food. They then travel to the coast packed in lorries supplied by the plantations; the lorries are covered with canvas so that the workers can see nothing of the countryside they are traversing. At the plantations the families are frequently separated. Living in huge single-room dormitories that hold as many as 400 or 500 people, they do the backbreaking work of tending the coffee and cotton plants. In the fall they return to the mountains, in the same lorries, to harvest the maize; then they usually return to the plantations. They are paid very little in the plantations, and some portion of what they are paid is stolen from them by the labor contractors, who are Indians who have learned to speak Spanish. Rigoberta's villagers do not speak Spanish. In fact, there are twenty-two Indian groups in Guatemala speaking different languages, so they have difficulty communicating with each other at the plantations, and they are vulnerable to being exploited by people in power whom they do not understand.

Rigoberta's life in the mountains has been a life of hardship; the maize is always in short supply, the work is devastatingly hard and the money is scarce. But it is a life of spiritual richness. Rigoberta is connected to her family and to her fellow villagers by the rituals of birth, of maturity, of marriage and of death. She and her compatriots reject many of the trappings of urban civilization—for example, they refuse to use mechanical grinders for their maize. The maize is not just sustenance; it is the spirit of life.

Her life has been more than hard, though; it has been calamitous. Although Indians make up 60 percent of the Guatemalan population, they are oppressed by the minority Ladino (mixed Indian and Spanish) population. She worked for a while as a maid in Guatemala City, where she was fed only table scraps and saw most of her wages confiscated to buy the clothes her mistress insisted she wear. Even the discrimination in the city would perhaps be bearable if her mountain home were a secure refuge—but it is not.

Chimel has often been attacked by the army. Indians have been killed and their belongings destroyed. Rigoberta helped to build a network of traps to keep the army from Chimel, and she led the villagers into mountain camps when the army was coming. But she and her *compañeros* had no guns or modern weapons; they had only staves and machetes.

As these confrontations proceeded, year after year, Rigoberta saw her family destroyed. One brother died of starvation at a plantation. Another brother was captured by the army when he was 16 and, along with dozens of young Indian men, was subjected to excruciating torture. She was present when he died: the army summoned the Indians from miles around to a town square where the prisoners were displayed, bleeding, disfigured and sick. She and her mother recognized the brother but could do nothing to help him. After the army commander gave the Indians a speech about the necessity of eschewing communism, Nicaraguans and Cubans, the young men were doused with gasoline and burned to death.

Rigoberta's father, Vicente Menchu, who had become a leader in the Indian resistance movement, was also burned to death when he and a group occupied the Spanish embassy in Guatemala City. Her mother was captured by the army, then raped and tortured to death.

Rigoberta is a Christian; she accepts the sacraments of the Roman Catholic church, and believes in Christ's divinity and sacrifice. The church she identifies with is the church of the poor, not of the clerical hierarchy. It is a church that coexists for her with the teachings of her Indian ancestors; she sees no need to reject her traditions in order to accept Christianity.

She has become a leader in the struggle of the Guatemalan Indians. Her life, of course, is continuously in danger. She has lived in exile, but has refused to abandon her country and her people. In 1992, she was awarded the Nobel Peace Prize for standing out "as a vivid symbol of peace and reconciliation across ethnic, cultural and social dividing lines, in her own country, on the American continent and in the world" (*New York Times,* Oct. 17, 1992).

The Third World

Carolina María de Jesús, Shahhat, Bernard Ouedraogo, Domitila Barrios de Chungara and Rigoberta Menchu are five among the 3.5 billion inhabitants of the Third World, the great majority of humankind, living for the most part in the continents of Asia, Africa and Latin America.

The name *Third World,* referring to the largest portion of the globe's people, is a recent usage, dating from the 1950's in France. It is actually a pun, based on the terms used to describe the three social classes that had political authority in the ancien régime of prerevolutionary France. The first estate was the Lords Spiritual, or the clergy; the second estate was the Lords Temporal, or the nobility; and the third estate was the bourgeoisie or commercial class. Political power resided in the hands of the first and second estates. Consequently, in eighteenth-century France, the term *third estate,* or *tiers état,* became a revolutionary slogan. The French Revolution, beginning in 1789, was fought to a large extent by and for the third estate, to establish liberty, equality and fraternity, to transfer political power away from a small oligarchy to the third estate, and thence to the people as a whole.

Alfred Sauvy and other French intellectuals, viewing the global forces that were emerging from the wreckage of the Second World War, coined the term *tiers monde,* or *Third World,* corresponding to the third estate of Europe two centuries previously. It connoted the majority, the dispossessed, the excluded—and it also connoted revolution. In the writings of revolutionary theorists Jean-Paul Sartre and Frantz Fanon, the term *Third World* became the banner of the hungry and the oppressed.

The pun is striking. In its origins, the term *Third World* carried with it a sense of opposition, tension and struggle. The Third World was a world excluded, subject to the power of alien rulers. The term itself called for change, for an extension of liberty and equality to those who did not have it. It set up an opposition between the rulers and the ruled. It drew attention to colonialism and imperialism and to their modern-day counterparts in a world of oppression and unequal power.

Over a few decades, the meaning of *Third World* has softened and taken on the connotation of "nonalignment." A conference of twenty-nine nonaligned nations in Bandung, Indonesia, in 1955 used *Third World* to mean the newly emergent nations of Asia, Africa and Latin America that were coming out of an era of colonialism into the status of independence. They were not to be aligned with either the first—western, capitalist—world or the second—eastern, communist—world. In this usage, *Third World* lost much of its meaning of confrontation and opposition. It became a more neutral term, one suggesting a different way, a social path lying somewhere outside the blocs of the post-war superpowers.

Third World can not be a completely neutral term, though, since its origins are, after all, revolutionary. It implies an opposition between the poor and the rich, and it also connotes hope. The third estate was, after all, empowered by the French Revolution, and went on to become the dominant force in French society. In a similar way, the term *Third World* carries with it the promise of change, the promise that those who are currently oppressed will eventually overcome their oppression and enjoy vastly better lives.

If there is a striking analogy between the world's poor of today and the third estate of prerevolutionary France, the analogy breaks down when it is extended to today's rich societies. The most privileged societies of the globe today are both secular and, for the most part, democratic. Accordingly, the Third World today is not confronted by a First (clerical) or a Second (aristocratic) World. In one of the great ironies of modern history, it is actually confronted by the successors to the victorious third estate. The French Revolution and the European industrial revolution, dating also from the eighteenth century, released forces of creativity, technology and expansion that completely transformed the European world and its offshoots. The medieval class system was blown away, and in its place the descendants of the third estate created a new class system: capitalism. It is this capitalist, industrial world, created by the third estate, that now confronts the Third World.

The Third World refers, then, to the poor of the world, those who are disenfranchised in an international system dominated by the indus-trialized countries: the north, the developed, the rich. The hopes that are inherent in the term *Third World* have for the most part not been fulfilled. As the twentieth century draws to a close, most of the people of Asia, the Middle East, Africa and Latin America have not drawn near to the people of the rich countries, in terms of either standard of living or political power.

The Extent of World Poverty

The Third World today covers most of the globe and embraces count-less cultures, religions, traditions and ways of life. Its achievements are monumental. Yet, there is a single characteristic that pervades the Third World, distinguishing it from the industrialized countries: widespread poverty. Not everyone in the Third World is poor: there are middle-class strata as well as pockets of luxury.[4] There are productive factories and sparkling computer centers. But the *favela* dwellers, the peasants, the underemployed and many of the industrial workers of the Third World subsist at standards of living that are low to the point of incomprehension for people living in the industrialized world.

Poverty can be thought of as an absolute condition, or as relative. Absolute poverty is a standard of living so pressing that it brings with it malnutrition and disease that seriously threaten life. The World Bank[5] has established two poverty lines. According to the first, anyone whose annual consumption fell below the equivalent of U.S.$370 a year in 1985 was considered poor. The second, more stringent poverty line was $275. Table 2.1 shows the World Bank's estimates of poverty in the Third World, according to these two standards.

Table 2.1   Poverty in the Third World

Region	Extremely Poor (below $275) Number (millions)	Percent of Population	Poor (below $370) Number (millions)	Percent of Population
Sub-Saharan Africa	120	30	180	47
East Asia	120	9	280	20
China	80	8	210	20
South Asia	300	29	520	51
India	250	33	420	55
Eastern Europe	3	4	6	8
Middle East and North Africa	40	21	60	31
Latin America and the Caribbean	50	12	70	19
All Third World	633	18	1,116	33

Source: World Bank, *World Development Report 1990* (New York: Oxford University Press, 1990), 29.

According to the higher (but still quite low) criterion, about one-third of the Third World's population lives in poverty. In Africa and in India, the proportion is closer to one-half. Almost half (47 percent) of the world's poor live in South Asia and another quarter in East Asia. One-sixth are in Africa, with about 5 percent each in the Middle East and in Latin America.

Most of the very poorest people are in rural areas—and in spite of the fact that they grow crops, they endure monotonous, unbalanced diets, inadequate caloric intake and malnutrition. They have lower health standards than urban people and less access to clean water and sanitation facilities. They suffer the diseases of the undernourished, and at each age their probability of dying is higher than among the rest of the population.

Poverty is not restricted to this most desperate stratum of human beings, however. A great deal of the world's poverty should be thought of in relative terms—that is to say, poverty is a relationship. One thinks of oneself as poor only if others are rich, and one's poverty is measured against that richness. The Pygmies of the Congo's rain forest, at least those who survive, live at a subsistence level and suffer from diseases that have been eliminated elsewhere, but they would not think of themselves as poor. They live in a self-contained society, hunting and gathering as their forebears did for centuries, in harmony with the forest and its spirits. But Carolina María de Jesús, who actually has access to more goods and services than the Pygmies do, is desperately poor. She lives in an urban society the benefits of which she is excluded from, and that urban society, São Paulo, Brazil, is itself bound to the international economic system but is for the most part excluded from its benefits.

Poverty in this relative sense is found in every country in the world. In the United States, millions of people live in a poverty that is frightening, scandalous and unfamiliar to almost all who surround them. Most receive income much greater than that of the typical person of Asia or Africa, but this does not mean that their poverty is any less real. The homeless living on the sidewalks in central cities or in temporary shelters, single parents in slum housing, the unemployed who have exhausted their resources, former farmers who ran deeply into debt before losing their patrimonies to foreclosure—these are some of the faces of poverty in one of the world's richest countries, and they demonstrate that income is not the universal criterion of poverty. What poverty really means is the inability to make choices. A family of four in the United States with $6,000 annual income is completely constrained in its choices and deeply impoverished, but in the world's low-income countries, where the average income per person was the equivalent of $320 in 1988, a family of four with $6,000 is privileged.

Although most poverty is relative, it remains the case that the people of the Third World are overwhelmingly poor—and the people of the industrialized world are, for the most part, not poor.

The *Third World* and *poverty* are both therefore terms of relationship. The Third World is the world dominated, the world excluded from power. The poor are the people on the bottom, the people denied the benefits of the society in which they live.

While income is not the heart of poverty, nevertheless it is revealing to reflect upon the staggering differences in income that exist in today's world. For example, in Britain in 1990 the average income per person was the equivalent of U.S.$16,100, while in the United States the figure was $21,790. In the poorest thirty-seven countries, with more than half of the world's population, the average income was $350, less than one-sixtieth of the typical U.S. income.

Figures like these are subject to many caveats; incomes are not directly comparable between different countries and cultures. In deriving per capita income figures like these, each country's national currency is converted to U.S. dollars according to the rates of exchange in international currency markets. These exchange rates are influenced by the cost of living in the different countries but normally do not reflect them exactly. Put differently, it is cheaper to live in some countries of the Third World than it is in the rich countries. A dollar, converted to rupees at the official exchange rate, will buy more rice in an outdoor market in Delhi, India, than it will in a neighborhood supermarket in Kankakee, Illinois. So the figures on comparative incomes may overstate somewhat the difference in average standards of living in different parts of the world. But not too much. There is a self-corrective mechanism in international currency markets, such that differences in costs of living tend to lead to compensating changes in exchange rates.

So while the income figures show that a typical person in the industrialized world is forty to sixty times better off, in terms of access to goods and services, than a typical person in the Third World, a better comparison of living standards might show a smaller gap. The economist Angus Maddison, who has spent a lifetime interpreting income data from different countries, estimates that the average standard of living in the rich countries is ten to twenty times greater than the average standard of living in Asia. Whatever the exact difference, it is huge.

Another way to see the inequity is to show the income accruing to each fifth of the world's population. In 1985, the poorest fifth received 1.6 percent of the world's income, and the richest fifth 74.2 percent:[6]

	Million Dollars	*Percent of Total*
Poorest fifth	230,396	1.6
Second fifth	316,254	2.2
Third fifth	497,128	3.5
Fourth fifth	2,595,577	18.5
Richest fifth	10,448,829	74.2
World Total	14,088,184	100.0

This is the overwhelming truth about the world we inhabit: the gap between the richness of the developed countries and the poverty of the Third World. The gap is so huge it is almost beyond our understanding. How can one imagine living for a whole year on the money one now spends in just three weeks? It would not be a matter of "belt tightening"; it would be a totally different and devastating life. In the United States, Canada or Britain, an ordinary family with one working parent typically lives in a house or an apartment with several bedrooms, a living room, a kitchen, at least one bathroom, running water and a heating system. There is a car, quite a lot of clothes, a radio and a television set, some books and enough extra money to eat out from time to time, go to the movies and take a vacation. The family members are generally in good health, and if they are not they have access to modern medical technology, the expense of which is usually insured. The poor in those countries lack this standard of living, but they are a minority. Many people have far more. Described this way it does not seem like a great deal. But for Carolina, Domitila, Shahhat, Rigoberta and the Mossi people it is a universe apart. It is not quite as incomprehensible to them as their situation is to us, since western popular culture— movies, magazines and television—has swept into most corners of the globe and created some impressions of middle-class life in the industrialized world. But it is so distinct from their situations as to be absolutely unattainable.

Among the poor of the world, a family typically shares one room —and in rural areas the room may provide a haven for farm animals as well. The family members do not have enough good food to eat. That is to say, they usually have enough to prevent starvation, but they suffer from dietary deficiencies of both calories and particular nutrients. There is not always enough to prevent starvation. They have few clothes, no private cars, no vacations and no money to spend on things beyond necessities. They experience perpetual insecurity, because they hardly ever have savings sufficient to tide the family through bad times. Above all, they are threatened by bad health: high infant mortality, less than full physical development of children, susceptibility to disease, uncertain life spans.

The pattern is far from uniform—there is every conceivable variation in the Third World as there is in the developed world. But no variation can conceal the basic fact of overwhelming poverty throughout much of Asia, the Middle East, Africa and Latin America: the almost unclothed people living in the streets of Calcutta and Bombay, the gaunt herders of central Africa whose fertile plains are slowly but inexorably eroding into desert, the peasants of northeastern Brazil driven from their homes by drought and landowners, the bark-clothed peasants of Mozambique fleeing from war zones.

The poverty of the Third World is not "traditional"; it is not an ancient way of life. The traditional cultures of the Third World are rich and various, and they are closer to the surface of everyday life than traditions usually are in the industrialized world where they have been suppressed. The old folkways of the Third World have little to do with poverty. The great religions of the Third World—Hinduism, Buddhism, Islam—are not apologies for poverty; they are integral worldviews that bind together the generations. The philosophies and customs that developed over the millennia led to a sense of belonging for people, not to a sense of exclusion. Scattered throughout the world are some significant groups of people living in completely traditional ways very much as their ancestors did—for example, in the rain forests of Africa, New Guinea and some parts of the Philippines. In learning about them we can discern something about the common heritage of the human race.

But the way these traditional people live is not typical of the widespread poverty that mars the face of the globe. The endless urban slums are not traditional; they are recent. The population explosion that magnifies the number of poor and threatens the very survival of the globe is a phenomenon of the last century, not of time immemorial. The poor laborers in the fields of tobacco, cocoa, bananas, cotton, rubber and sugar are not obeying traditional cultural imperatives; they are producing export crops for sale in the prosperous markets of the United States and Europe.

Traditional cultures generally had low standards of living by comparison to life today in the rich countries. Life in traditional societies may even have been for the most part, in the words of philosopher Thomas Hobbes, "nasty, brutish, and short." But people living in traditional societies were not poor in comparison to the people around them with whom they had contact. In contrast, today's poor in the Third World are centrally connected to a changing world—their cities, their farms, their mines, their slums all grow and change rapidly, all responding to the dynamic demands of a growing world economy. The process that transformed the world, that gave us jet airplanes, computer technology and California suburbs, transformed the Third World also, creating the new phenomena of massive urban and rural poverty.

The world is not, of course, neatly divided into two categories of countries, rich and poor. There is a spectrum, and within the spectrum there are intermediate cases. Estimates of average income per person nevertheless convey a picture of a very skewed distribution of the world's resources. At one end lie thirty-seven countries with more than half the world's population, approximately 3.1 of the world's 5.3 billion people, with an average income per person in 1990 of U.S.$350. This group is dominated by the two largest countries: China (about 1.1 billion people, average income of $370) and India (over 800 million people, average income of $350). It includes the poorest countries of Africa

(Burkina Faso, Chad, Ethiopia, Madagascar, Malawi, Mozambique, Sierra Leone, Somalia, Sudan, Tanzania, Uganda and Zaire) and the poorest countries of Asia (Bangladesh, Bhutan, Laos and Nepal), with per capita incomes of under $250. Above the poorest half of the world's population lies another quarter, the more fortunate countries of the Third World, with per capita incomes ranging from $630 to as high as $6,000. Prominent in this intermediate group are the Philippines ($730), Colombia ($1,200), Thailand ($1,420), Argentina ($2,370), Mexico ($2,490), Brazil ($2,680) and South Korea ($5,400). Some Middle Eastern oil-exporting countries have such high incomes as to be appropriately included in a separate category.

The industrial market economies have average incomes ranging from Ireland ($9,550) through Britain ($16,100), Canada ($20,470), the United States ($21,790), Japan ($25,430) and the highest, Switzerland ($32,680). Because of differences in accounting methods, comparable figures cannot be calculated for Russia and most of the former Soviet bloc countries, but estimates have been made for Hungary ($2,780) and Czechoslovakia ($3,140).

These average income figures are startling, but of course they conceal much more than they reveal. An average is just that, an average. The fact that India has an average income of $350 does not mean that all Indians enjoy an income of $350. The majority of Indians have less than $350 a year, and a substantial number of Indians very much less. Correspondingly, there are middle class and even wealthy Indians who command a great deal more of the country's economic resources.

The distribution of incomes between different groups has been surveyed in a number of Third World countries, but it must be conceded that the data are generally quite suspect. The surveys have been taken in different years, with different concepts and statistical methods used, and differing degrees of accuracy. Consequently international comparisons are perilous.

Nevertheless, the latest data available appear to confirm what has sometimes been called the Kuznets Curve: that is, as countries' average incomes rise from the very poorest levels, income distribution first becomes more unequal, then more equal. The surveys that have been collected by the World Bank from forty-one countries show the following pattern in the proportion of a country's income that is received by the poorest 20 percent of the population. In countries with average incomes of under $1,000, the poorest one-fifth of the population earns 7.2 percent of the national income. In countries that have between $1,000 and $5,000 average income, the poorest one-fifth receive 5.3 percent of the income, and in countries above $5,000, they receive 6.2 percent. The point is this: wide discrepancies between rich and poor are not just a phenomenon of advanced capitalist countries like the United States; they are found, and to an even greater extent, in the poor countries of the world. Poverty is never shared equally. Moreover, it appears that when economic growth takes place in poor countries, it does not usually improve the status of the poorest; rather it raises the rewards of upper-income groups, and leaves the poor further behind.

Poverty is not shared equally by the sexes. Women receive less health care than men, and consequently their death rates are higher. They receive less schooling, and consequently their illiteracy rates are higher. They perform work that is on the whole more tedious and of lower status than men's work. They receive less compensation. They usually work longer hours, because in addition to their work outside the home they are almost always solely responsible for all of the work inside the home. To take an example, a female lace maker in the Narsapour region of India works 8 hours a day in her home (her so-called "leisure" time), for an average daily salary of 0.56 rupees. This is only one-third of the wage estimated as necessary for subsistence, 1.6 rupees. It contrasts with the minimum wage in agriculture of 3.4 rupees for men. Her husband typically earns three times as much as she does. To see how little her earnings amount to, they can be compared with the cost of a sari, of between 30 and 70 rupees. That is to say, she works between 2 and 4 months to earn the money to buy a dress. Her total work day lasts 15 hours, not 8, because of the 7 additional hours she spends on housework.[7]

Some countries of the Third World have done better than others in attacking and alleviating the most serious poverty. The United Nations Development Program (UNDP) has ranked countries according to a "human development index," based on health conditions, literacy and access to goods and services.[8] It has found that a high ranking on this index is not necessarily associated with high average incomes. Some countries with strong performance in human development are Malaysia, Sri Lanka, Thailand, Tunisia, Botswana, Zimbabwe, Uruguay and Costa Rica. Correspondingly, however, other countries, including some with quite strong economies, have done much less for their people, among them Brazil, Nigeria and Pakistan.

Communist and socialist countries appear to have faced more obstacles to overall economic growth than have their capitalist counterparts, but on the whole they have done a better job of eliminating the worst features of poverty. We do not have actual data on income distribution that would allow us to compare the share of income going to the poorest 20 percent of the population in China or Cuba, for example, with India or Mexico, but we do have indirect evidence. Life expectancy at birth is higher in China (70 years) and Cuba (76 years) than in most neighboring countries (India's is 59, Mexico's 70), indicating a higher level of public health and medical care. Infant mortality is lower, and the proportion of children in school is higher. This is not to say that poverty has been abolished in communist countries—China is still a desperately poor country—but rather that they have had some success in addressing the worst manifestations of poverty.

Still, none of the differences between and within countries should obscure what is common. Despite the huge cultural and economic differences between a *favela* dweller in São Paulo, a nomad herdsman in the Sahel desert and a peasant growing rice in India, one feature they all share is insecurity. When times are good—when the rains fall, when the market price is high—the family can be fed and a few improvements made to the dwelling. But bad luck may strike at any time and wipe out the chances for survival itself. When times are bad in Africa, in India, in China, thousands starve to death. The consciousness of imminent disaster, a fear of what the future will bring, has been found by social scientists to be pervasive among the world's poor, and for good reason.

The poor are undernourished—that is to say, with less caloric intake than they need—and malnourished—with less protein and vitamin intake than they need. As a consequence, many of their children do not achieve full physical and mental development. They are susceptible to disease and premature mortality at much higher rates than are the people of the richer countries. There have actually been dramatic improvements in health and longevity in the Third World over the last 50 years as the benefits of public health and sanitation measures have been extended throughout the world. Yet, large differences between the developed and the developing countries still exist, in part because of the uneven distribution of medical services, but in larger measure because of persistent dietary deficiencies. Some summary figures show the picture.

In sub-Saharan Africa, the infant mortality rate (babies who die before their first birthday) fell between 1965 and 1990 from 157 per thousand to 107. In India the fall was also significant, from 150 to 92; and in China more dramatic still, from 90 to 29. But in the industrial world as a whole, the infant mortality rate was 24 per thousand in 1965, falling to 8 per thousand, or less than 1 percent, in 1990. Another statistical indication of health is life expectancy at birth. In 1990 in the United States and Britain, the average life expectancy was 76 years; in Laos it was 49, in sub-Saharan Africa 51, in India 59, in China 70.

Caloric intake is substantially different in different areas of the world. In the industrialized countries in 1989, the average person was supplied with 3,409 calories per day. Since the average daily caloric requirement is about 2,500, this represents a surplus of over one third, and indicates both food wastage and also considerable obesity. In fact, some of the most serious health problems in the industrialized countries are the result of overeating and improper eating, combined with lack of exercise. In Africa the caloric intake was 2,112, a figure that had barely improved in 24 years, and which represented just 85 percent of requirements. In India, average caloric intake was 2,229, or about 89 percent of requirements, and in China 2,639, or 105 percent. Again, these are averages, and one must remember that a large portion of the population falls below them. The UNDP estimates that 800 million people in the Third World are hungry.

Disease is far more prevalent in the Third World than in the rich countries. Surveys in Latin America and Africa have shown that fully 90 percent of the people studied were infested with some form of parasite. In Peru, for example, 113 out of 122 men sampled in the armed forces had a parasitic infection. Ninety percent of people in an area of East Africa were found to have beef tapeworms. The prevalence of tropical diseases like hookworm, bilharzia, filariasis and schistosomiasis is almost universal in some areas.[9] These diseases are typically associated with pain and loss of strength, and sometimes with early mortality.

Another indicator of differences in health is population per physician. For 1984 the figures collected by the World Bank are: industrial countries, 450; sub-Saharan Africa, 23,850; India, 2,520; China, 1,000. The figure for Africa speaks for itself. The figures for China and India are actually improvements over the last two decades, and show considerable recent investment in health care by both those giants. Still, they lag considerably behind the rich countries. The UNDP estimates that only 61 percent of the people in the Third World have access to primary health care services.[10]

Illiteracy is widespread in the Third World. While schooling has expanded rapidly in the last several decades, still one-quarter of the men and fully one-half of the women are unable to read or write. Between 900 million and a billion people are illiterate, three-quarters of them in the five largest Asian countries.[11]

These are the bare facts of living standards in the Third World—low average incomes, substantial numbers living in the direst and most life-threatening poverty and an incredible gap between the poor and the economically developed countries. It would not be correct to call this picture a crisis, because it persists from year to year. It is a tragedy.

The causes of the world's poverty are many; they are explored in the chapters that follow. At the very root, however, the problem is simple to understand: it is a question of power. Poor people are poor because they are powerless. The essence of poverty is the relationship between the poor and the rich, and the essence of that relationship is power. Sometimes the power is transparent. When Domitila is attacked in prison, and when Rigoberta's family is murdered, we have no difficulty in recognizing the abuse of power that is concentrated in a few hands. Yet, even when the power is concealed or employed indirectly, it is no less present. Shahhat lacks the power to change his life as the forces of capitalism change the world around him. Carolina lacks any power to bring about changes within Brazilian society. They are victims of their powerlessness, just as surely as are those who are physically attacked. If Bernard Ouedraogo is successful, it will be because he has helped his people to reclaim some of the power that has been stolen from them.

Poverty Is Growing

As the years pass, the problems of poverty in the Third World are getting worse, not better. There are more poor people, and in many cases their prospects are getting dimmer.

The picture is not uniform. There are important exceptions, particularly in large parts of Asia where the living standards of the poorest appear to be improving. The two most notable exceptions are China on the one hand and a group of four export-oriented countries on the other: Taiwan, South Korea, Singapore and Hong Kong.

China has experienced extraordinarily rapid economic growth since the mid 1960's, and because the rate of population growth has fallen, most of this economic growth has been translated into improvements in the standard of living of the people. China has a relatively equal distribution of income, and it appears that many of the poorest have shared in the improvements. In spite of the progress, however, China is still a very poor country. Moreover, there is serious concern for the future. Much of the improvement in living standards in China has probably been associated with a liberalization of the economy, a freeing of enterprise from the heavy controlling hand of the Communist party and an opening of the country to foreign ideas, technology and investment. As the decade of the 1990's proceeds, there is fear that a more authoritarian political structure may damage the prospects of further economic growth.

The four smaller Asian countries that have done well economically —sometimes dubbed the "newly industrializing countries," or NICs— are also countries with relatively equitable distributions of income among their people. They have built their success upon a strategy of producing manufactured goods, many of them embodying high technology, and exporting them to the United States and other rich countries. Their rapidly developing manufacturing sectors have pulled up the living standards of people throughout their countries, and as a consequence comparatively few of their citizens now live in desperate circumstances.

China, Taiwan, South Korea, Singapore, Hong Kong and a few other countries are exceptions, though, to the general experience of the Third World since the 1960's. From what one can tell, there are more poor people than ever before.

Again there is the caution that the data are most imperfect, and there is consequently a great deal we do not know about the material conditions of people's lives. Some things we do know, however. The populations of most Third World countries are growing so fast that they double within 20 to 40 years. Between 1965 and 1990, about 1.5 billion people were added in the Third World. Unless there has been an extraordinary reduction in the proportion of poor people—and there is no indication that such a reduction has occurred—the number of poor people must have increased greatly. But there are more reliable indicators than this that the problem of world poverty is worsening.

In many Third World countries there has been only very slow economic growth in recent years. Without the growth of production there can be no growth in overall incomes and hence very little chance that the poor can benefit. Leaving aside the exceptional case of China, and also the large country of India (where there has been moderate economic growth since 1965), the World Bank reports that on average in the Third World there was slow economic growth between 1965 and 1980. During the 1980's, the growth in output per person fell in half. In many Third World countries in the 1980's, production and income grew slower than the population, leaving the typical person with less.

The area with the worst problems was sub-Saharan Africa, where output per person fell by about 1 percent each year during the 1980's. Most Africans are substantially worse off today than their parents were at the time of national independence, around 1960. In Latin America and the Caribbean, average incomes fell by about 0.5 percent each year during the 1980's. In Asia the picture was better, with the strong performance of China, Taiwan, South Korea, Hong Kong and Singapore and the reasonably rapid economic growth of India and Pakistan.

Even in the countries where there was overall economic growth, however, there was probably not much reduction in poverty. The Kuznets Curve, after all, shows that most economic growth accrues to the benefit of the high-income people in a country, leaving the poor farther and farther behind. This appears to be exactly what has happened. In a survey of what little statistical information exists on trends in world poverty, the World Bank[12] reports a worsening picture. It estimates that in the decade of the 1970's, the number of people with seriously inadequate diets increased from 650 million to 730 million, and that since 1980 the increase has been faster. In twenty-one of the thirty-five lowest-income countries, the average supply of calories per person fell between 1965 and 1985. While few Third World countries have comparative data on poverty in different years, it is estimated that the number of poor people was increasing in the mid-1980's in Brazil,

Chile, Ghana, Jamaica, Peru and the Philippines. Improvements in health that had seemed to be well established in the 1970's were reversed in the 1980's.

Mexico is a terrible example of the collapse of the standard of living in the 1980's. For the 15 years prior to 1980, real income per person grew at more than 3 percent a year; in the 1980's, it fell at a rate of almost 2 percent a year. Wage earners were hardest hit, with the purchasing power of wages falling almost in half. The *New York Times*[13] reports that milk consumption plummeted in the 1980's while families used soda pop as a substitute (because it is cheaper than milk and does not require refrigeration), with disastrous consequences for nutrition. A Mexican government study has reported that only 20 percent of rural children under 4 years of age are of normal weight and height. Mexico was particularly hard hit by the collapse of oil prices and the debt crisis of the 1980's, but many other countries, in Latin America and elsewhere in the Third World, shared its distress.

Many people thought, and still think, that the inequities in the world, while major, are diminishing and will continue to diminish as modern technology spreads throughout the world. Perhaps they will, but not if current trends continue. The progress of South Korea is exceptional, not common. Much more typical of the desperate situation of most Third World people are the experiences of Bangladesh, El Salvador and Zaire, where incomes are stagnant or falling and health is precarious. The prospect of an end, or even a reduction, in world poverty is not in sight.

The Betrayal of Responsibility

The people in the rich countries bear some responsibility for the poverty of the Third World. There are two dimensions to this responsibility. There is a difficult set of questions related to causality: how did the economic progress of the rich countries help or hurt the prospects of the poor, how did the empires of the rich impact the lives of the poor, how are the policies of the rich today affecting the standards of living of the Third World? These complex questions are addressed in the next and subsequent chapters.

There is a much simpler dimension to the responsibility of the rich, however, and it is a dimension completely independent of one's answers to the questions posed in the previous paragraph. Living in a world of obscene inequality, the privileged have the moral responsibility to do what they can to improve the lot of the less privileged. This responsibility arises from the common humanity of all people; we are a single species. It is a responsibility recognized by most ethical and religious systems. It is a responsibility willingly embraced by many people and institutions in the rich countries. Taken as a whole, however, and with those honorable exceptions, the rich countries have rejected and betrayed their responsibility to the Third World.

For many reasons, most people in the privileged countries remain impassively unaffected by the tragedy that surrounds them. They have few impressions of the Third World, and those they have evoke fear rather than empathy or identity. Amazingly, they often view the Third World as powerful and hazardous to them. The television brings threats into their living rooms. In recent years the strongest image of the Third World on the screens has been that of the terrorist, the madman, the destroyer of civilized values and innocent bystanders. One sees the insurrectionary colonel, strutting and posturing. One is shown the fundamentalist Islamic fanatic, exhorting the population to suicide missions. One hears of the communist revolutionary guerrillas who defeated the United States in Vietnam and threatened it in Central America. One is told about the one-party state, intolerant of dissent, with its political prisoners and torturers. One hears the rhetoric of confrontation, grievance and blame. One fears the explosive on the airplane.

These aggressive images are not entirely fantasies. The Third World has its terrorists, its revolutionaries and its combative rhetoric. All are quite real. But what is so destructive about these images is that they blot out the much more universal issue in the world—the issue of poverty, with its attendant hunger, disease and premature death. As a consequence, many, perhaps most, people in the rich countries simply do not know or care about the desperate situation of their sisters and brothers.

They avoid grappling with the inequity on the planet because a full understanding of it would seriously threaten the senses they have of themselves. Most people in North America and western Europe do not think of themselves as rich beyond imagination, and certainly not as oppressors. Quite the contrary, they see themselves as comfortable, perhaps, but still struggling to make ends meet, financially insecure, hoping to do a bit better in the future. Most see themselves in the position of the little guy, fighting for some advantage against forces that are more powerful.

In their own societies and daily lives, that kind of an attitude makes sense—but from a global perspective it is nonsense. Almost everyone in the United States, for example, lives a life of incredible luxury, compared to almost everyone in the Third World. There are exceptions —the very poor in the north, the very rich in the south—but not many. If Americans and Europeans were to think of themselves in this sort of global context, as constituting the world's privileged, they might then face painful questions relating to their responsibilities. They might have to ask themselves: Where does their responsibility lie? Does their material comfort require others to be poor? Are they making world poverty worse, or are they part of the solution? Should they try to be part of the solution? What solutions might there be? Will an attack on world poverty require sacrifices from them? What kind of sacrifices?

These are questions most people in the developed world would prefer to avoid. It is stretching an analogy only a bit to recall the "good Germans" of the 1930's and 1940's who knew nothing about the Holocaust being perpetrated by the regime to which they gave loyalty, because they did not want to know. If people today know nothing about the hunger and disease of India, Zaire, Cambodia and Haiti, it is in large measure because they would prefer not to, because the knowledge would powerfully threaten their rather complacent senses of themselves. If they turn their backs on the majority of the world's population, and address only their own problems, it is because it would be shocking and dangerous to do otherwise.

The privileged are turning their backs. The people of the developed countries, having achieved a comfortable standard of living, are largely oblivious to the fate of the world's majority, and to their own responsibility for that fate.

One should not overstate the argument. People in the rich countries will not solve the problems of the Third World by themselves. The destiny of the Third World is in the hands of its members, to make of it what they will. It is they who will determine their future, not North Americans or Europeans. To think otherwise is to perpetuate a peculiarly modern form of cultural imperialism, to conceive of the rich as puppet masters, manipulating the strings that make the rest of the world dance. They do not. But the prosperous countries and their institutions—their governments, their armed forces, their corporations, their voluntary associations—powerfully affect the constraints within which the Third World will determine its future.

On the whole, the rich have been the enemies of the poor in the past and continue to be today. Not unambiguous enemies: rich countries and the people in them have had generous intentions, they have provided useful aid and they have initiated hopeful partnerships. There have been moments in American history when the nation seemed to reach out in a gesture of common humanity—moments such as the early 1960's, when President Kennedy touched the spirit of a generation with the Peace Corps and the Alliance for Progress in Latin America. In retrospect these initiatives seem flawed, even tainted with dubious motivations, but at the time, the intentions of many Americans were genuine. In the late 1970's, President Jimmy Carter drew his country's attention to the millions oppressed by human rights violations.

But the promises inherent in these gestures have not been kept. Even while they were being made, they were contradicted by the exigencies of anticommunist geopolitics and by economic policies at home that neglected the welfare of the world's poor. And in the 1980's even the generous gestures were forgotten, as the developed countries for the most part abandoned the Third World to stagnate in a swamp of debts.

There is plenty of responsibility to share for the poverty of the world's poor, and Third World leaders can claim a lot of it. Military regimes have attacked their own people, protected the exploiters of their own poor and squandered billions on armaments. Nationalist leaders have wasted resources on flashy, self-serving projects. Voices of the needy have been squelched. The principal drama of the Third World rests in the Third World, among its own peoples, in the struggle to address their pressing problems and avoid the traps that threaten to submerge them.

But the rich countries could help. Having played a central role in the creation of the world's inequities, they could allow themselves to be used constructively. They will not help by being missionaries, by trying to bring the ideology of free markets, or even democratic institutions, to the Third World. The people of the Third World will do that well or badly by themselves, and there is not very much that the rich can do about it. Their responsibility is to reform their own institutions, to lend a hand that is open and not clenched, to be helpful and not harmful to the world's poor. This is a task that is achievable; and it is also respectful of the Third World, not manipulative.

Suggestions for Further Reading

Bisilliat, Jeanne, and Michèle Fieloux. *Women of the Third World, Work and Daily Life.* Translated by Enne Amann and Peter Amann. Cranbury, N.J.: Associated University Presses, 1987.

Berger, Peter. *Pyramids of Sacrifice.* New York: Basic Books, 1975.

Galbraith, John Kenneth. *The Nature of Mass Poverty.* Cambridge: Harvard University Press, 1979.

Grant, James P. *The State of the World's Children, 1982–83.* New York: Oxford University Press, 1982.

Harrington, Michael. *The Vast Majority: A Journey to the World's Poor.* New York: Simon and Schuster, 1977.

Hartmann, Betsy, and James K. Boyce. *A Quiet Violence: View from a Bangladesh Village.* San Francisco: Institute for Food and Development Policy, 1988.

Lewis, Oscar. *The Children of Sanchez: Autobiography of a Mexican Family.* New York: Random House, 1961.

Notes

1. Her diaries have been collected in Carolina María de Jesús, *Child of the Dark*, translated by David St. Clair (New York: E. P. Dutton and Company, 1962). The entries, particularly the later ones, should be read with some care and skepticism, since they were apparently extensively edited by a local reporter for publication. The earlier entries, including those quoted here (from *Child of the Dark*, pp. 17, 18, 47), convey a sense of immediacy and authenticity, however.

2. Ouedraogo's story is told in Peter Adamson, "The Rains," in James P. Grant, *The State of the World's Children, 1982–83* (New York: Oxford University Press, 1982), 45–128; the excerpt provided appears on pp. 117–18 of that book. Further details appear in Frances Moore Lappe, Rachel Schurman, and Kevin Danaher, *Betraying the National Interest* (New York: Grove Press, 1987).

3. Her book, edited from tapes by the Brazilian journalist Moema Viezzer, is Domitila Barrios de Chungara, *Let Me Speak: Testimony of Domitila, a Woman of the Bolivian Mines* (New York: Monthly Review Press, 1978). The quote at the end of Domitila's story is from *Let Me Speak*, p. 41.

4. In fact, *The Economist* of August 6, 1988 estimates that the Indian middle class is almost equal in number to the total populations of Britain and France.

5. World Bank, *World Development Report* (New York: Oxford University Press, 1992). Except where noted, the data in this chapter come from this source.

6. These estimates are from Ruth Leger Sivard, *World Military and Social Expenditures 1987–88*, 12th ed. (Washington, D.C.: World Priorities, 1987), 21.

7. The Narsapour example is described in Jeanne Bisilliat and Michèle Fieloux, *Women of the Third World: Work and Daily Life*, translated by Enne Amann and Peter Amann (Cranbury, N.J.: Associated University Presses, 1987).

8. United Nations Development Program, *Human Development Report 1990* (New York: Oxford University Press, 1990).

9. See Andrew Kamarck, *The Tropics and Economic Development: A Provocative Inquiry into the Poverty of Nations* (Baltimore: The Johns Hopkins University Press, 1973), chapter 7.

10. See note 8.

11. See note 8.

12. World Bank, *World Development Report* (New York: Oxford University Press, 1988), 4.

13. "Mexico Feels Squeeze of Years of Austerity," *New York Times*, July 25, 1989.

CHAPTER THREE

Explanations of Underdevelopment

By dependence we mean a situation in which the
economy of certain countries is conditioned by the
development and expansion of another economy to
which the former is subjected.
                              —Theotonio Dos Santos

The tragedy of the dependency perspective lies in
its assumption that the world-system must be transformed before meaningful internal changes can
occur. If one begins with such a pessimistic assumption, the task becomes so daunting that politically
innovative strategies are dismissed in favor of symbolic
jousting at transnational windmills.
                              —Paul M. Lubeck

There could be no greater slur inflicted on our capabilities: we are nincompoops, we are unable to ensure
a local supply of exploiters, the process of exploitation
has to be initiated elsewhere. . . . This itself is neocolonialism of a sort.
                    —*Economic and Political Weekly,*
           India (quoted by Blomstrom and Hettne)

HOW ARE WE to understand the tragedy described in Chapter
2, the massive and swelling poverty that plagues the Third World, side
by side with the unconstrained growth of the industrial countries? Why
has social change in the Third World come so often to a dead end?
Social scientists have advanced some answers to these questions, but
their answers are not simple—and in some respects they are contradictory. They can be grouped into three different schools, sometimes
called modernization, dependency and Marxism. This chapter ex-
plores these three schools, searching for clues to explain why the
promise of a better life has been empty for so many people.

Dependency theory asserts that economic growth in the advanced
capitalist countries created Third World poverty in its wake. The argument is not simply that the Third World is poor in comparison to the

industrialized world; rather it is that the development of the industrial system in Europe and North America fundamentally changed and impoverished most of the societies of Asia, Africa and Latin America. Theorists of this persuasion argue, therefore, that poverty in the Third World cannot be understood without reference to the entire international order.

This argument has been developed in detail by social scientists in the Third World as well as in the developed countries. Different writers in the dependency school have different approaches, and some of the debates are quite significant,[1] but the school is united in seeing the structure of modern Third World societies and the problems that beset them as responses to the capitalist growth of Europe and North America.

The dependency school stands in opposition to the argument that the origins of poverty are to be found internally, within the social structure of the Third World countries themselves. There are two quite separate variants of this internal argument: modernization theory and classical Marxism.

Modernization theory is the dominant philosophy of social scientists in the developed countries; it is the worldview that most of them adopt in their attempt to understand the origins of poverty and underdevelopment, and it includes very few hints that the rich are responsible for the plight of the poor. Modernization theorists focus upon deficiencies in the poor countries—the absence of democratic institutions, of capital, of technology, of initiative—and then speculate upon ways of repairing those deficiencies.

The other internal school is Marxist. The Marxists focus their attention upon the class structure in poor countries and the mechanisms that exist for exploitation, that is to say, for the appropriation of surplus production by the dominant class. If the dominant class is capitalist, then the exploitation and the appropriation of surplus may be accompanied by economic growth. If, however, the class structure of the country is feudal or some other noncapitalist type, then the surplus is likely to be wasted and the country mired in stagnation.

This nomenclature is all a bit confusing, because in fact many of the dependency theorists consider themselves to be Marxist, and in truth one would have to acknowledge that some of the most creative Marxist thinking in recent decades has come from within the dependency school. The sociologist Aiden Foster-Carter resolves the problem by referring to the dependency school as "neo-Marxists."

Modernization Theory

Modernization theory is the mainstream school of scholarship about poverty and economic, social and political development in the countries of the Third World. A great deal of useful, even brilliant, work has been carried out within this framework. The adherents of this approach do not actually see themselves as a cohesive school; they are more inclined to emphasize the disputes between themselves and to dismiss the dependency school and the Marxists as irrelevant, or excessively doctrinal or political. There are a number of common elements to the modernizationists' analyses, however, and they can be usefully drawn together.

An important idea in this school is the concept of the "traditional" society. The modernizationists think of today's Third World societies as being largely traditional; they also think of western Europe as having been traditional in the long period before the era of modern economic growth and cultural change.

According to this view, the essence of a traditional society is that it is stagnant and unchanging. Its values are spiritual values, not the values of individual self-betterment. Its rhythms of life are circular, not linear and progressive; one returns always to the same place. The traditional world is emotionally comfortable, a world in which each person has a place that is secure, a place in the family among the pantheon of ancestors. The traditional person identifies with his or her ancestors, and emulates them. Daily work is carried out just as it always has been, not to secure a profit but to perform one's duty, to maintain one's place in the society. Nothing is innovative, and there is no attempt to "better" one's lot. There is no real distinction between daily life and spiritual life—it is all one. Almost any religious system can serve as the basis for a traditional society. Referring to French Canada of the nineteenth century, the historian A. R. M. Lower wrote:

> The life of the peasant is a series of ritual occasions, planting and harvesting, being born, coming of age, begetting, dying. . . . All are one family, interrelated if not in this generation, in the last or the next. All give unquestioned obedience to the great mother goddess, the earth-mother, who can easily be made to wear a Christian dress. . . . His religion is among the simplest and oldest of all creeds, Catholic almost by accident.[2]

The picture of traditional life painted by the modernizationists is not a negative one. It is an integrated life, in which the spirit, the family, the larger group and the work tasks all combine to form a seamless whole, a life in which there is no estrangement, no alienation. From an economic point of view, however, it is a poor, subsistence life, a life that has no hope of accumulation, income and wealth. There is no sense of progress. When time is circular, when the most honorable task is to imitate one's ancestors, there can be no breakthroughs, no fundamental changes, no development.

Historians in the modernization school argue that about 500 years ago, most people everywhere in the world were poor, living in traditional social arrangements. There is scholarly disagreement as to whether average standards of living in western Europe were the same as, or higher than, average standards of living in Asia at the same time.[3] Whatever the answer, there is no question but that most people, everywhere in the world, lived at a very low standard, compared to the norms in today's wealthier countries.

There were sparks of scientific discovery in widely scattered parts of the world—in the Middle East, in China, in Africa and in South America. For a variety of historical reasons, however, scientific inquiry led to consistent technological innovation principally in western Europe. Science and the entrepreneurial spirit combined to produce little pockets of productivity: higher yields per acre of crops, for example, more seaworthy ships, advancements in weaponry, more efficient techniques for artisans. These pockets of productivity grew, widened and deepened, gradually transforming the societies of Europe, and later of Europe's offshoots in North America and elsewhere. The engine of this economic growth was capitalism.

To understand the modernizationists' view, one must know what they mean by capitalism. The term *capital* is actually used in diverse ways by different groups of people. In common parlance, capital is often synonymous with *money*, as when a broker says, "I have some capital to invest in the stock market." But this is not how the word is used by modern social scientists.

For mainstream economists (often called "neoclassical" economists), capital is a means of production, that is to say, something that is used in the production of other things. To distinguish it from other means of production, such as land and labor, the term *capital* is reserved for those means of production that have themselves previously been produced. Included in the capital stock are factories, machines and tools that have been produced at some prior time and that are currently used for making goods and services. Capital can include highways, trucks, harbors, airplanes and even inventories. Natural resources, like deposits of iron ore, are not considered to be capital because they have not been produced.

For mainstream economists, capitalism is the social system under which this capital is privately owned. At the center of this view of capitalism is the market, the institution in which sellers and buyers come together on a voluntary basis to exchange goods and services in return for money, at a price. The privately owned capital is used to produce the goods and services that in turn are sold in markets, at prices that are determined through the interplay of supply and demand.

Included in this view of capitalism is an important role for the government. Earlier generations in Europe and North America, influenced by the laissez-faire ideas of Adam Smith and his followers, may have argued that government was a threat to capitalism, but in the modern world it is clear that governments are central partners in most capitalist systems. In the archcapitalist United States, for example, about one-third of the goods and services produced are paid for by governments at all levels. Governments in capitalist countries build the infrastructure—the roads, airports, waterways, educational systems— that are needed to maintain the system; they endow the military; they regulate the private sector through a series of rules, subsidies, price controls and oversight agencies; and they patch up the loose ends of the system with welfare programs. In the Great Depression of the 1930's, there was a danger that the capitalist societies of North America and Europe would collapse because of their own rigidity; they were saved first by the Second World War and after the war by government economic policies and by the development of public welfare programs. Governments in the capitalist countries learned to spend, tax, regulate, legislate and produce in ways that supported the capitalist system and that compensated for its unevennesses and shortcomings. Capitalism today in no way implies the absence of government activity; what it implies is that governments support the system of the private owner-ship of the nation's productive capacity.

Economic historians in the modernization school argue that innova-tion and technological growth became self-sustaining in Europe because they were embedded in the capitalist system. Individual capi-talist entrepreneurs were in competition one with another. Each knew that if he did not struggle aggressively, his competitors would overtake him, capture his market and ruin him. So each capitalist had to be at the forefront, working as hard as he could to develop better products and to expand his output. Each tried to enlarge his profits, by keeping costs low while increasing revenues. The capitalists used those profits in part for their own consumption, but to a much greater extent for investment in more capital equipment in order to produce more goods.

Growth became the only constant; the fundamental tenet of Euro-pean societies during the industrial revolution was that each genera-tion would outperform its parents in terms of production, wealth and, eventually, standard of living. According to the people who view the growth process through these lenses, each feature of the capitalist sys-tem conspired to promote growth. Workers who were mobile and unencumbered by artificial restrictions sought out employment where they could be most productive and earn the best wages. Financial insti-tutions searching for the highest rate of return on their funds invested in the most promising new activities. Firms that were in competition with each other cut costs and thereby promoted efficiency. Particularly important was the role of entrepreneurship: the lure of profits drew adventurous people into uncertain, risky projects, thereby creating wealth and eventually raising standards of living.

Initially the workers were excluded from the benefits of the industrialization process, working long hours for minimal wages in health-threatening environments. Conditions in the early European factories and the towns that surrounded them were frightening. Contemporary economists in the nineteenth-century British "classical" school actually predicted that the poor would remain poor while growing in number, surviving at little more than a subsistence level. Modern scholars in the modernization school stress, however, the fact that these predictions proved false. As history unfolded in twentieth-century Europe and North America, wealth was increasingly distributed among the population, not equally, of course—not even equitably—but widely as workers were drawn into the productive sphere to enjoy the benefits of the quickly advancing technology. Pockets of poverty remained, but they were scattered, and to a large extent they occurred not among the working people but among those who for one reason or another were not able to work. The undeniable poverty that still exists within capitalist societies should not, say the modernizationists, obscure the fact that the capitalist system has created much higher overall levels of production, income and wealth for most people than have ever been known before.

Many social scientists emphasize the political modernization that accompanied the economic modernization. Feudal autocratic monarchies were challenged by representatives of the people and eventually displaced—in some cases gradually over centuries as in Britain, in other cases through revolution as in France. Individual freedoms were ensured—of association, of speech, of religion. Representative forms of government were established, and the principle that governments are to be democratic, that they are responsible to the people, was won. Political parties were formed and free elections regularized. The rule of law was made supreme and the independence of the judiciary guaranteed. The exact form of government differed in each country of the modernized world, but the common element became democracy. Political modernization and economic modernization went hand in hand, inseparably, both exalting the position of ordinary people to a status not known in previous regimes that were both poorer and more despotic.

According to at least some of the modernizationists, capitalism was as responsible for political freedom as it was for the wealth of the developed countries. Capitalism, they argue, is a system of decentralized power, with many different people controlling the wealth of the country. In a socialist or autocratic system, economic power is centralized, and as a consequence only one political voice is tolerated. But the dispersion of wealth among many capitalists, and eventually among the workers as well, allows for a variety of political power bases. Politicians and competing political parties can turn to any number of sources for financial support, and so diversity and debate are kept alive. The two phenomena, capitalist economic development on the one hand and political freedom and diversity on the other, are so closely connected to one another as to be inseparable. Capitalism needs political freedom, say the modernizationists, in order to preserve the openness required for the flourishing of entrepreneurial innovation, and a liberal political order needs the diversity of power centers that only capitalism can provide.

The modernizationists argue that the poverty and backwardness of the Third World can be understood simply as the failure of those societies to kindle the same sparks of creativity. The Third World was left behind at the starting block; it neglected to transform itself. Without a commitment to science, to free enquiry, to technology, to the spirit of enterprise and competition, to democracy and the rule of law, it stagnated as it had for centuries, while the societies of the northern hemisphere grew both economically and morally.

According to this way of looking at the world, then, there are two poles: "modern" and "traditional." The modern world is what economists sometimes call "rational." It is inhabited by people who are constantly trying to do the best they can for themselves, to "optimize," to "maximize." The modern world is based on research and development and on the goal of efficiency. It is driven by the search for profit and wealth as people take risks to do things in new and better ways in the hope of improving their lot. It is based on competition and on the laws of the marketplace that reward success. The modern world is forward-looking, committed to growth and to improvement.

The modernizationists argue that the task before the underdeveloped countries is to transform themselves from tradition to modernity, that is to say, to follow in the footsteps of the now developed countries. The title of the influential book by Nobel Prize–winning economist Theodore W. Schultz is revealing: *Transforming Traditional Agriculture.* Schultz paints a picture of traditional agriculture as being in a state of equilibrium in which little changes, and little can change because the ancient folkways are perfectly adapted to providing as much security as possible in an inherently dangerous world. To transform this traditional world, he maintains, new opportunities must be provided to peasants, new incentives, new rewards, new technologies, new knowledge. With these new stimuli, the traditional, unchanging subsistence peasant can be converted into a productive, surplus-creating, modern farmer.

Fortunately, argues the modernization school, there is every chance that the world's poor countries can succeed in this transformation from the traditional to the modern, because they have an advantage the Europeans lacked. They can follow in the footsteps of those who have come before. In fact, since the path to modernization is now charted, the poor countries can avoid some of the false starts and dead ends that delayed the progress of the pioneers. Furthermore, the rich countries can lend a helping hand to the poor, offering them technology, markets, capital and encouragement.

People who see the world through the lenses of modernization theory often think in terms of stages, through which all countries must pass on their journey to a high standard of living. Some of these sets of stages are fairly simple and obvious—for example, agriculture to industry to services, or rural to urban to suburban. One of the more powerful, although more complex, stage theories of modernization was presented in Walt Rostow's book, written in 1960, *The Stages of Economic Growth*. Rostow used the metaphor of the take-off of an airplane, identifying five stages corresponding to the take off:

1. *The traditional society.* The airplane is at rest. The society is in a pre-scientific culture, with the great majority of the population living in a traditional way at a bare subsistence level.

2. *The preconditions for take off.* In this stage the equilibrium of the traditional society is challenged—perhaps by science, or by foreign commerce, or by invasions. The traditional organization of the society is upset, and the opportunity is presented for fundamental social change. But at this stage it is only an opportunity; the forces of tradition may yet reassert themselves and prevent further modernization.

3. *The take-off.* "We come now," wrote Rostow, "to the great watershed in the life of modern societies. . . . The take-off is the interval when the old blocks and resistances to steady growth are finally overcome."[4] The take-off occurs when political power accrues to a group that regards economic growth as its main business; when the country's savings rate, as a proportion of national income, doubles; and when modern technology is applied to a few leading sectors, both agricultural and industrial.

4. *The drive to maturity.* This stage corresponds to the increase in altitude of the airplane. It lasts perhaps two generations, and it is the period in which economic growth spreads from the initial few leading sectors to a wide range of activities. The country becomes an active participant in international markets, exporting new goods and producing for domestic use goods that were formerly imported. As the country reaches maturity, it is able to use modern technology to produce, if not every good in the world, then at least every good it chooses to.

5. *The age of high mass consumption.* This stage corresponds to the high altitude, high speed, long-distance flight of the airplane. In this fifth stage, the fruits of growth are finally transferred to the mass of the population. No longer are the people called upon to sacrifice for future growth. Now their broad standards of living rise, steadily and

predictably—and the country has sufficient wealth to turn its attention to social welfare, that is to say, to extending the fruits of growth in at least a minimal way to those people who were not able to participate directly in the growth.

In the period since Rostow's book appeared, there has been an enormous amount of creative scholarship in the modernization school—by sociologists, psychologists, historians, economists and political scientists. What remains constant throughout this literature is the idea of two poles, tradition and modernity, with the transition between them seen as the task of our age.

For some writers the issue is primarily one of individual psychology. In the traditional society, they believe, people are rooted in ancient ways of relating to each other and conceiving of problems. They venerate their ancestors and think of time in a circular, repetitive way. The transformation to modernity requires a breaking of these ways of thought, the creation, for example, of a "need for achievement" in psychologist David McClelland's phrase, a celebration of individual success as opposed to group affiliation.

Other writers view the tradition-modernity dichotomy from a more social, political point of view. A traditional society may be one in which the ruling group uses its power to confiscate the wealth of the country and uses that wealth in support of itself, for example, in ostentatious consumption. What is needed is a class of entrepreneurs who will mobilize the country's wealth for productive investment, to create the technology and the capital needed for growth. Everett Hagen has suggested that the entrepreneurs may come from a minority group whose progress towards positions of power in the traditional society has been blocked.

Still others, like Theodore Schultz, see the problem as one of economic incentives. It is rational for people in traditional societies to avoid change and progress, since change entails risk, and risk in turn leads to the possibility of disaster, a possibility all too imminent for people living at a subsistence standard. So, the transformation out of tradition requires that there be low-risk opportunities and incentives provided to people, so that they can opt for higher productivity and incomes.

Opinions differ as to whether the impetus for modernization comes from within the society or from without. From within, it may come from a class of "new people," not formerly part of the power structure. Or it may come from a formerly elite group in the traditional society that has been displaced. Proponents of external sources of change point to the technology that is available from the more advanced countries, to colonialism and imperialism that disrupted traditional societies, to international corporations that seem to jump national boundaries without noticing them, to foreign media, to travel and to trade. Any of these groups or forces can upset the equilibrium of traditional societies and set them on the road to change and modernization.

So, modernization theorists have a variety of approaches for understanding social change, but the central idea remains that the task before the world is the transforming of traditional societies. It follows from this that the main unit of analysis in modernization theory is the nation. Rostow wrote, "The whole transition we are examining took place historically within a system of nation states and of national sovereignty,"[5] and this perspective has not changed. In the modernization school, each country can be looked at separately. The first airplane to take off from tradition was Britain's, in the late eighteenth century, and it was followed over the next century by France, Germany and other European countries, and by the United States, Canada and Australia. The twentieth century saw the take-off of Russia and Japan, and several smaller Asian countries.

The rest of the world's fleet is still at the airport, to continue with Rostow's analogy. The airplanes of the Third World are grounded. Their countries are still stagnant, still traditional, as they have been for centuries.

The challenge to modernize is one that faces each country separately, as it tries to get its airplane into the sky. What Britain, the United States and Japan did, now Zimbabwe, Colombia and China can. Their methods may differ somewhat, depending upon national factors, but in each case they must find a way to break away from the fetters of tradition, to free the innovative spirit, and to direct their human, physical and financial resources towards productivity and growth. Their task is to follow the example of those airplanes that have already taken off, perhaps not in every detail, but in broad measure.

As the countries of the Third World struggle to get their planes into the air, the now rich countries can show them the way, and they can also offer tangible assistance. In fact, according to this way of looking at the issue, the industrial world can be of the greatest help to the Third World by itself growing quickly and creating and diffusing the technology needed by the Third World. The corporations of the rich countries can utilize that technology in their branch plants in the poor countries. The financial institutions of the rich countries can provide funds for the economic development of the poor. And the affluent consumers of Europe and North America can provide expanding markets for the exports of Asia, the Middle East, Africa and Latin America.

It is a benign picture. With just a bit of imaginative license one can see long ropes attached to the tails of the rich countries' speeding supersonic jets, ropes with hooks trailing at their ends. The hooks are dangling free, but they are out there, waiting to be snared by any of the grounded planes that choose to move into position. Once snared, the planes of the Third World will be pulled into flight.

What could go wrong? Two things. First, the planes on the ground may choose not to snag the offered hooks. In Rostow's terms, they may not develop the preconditions for take-off—the education, the legal systems, the political systems and the mobility needed for growth. They may allow their populations to grow so fast that they lack the stamina for take-off. Second, the planes that are already flying may slow down and lose the power to lift the grounded planes into flight. This is a very important proposition of modernization theory: the already developed countries must continue to grow if they are to assist the poor. Without growth in the developed world, there will be no new capital for investment in the Third World and no expanding markets to stimulate Third World exports and economic development.

So, there is no conflict between the rich and the poor as seen through the prisms of the modernizationists. There is no ethic, for example, that the existence of great wealth in a sea of poverty might be unstable, or immoral. There is no fear that the world's benefits may be limited and that therefore the accumulation of wealth in some hands destroys the promise of advancement for others. Quite the opposite. As modernization theorists describe it, part of the world has raised itself from poverty to affluence; now the rest of the world has every opportunity to do so and can even turn to the developed countries for assistance.

The modernization view of the world is not without its moral imperatives for the rich. If the poor countries are to modernize, it is important that the rich countries not turn their backs on them. Foreign aid, foreign investment, planning assistance, expanding markets, technology transfer, even the Peace Corps—all these are productive connections between the rich and the poor that the rich should nurture. In other words, proponents of modernization stress government policy. In fact, many of them are most comfortable in the role of advisers—to their own governments, to Third World governments and to international agencies.

This aspect of the modernization school can hardly be overstressed. As scholars, its practitioners are interested in identifying root causes of growth, historical patterns and sound predictors. But the analysis usually comes around, in the end, to government policy—and for many in the school it is not at all unfair to say that the scholarship serves primarily as backdrop and justification for policy recommendations. An important part of their agenda is to participate in the councils of state, to influence development policy. It was no accident that Rostow himself became one of the closest advisers to President Lyndon B. Johnson.

Many of the insights that the modernizationists have had into government policy have been very fruitful. Economists in the school have advanced important propositions about trade and tariff policy, about planning techniques, about agricultural pricing policies, about the use of monetary, fiscal and financial policy in poor countries, about appropriate technology, employment policy and much more. Demographers and public health professionals have helped establish family planning programs. Consultants expert in such fields as political systems, legal systems, medicine, labor unions, cooperatives, and media have lent their advice, some of which has been useful and well taken.

It is a bit dangerous to put a political label on the modernizationists, but for most of them "liberal" fits pretty well. They are not conservative; that is, they do not regard the current state of the world as optimal. Neither are they radical (or Marxist, or socialist); that is, they see no need for fundamental political and social change in the rich countries, nor for revolution in any country. They are reformers. They are on the side of the world's poor, and they think that more can be done to help them. What is needed, they think, is better policies, more technology, more aid, freer markets, sounder planning. Most importantly, they see no necessary conflict between the world's rich and poor, between the capitalist markets of the industrial world and the traditional societies of the Third World. The ideal is partnership and the serving of mutual interests.

Dependency Theory

Dependency theorists critique the modernization school. They believe that the growth of today's rich countries impoverished the Third World and that the forces of international capitalism still block its progress.

Dependency theory is an outgrowth of Marxism; in fact, many of the central ideas of dependency find their original expression in a 1957 book by Paul Baran, the leading American Marxist economist of his generation, entitled *The Political Economy of Growth.* It was at the hands of Latin American social scientists, however, that *dependencia,* as they called it, became a major intellectual movement. The most important precursor of the dependency school was Raúl Prebisch, an Argentincan economist who was secretary of the United Nation's Economic Commission for Latin America (ECLA) in the 1950's, and of its Conference on Trade and Development (UNCTAD) in the 1960's. The ideas of dependency were later developed by Celso Furtado, Theotonio Dos Santos, Osvaldo Sunkel, F. H. Cardoso and other Latin American social scientists. Outside Latin America, the most important writers have been Samir Amin of Senegal, André Gunder Frank of Germany and Immanuel Wallerstein of the United States. To a major extent, therefore, dependency theory has been a product of the Third World itself; this is one important respect in which it differs from the modernization perspective, which has been developed almost exclusively in the major universities of the developed countries.

For the modernization theorists, underdevelopment is a state, or a condition; it is synonymous for most writers with tradition. For those in the dependency school, underdevelopment is a process. Underdevelopment is not just the failure to develop; it is an active process of impoverishment. Aiden Foster-Carter put it nicely when he described André Gunder Frank's use of *underdevelop* as a transitive verb, as in "I underdevelop you."

It is simply not true, argue the dependency theorists, that Third World societies are in a primitive, unchanged state. Quite the opposite. They have been formed, even created, by their interaction with the world's rich (and, not incidentally, capitalist) countries.

Dependency theorists acknowledge that prior to the sixteenth century, that is to say, before the era of modern economic growth, the world's major regions were essentially unconnected one to another. In that "premodern" period, it may make sense to think of the societies of today's Third World as having been "traditional." Prior to the sixteenth century, the empires of the world were not global in scope. But in the sixteenth century, argues the most influential social historian of the dependency school, Immanuel Wallerstein, capitalism started to develop as a world system. Capitalists from Europe began to seek profits in every corner of the globe. In fact, the search for profits, through the production of agricultural goods for sale in faraway markets and through long-distance commerce, became the dominant world force. Europeans seeking profits gradually came to control the rest of the world, sometimes formally and administratively through colonial empires—but also informally and commercially, without legal administrative control but with the economic power to strike unequal bargains.

From the sixteenth century on, capitalist markets dominated the world, and these capitalist markets fundamentally changed the social structures of the Third World. The process continued for over four centuries and continues today. Dependency theorists argue that although the era of formal colonial empires is almost past, still "neocolonial," capitalist domination remains, and Third World social structures continue to be dependent upon the industrial world. The workers of the Third World produce raw material exports for the rich countries. They work for foreign companies, and they are caught up in the geopolitical power struggles of the economically advanced countries. They are required to speak the languages of the colonial powers and to use their currencies.

It is not the case, then, that the poor countries are in some sort of primitive, unchanged state. For better or for worse, they have been changed by centuries of contact with the world's rich countries. And for the most part, say the dependency theorists, for the worse. The poverty of the Third World is not traditional, and it is not accidental. It is the necessary companion to the richness of the developed countries. As a condition for its own development, the industrial world required cheap raw materials from the Third World. The expansion of the industrial world therefore shaped the structure of the emergent Third World, deforming it, impoverishing it and rendering it incapable of balanced development.

An example will show how the dependency school sees the process as having worked. A generation ago, Eric Williams, a young West Indian who was later to become prime minister of the newly independent country of Trinidad and Tobago, argued that the slave trade between Africa and the Caribbean islands was responsible for the emergence of a commercial middle class in Britain. British ships brought slaves, captured in the interior of Africa and traded at its shores, to the Caribbean; there the ships exchanged their cargoes for the sugar grown by the slaves on plantations. The sugar and molasses were then either exported back to England or traded for farm products in the North American colonies that were in turn sent to England. The trade provided rich profits that were invested in British enterprises, as well as cheap food that was needed for a growing British industrial work force. Both the profits and the cheap food were the basis for the British industrial revolution, and consequently for the growth of a bourgeois middle class in the imperialist country.

This example shows the essence of the dependency approach, the actual creation of underdevelopment. The requirements of British capitalism led to the corruption and despoliation of the African population. Dependency theorists would say that it is wrong to see West African societies of the twentieth century as essentially traditional, since they were fundamentally uprooted and changed by centuries of the slave trade. In addition, British capitalism led to the dominance in the Caribbean region of a plantation sugar system that met no local need, and that actually depended for its commercial success upon the continuing poverty of its labor force. The plantations of the Caribbean are not traditional; they were instituted to meet a need in the economically advanced countries, and they persist to this day for that same purpose. The profits of the triangular trade accrued in Britain, where they were reinvested and where they eventually raised the average standard of living in the metropolitan center. The Third World was left with skewed, impoverished economies and devastated populations—while the core of the world system gained comfort and prosperity.

In other regions of the Third World the details of the history are different, but the broad outlines the same, claim the dependency theorists. Workers were organized into labor gangs on plantations to produce rubber, cotton, cocoa, jute, sugar, tobacco and many other products for use as either raw materials or consumer goods in the rich countries. Peasants were attracted or forced out of their subsistence cultures and into the production of agricultural goods for export, and they thereby became vulnerable to the fluctuations of world markets. Mines produced bauxite, tin and many other minerals for the industries of Europe and North America. In all of these cases it was essential for the success of the capitalist system that labor earnings stay low in the Third World, so that imports into the core countries could remain cheap and profits correspondingly high.

Dependency theorists argue that the particular legal structure of colonialism was not of primary importance. In some cases, the Third World area was ruled as a possession of a European power. In other cases, the Europeans exerted indirect economic control over nominally independent countries. The end result was much the same whether in the British Raj of colonial India or in the independent countries of nineteenth-century Latin America. The world was integrated into a single trading system, with the advancement of the rich countries at the capitalist core being contingent upon the impoverishment of the Third World.

Dependency theorists see the same sorts of exploitative processes occurring in today's international economy. They have been particularly critical of the role that multinational firms have played in recent decades in the Third World. A typical multinational, with its head office in the United States, Europe or Japan, may control operations in dozens of separate countries. Its size and power are such that it can dominate a weak, host Third World country, bargaining from a position of strength for concessions, distorting the structure of the domestic economy, creating vast income gaps and imposing its own priorities, to such an extent as to render the country incapable of genuine development. Dependency theorists also criticize the tariff policies in the rich countries that dictate the sorts of industrial patterns that poor countries are able to choose. They see the great banks of the rich countries sucking resources out of the Third World, and they fault international economic agencies like the World Bank and the International Monetary Fund for imposing policies in the Third World that are favorable to the rich countries.

The dependency school does not focus solely upon the export industries of Third World countries. Initially, the Third World was underdeveloped as its workers were forced into low-wage occupations to produce goods for export to the rich core countries. In the last several decades, however, there has been considerable industrial development in much of the Third World designed for the production of goods to be sold within the poor countries themselves. The dependency theorists see even this industrialization as being weak, subservient to the rich countries and incapable of leading to real improvement for the masses of poor people. The industries are very often controlled by foreign owners. They produce goods only for the rich minority of local people, and they use modern technology that is so labor saving as to employ very few people. Many workers are attracted into the cities in the hopes of getting a relatively good job in one of these new factories, but there are few jobs available, and the consequence of the industrial expansion is therefore often massive unemployment, an increase in urban poverty and an even greater gap between the rich and the poor.

The dependency school recognizes a growing bourgeoisie, or capitalist class, in most Third World countries, but it does not believe that this class has the independence and strength to lead the Third World to sustained growth, as the capitalist class did in the core countries. The Third World capitalists are themselves a dependent class, responding primarily to foreign signals and incapable of undertaking the risks and responsibilities needed to transform their countries in any fundamental way. André Gunder Frank offered the model of a descending series of power centers. At the core in Europe and North America lie the real powers—then in the Third World capital cities there are groups of people who are dependent upon the foreigners but who in turn dominate leaders in the provinces; in turn, the provincial leaders are dependent upon the capital city groups but themselves dominate local groups, and so on.

Much of the analysis in the dependency school has to do with what its adherents call "unequal exchange." In international trading markets, Third World countries are seen as giving up much more than they get. Raúl Prebisch and many of the writers who followed him have focused, for example, upon what they see as the declining "terms of trade" for the Third World. They see the relative prices of Third World exports falling over time and the prices of their imports from the industrialized countries rising. The consequence is that it takes more and more pounds of coffee, for instance, to buy a tractor. Brazil can be very successful at increasing yields and producing more coffee, but in return for the sale of that coffee it will get fewer, not more, tractors. Therefore, because of its commitment to trading relationships with the rich countries, Brazil makes itself poorer.

The dependency theorists argue that there is a circular trap causing the declining terms of trade. Prices of Third World exports are low because wages in the Third World are low, while prices of industrial goods are rising because wages in the rich countries are high and rising. In turn, wages in the Third World are low because the terms of trade are moving against the Third World, and wages in the industrial world are high because the rich countries have been able to exploit the poor. Exploitation creates poverty, which permits more exploitation, and the circle goes round.

André Gunder Frank and some others in the dependency school

have concentrated not so much on the allegedly declining terms of trade as on the removal of the economic surplus from the Third World. Profits and savings that might have been used productively in the poor countries are siphoned off to the rich countries, in a reverse Robin Hood maneuver, stealing from the poor to give to the rich. Frank argues that the plunder of the Third World began with the discovery of gold and silver in Latin America in the sixteenth century, and it continues today. Multinational corporations, he says, bring little new money into a Third World country when they invest in a new factory; instead they borrow the money locally, from savers in the Third World country itself. When their enterprises make profits, however, they repatriate those funds back to their home countries. The consequence of international investment is that the Third World loses resources.

There is another strand within the dependency school that does not focus on unequal exchange, and that is even willing to admit that the international economic system may lead to the creation of some new wealth in the Third World rather than simply to its expropriation. These theorists believe that the heart of underdevelopment today lies in the creation of a rigid, unproductive social structure in the Third World, a social structure dominated by the puppets of the rich countries. This relatively small group of local people controls the agricultural and industrial development of the Third World. These people benefit, indeed grow rich, off their relationship with foreign companies and foreign investors, but they keep their gains to themselves. Connected as they are to the foreigners, they are unable to expand the development effort in ways that would improve the living conditions of the people as a whole.

Most members of the dependency school claim that economic subservience leads very often to political subservience. Groups in power in the Third World serve essentially at the convenience of the political and business power centers in the core of the international capitalist system. The core states support clients in the periphery who can be counted upon to serve their interests, in broad outline if not in every particular. The U.S. government, for example, heaps military and economic aid upon regimes in Third World countries that favor private enterprise and that welcome American business investors. If and when these clients are displaced by groups that have the welfare of the local people closer to heart, they are attacked by the core in all sorts of ways, including militarily, as in Chile in the early 1970's and in Nicaragua in the 1980's.

It is therefore pure ideology, say the dependency theorists, to regard Third World societies as traditional, primitive or unchanged. They have been formed by capitalist development just as surely as have the rich countries—only in their case they have been underdeveloped, impoverished and made less capable of meeting the needs of their people.

The analysis of the dependency school contradicts one of the principal intellectual achievements of mainstream classical and neoclassical economic theory: the doctrine of comparative advantage. This doctrine teaches that trade is to the advantage of all participants; the more trade and the fewer restrictions on trade the better. Each country in the world will be better off to the extent that it concentrates on producing those goods at which it is relatively most efficient, exporting its surplus production of those goods and importing from abroad for its other needs. A country that cuts itself off from international trade and tries to be self-sufficient in all products will end up being inefficient, and poorer than it need be.

The doctrine of comparative advantage is logically correct; when formulated in mathematical terms it is unassailable. But seldom, in the almost two centuries since it was discovered, has it proven persuasive to economically backward countries, that is, to countries trying to catch up with the world leaders. In the nineteenth century, both Germany and the United States imposed tariff barriers to restrict trade and keep cheap British imports out of their countries. They were willing to sacrifice cheap consumer goods for their population in order to create domestic markets sufficient for the growth of their own industrial plants. Similarly, in the Third World today, dependency theorists look with a very skeptical eye at the supposed advantages of free trade in international markets. Writers like André Gunder Frank deny all of the propositions of comparative advantage theory, arguing that international trade and investment actually suck resources out of Third World countries. Others agree with mainstream economists that free trade has some advantages in that it provides relatively cheap consumer goods to the local populations, but they argue that the costs are too high.

The principal problem with the doctrine of comparative advantage, say its critics, is that at the present time the comparative advantage of Third World countries lies in products that in the long run will do them no good at all. For example, the immediate comparative advantage of Honduras may be in the production and export of bananas. Honduras has the best climate for bananas, the best land and long experience in the cultivation of the fruit. The incomes of Hondurans at the present time will be maximized if they concentrate most of their energy on bananas. If they devote themselves to manufacturing, they will founder, because they have limited skills in manufacturing, because they lack a large domestic market for manufactured goods and because the rich countries can produce manufactured goods far more efficiently than they can. Yet, if they follow this prescription and stick with bananas, they will be consigning themselves to poverty for the indefinite future, say the critics of comparative advantage. A labor force concentrating on bananas will always remain unskilled and will never develop the capability to increase the standard of living of the country. It would be far better to seal the country off against imports of manufactured goods and get started right away on a local manufacturing sector. In the short run, Honduras will not be very successful at it, but over time its people will develop the skills needed to bring high productivity to the country. International trade with the rich countries leads only to disaster; it is far better to proceed along a course of autonomous self-sufficiency or of trade with other Third World countries.

Modernization theory sees capitalism as a creative force that was historically responsible for the growth of the developed countries and that is potentially capable of impelling the Third World to higher standards of living. The only problem, the modernizationists would say, is that it has not really been tried in the Third World.

Dependency theory comes to the opposite conclusion about capitalism. It sees international capitalism as the ruin of the Third World. Far from being a stranger to capitalist ways, the Third World has been intimately involved in the capitalist system for centuries. The economic growth of the world's rich countries is seen as having been dependent upon the accumulation of capital, and to a large extent this accumulation came either directly or indirectly from the Third World. The profitability of firms depended upon the wedge between the selling price of their goods on the one hand and the costs of inputs on the other. It was critically important that costs be kept low, and this became the function of the Third World: to provide the raw materials for industrialization at cheap prices. So, vast portions of the land and labor power of the Third World were turned over to the production of industrial raw materials and food for the labor forces of the industrial factories. Sometimes the plantations and mines were established by force against the resistance of a recalcitrant local community, but more often they were established through the normal market mechanisms of capitalism, by offering monetary incentives to entrepreneurs in poor countries to meet the needs of growing markets in Europe and North America. What was most important in this process was that living standards in the Third World be kept low, so that the prices of the goods produced in the Third World could be kept low, so that the costs of production of the capitalists could be kept low and profits kept high.

The modernization school sees the rich countries as at least potentially the salvation of the poor. The dependency school sees them as the main obstacle to the well-being of the poor: the industrial world is the cause of the underdevelopment of the Third World. It will come as no surprise, then, to learn that the political allegiances of the two schools are different. While modernization theorists are by and large liberal and procapitalist, dependency theorists are socialist and frequently revolutionary.

Although there is a fair consensus among the dependency theorists about the diagnosis, about the origins of poverty in the Third World, they have any number of prescriptions and ideas about the best form of response today. And not all of the responses are anticapitalist.

One view held by some in the dependency school is that the best course of action for the Third World is to fight fire with fire, to transform capitalism from the enemy of the Third World to its savior. Whatever damage international capitalism may have caused in the past, the Third World should use the forms of capitalism today to break out of its dependent state. There are success stories in this mold. Japan emerged from the devastation of World War II with an aggressive capitalist economy that incorporated some of the communitarian forms of its previous feudal structure, and over the course of several short decades of remarkable growth, that nation has overtaken the living standards of the original core capitalist countries. Coming along a little later, Singapore, Hong Kong, Taiwan and South Korea have all embarked on the same path, unleashing the creative spirits of capitalist entrepreneurs to develop manufacturing sectors that are challenging the northern societies.

But this strategy is regarded with suspicion by most in the dependency school. While capitalism may be having some success in scattered parts of the Third World, it is also reproducing the tensions and inequities that are found in the economically advanced countries. Since capitalism is based upon competition, it will lead inevitably, they feel, to greater chasms between the haves and the have-nots within each country, and increased exploitation. Capitalism is not, they argue, a strategy that can work for the great majority of the world's poor.

There is a liberal wing of the dependency school that argues that capitalist free enterprise should remain, but that it should be subject to strong guidance and even control by the central governments of Third World countries. This would ensure that it is directed to serving the real needs of the people and not the external demands of foreign markets. Proponents of this view argue for tariff barriers against foreign imports, effective government economic plans, public financial institutions that favor some sectors against others, and so on.

Most of the dependency school adherents regard these measures as halfhearted and naive. They call for full socialist revolutions in the Third World and the expropriation of private enterprises, both foreign-owned and domestic, so that the people as a whole, acting together through their governments, can combat the destructive forces of capitalism. For still others, the focus of the socialist revolution is not on the Third World at all but on the rich countries, where the source of the problem really is. And for another group, the problem can never be resolved on a national level since it is global in scope: the long-run goal is a socialist world government that will completely change the dynamic of international relations and permit the creative development of Third World societies.

Marxism

The legacies of Karl Marx are almost infinite, and some of the most vitriolic debates in the history of scholarship have been between contending schools of Marxists, each claiming to be the true interpreter of the teachings of the nineteenth-century master. The conflicts have carried over into the study of the development of the Third World. Many of the dependency theorists consider themselves to be Marxist, writing in the tradition of Marxist scholarship and using well-known Marxist categories. But some of the dependency theorists, people like Raúl Prebisch and Celso Furtado, for example, are not Marxists. Moreover, dependency theory has been attacked since the 1970's by rather more orthodox Marxists who argue that it has abandoned the central tenets of Marxism, and that in consequence it deals only with surface phenomena, not with the true underlying causes of development and social change—hence the label "neo-Marxist" that is now sometimes used to refer to the dependency school.

There has been a resurgence of Marxist thinking about the Third World, to such an extent that one can now say that it represents a separate school, a school that is antagonistic to both the modernizationists and the dependency theorists. At the basis of this Marxist school is the analysis of the class structures of Third World societies, rather than the growth of resources and technology (as in modernization theory) or foreign domination (as in dependency theory).

Three principal conclusions distinguish the Marxists from the neo-Marxist dependency theorists. First, Marxists argue that the fundamental forces for social change lie internal to the Third World societies, not external to them. Second, they argue that capitalism is quite capable of producing growth in the economies of the Third World. And third, they argue that imperialism, both in its historical form and in its current neocolonial form, is often an agent of progress, that it may operate in such a way as to propel Third World societies on the path to capitalist growth. In all of these conclusions, the Marxists lie closer to the modernizationists than they do to the dependency theorists, but it must quickly be added that the Marxists look at the Third World very differently from the way the modernizationists do.

At the basis of Marxist thinking lies the idea of the mode of production,[6] that is to say, the class structure that exists in a society and that leads both to production and to exploitation of the working population. Marx identified different modes of production, each with its characteristic class structure. For example, a slave society was one mode of production, with two basic classes: slave-owners and slaves. The slave-owners owned all of the means of production, both human and non-human. In spite of the fact that the slaves produced everything, they were given only enough subsistence to reproduce themselves; the remaining product was expropriated from them and used for the consumption of the slave-owners as well as for the reproduction of the nonhuman means of production.

Feudalism was the mode of production characteristic of medieval Europe, after the slave systems of the ancient world and before capitalism. In feudalism the two basic classes were the nobility and the serfs. The serfs performed the work on land that was held in common by them, and they were exploited by being forced to transfer some portion of their produce and/or their labor time to their lords.

Capitalism, as Marx described it, was the mode of production that grew out of European feudalism. The feudal classes were transformed into capitalist classes by the process of the "alienation" of labor. In feudalism, serfs had customary rights to the use of the land and the tools needed to produce agricultural output. When feudal lords discovered, however, that they could make monetary profits by using the common lands for the grazing of sheep and the selling of wool to textile merchants, they "enclosed" those common lands, that is, they fenced off the land and drove the serfs from it. This was the alienation, or separation, of labor from the means of production. In feudalism, workers had assured access to land and to tools; it was their birthright. Capitalism arose when the workers lost this access and were left with nothing but their own hands.

Thus arose the two fundamental capitalist classes: the working class, which did not own or have access to any of the means of production and which therefore had to enter into a wage contract with the capitalist, and the capitalist class, which owned the means of production and hired the workers for wages. Capitalist exploitation occurred through the wage, which represented much less than the full value of what the workers produced. The capitalists expropriated this surplus value, that is, the value produced by the workers over and above the wage. They used the surplus value primarily to reproduce more capital—adding to the means of production, hiring more workers, expropriating more surplus value and increasing profits.

It followed from Marx's analysis that capitalism was a tremendously powerful engine of growth. The capitalists, in competition one with the other, vied to increase their surplus expropriation and outproduce each other, and in so doing they greatly increased the productive capability of their countries. It was not a pretty process. The creation of a capitalist labor force in the first place, by enclosure or related means, always entailed the destruction of a precapitalist (or "traditional," to use the modernizationists' term) way of life, and often entailed the letting of massive amounts of blood as well. The human devastation that followed the birth of capitalism, chronicled in the first volume of Marx's *Capital*, is a powerful antidote to the smooth, benign and mathematical growth models of modern neoclassical economists. Once capitalism was established, its progress was always uneven, between countries and also within countries. Some countries, areas, industries and people jumped ahead, and some were left behind, even destroyed. Workers were exploited to unbelievable lengths in the first factory and mill towns; there were dismal generations of long hours, low pay, child labor, malnutrition and disease.

Eventually, in the most advanced capitalist countries, the benefits of increased production were extended to many of the workers. This was not, however, a development that Marx himself foresaw, writing in the middle of the nineteenth century. He predicted instead that the contradiction between ever richer capitalists and ever poorer workers would eventually lead to the collapse of the capitalist system and its replacement with socialism, by which he meant essentially the end of class warfare and exploitation and their replacement by a system in which the benefits of production were shared equitably.

The modern Third World Marxist school returns to many of Marx's views about nineteenth-century European capitalist development. It argues that capitalism can develop in the Third World and is, in fact, developing in many areas of it. That is to say, Third World countries can have their own, autonomous capitalist classes, capable of producing, reproducing and growing, just as the capitalist classes did in the currently advanced countries. Modern Marxists do not see capitalism in the way the dependency theorists do—as a global system with all of the power and the benefits accruing to the core countries and only poverty, underdevelopment and weakness in the Third World. They fully understand that Third World countries are intimately involved in international networks of trade, investment and finance, but they argue nevertheless that there is internal autonomy, that the local capitalist classes may have their own power and not simply be subservient to the international system.

The Marxists recognize other possibilities. The capitalist class may be dependent upon foreigners, and incapable of leading its country to economic growth, but if so this is a consequence of its own internal weakness vis-à-vis contending classes at home.

The Marxists do not, of course, see capitalism as the only mode of production that may increase productivity in the Third World. Countries may opt for socialism; the socialist regime may be capable of mobilizing the peasantry and working classes for development, or again it may be too weak to be successful. The point is that the source of the strength or weakness of the dominant class must be sought internally, in its relationships with other classes, not externally. To quote Agustín Cueva:

> Dependency theory holds that the nature of our social formations is dependent on how they are integrated with the world capitalist system. But, is it not more correct to state the inverse? Is it not the nature of our societies that determines their links with the capitalist world? Thus, for example, if Bolivia after the 1952 revolution had followed a similar course to that of the Cuban Revolution, it would not today be a dependent country.[7]

The argument between the more orthodox Marxists and the dependency school over the role of wage labor in capitalism is particularly interesting. A classic Marxist definition of capitalism is that it is a system of wage labor. Since the working class is free, and since it does not own the means of production itself, workers must offer their labor power to the capitalists in return for a wage. In most Marxist writing, the wage contract is the source of class conflict between workers and capitalists. The workers produce all of the value, but the wage they are paid represents only a fraction of that value—hence the stage is set for protracted struggle as the workers try to increase their share and the capitalists resist.

The dependency theorists have either explicitly or implicitly rejected the identity of capitalism with a wage labor system. Immanuel Wallerstein, the intellectual leader of a variant of the dependency approach known as "world systems analysis," has made the case most clearly. From the sixteenth century on, he argues, it is important to see capitalism as a world system, not just as the national system of several countries of Europe. The core of the capitalist world system was in western Europe, where a regime of wage labor grew up. This core gradually exerted its dominance over the rest of the world, beginning with eastern and southern Europe, and eventually extending its influence throughout Asia, the Middle East, Africa and Latin America. In time, most of what is now the Third World became integrated into the capitalist world system, providing food, raw materials, markets and profits for the core countries. The Third World was a component of world capitalism, but for the most part it did not have a wage labor system. The Third World had all sorts of other arrangements for securing a supply of labor, including slavery, peonage, indentured servitude, sharecropping and independent peasant production. The fact that the Third World had different, nonwage ways of dealing with labor did not mean that it was any less a part of the capitalist system. So, according to the dependency school, what is unique about capitalism is not wage labor, but the private ownership of the means of production by a class of profit-seeking capitalists, and the buying and selling of the goods they produce through markets. Like the mainstream, neoclassical modernizationists, the dependency school sees capitalism as essentially a system of market relationships, not a class struggle mediated by the wage contract.

The Marxists are not persuaded by this argument that capitalism is consistent with any and all forms of labor organization. They maintain that such a position is equivalent to saying that the defining characteristic of capitalism is the market. Nonsense, they say, markets exist in almost every social system. Ancient Athens, which was a slave society, had a thriving market. The defining characteristic of capitalism is the class struggle between workers and bosses. This class struggle occurs when workers are alienated from the means of production and are therefore compelled to work for wages for the capitalists. And the class struggle is essentially an internal, national phenomenon.

One subject on which the Marxists and the modernizationists differ in interesting ways is the role of governments, and government policies, in the Third World. Western economists and other social scientists in the modernization school spend a good deal of their time identifying "obstacles" to development and then recommending government policies that can overcome those obstacles. The implied assumption is that the government stands separate from the society, and that by making the right choices it can steer the country around the obstacles to development. A typical obstacle might be that the country's manufacturing sector is hampered by insufficient markets, so that it cannot produce on a scale large enough to become efficient. Government policy can address this problem, perhaps by erecting tariff barriers to keep out foreign manufactured goods that take away markets, or perhaps by negotiating with rich counties to reduce their tariffs so that the Third World manufacturers can enjoy expanding markets abroad. For the modernizationists, the government is not a part of the problem; the government can be the solution to the problem if it adopts the right policy.

The Marxists see the government not as a neutral and beneficent outsider, but as an integral part of the social structure of the country. The government is generally controlled by the ruling classes, and government policies are an expression of the interests of those classes. The dominant classes may or may not be capable of progressive development. If they are, government policies will help to move the country forward, and if they are not, government policies will be harmful to development. It would be a mistake to see the government as standing in opposition to the dominant groups in the society and able to use its policies to direct development in a way not wanted by those groups. Unlike the modernizationists, therefore, the Marxists do not see government policies as fundamental.

While the dependency model dominated thinking about development in Latin America in the 1960's and early 1970's, it did not prove to be all that attractive to social scientists in Africa and Asia,[8] and even in Latin America it has met increasing resistance from the left in recent years. Correspondingly, the Marxists' investigations of social change in the Third World have become increasingly lively.

In Kenya, for example, there has been a very interesting debate about the mode of production. Some writers believe that in the era before western imperialism, Kenya had a sort of capitalist society, with wage labor. Others have identified different modes of production. Goran Hyden claims that Kenya had what he calls a "peasant mode of production," with small household units of production. Marxist students of Kenya view British imperialism ambivalently. While imperialism exploited the Africans, it may also have broken down a stagnant mode of production and opened the way for capitalism. When Africans regained control over their country after the independence movement, they were able to build a capitalist system upon the remnants of imperialism. Paul Lubeck writes:

> The brutal intrusion of white settler agriculture undermined many precapitalist institutions and practices that otherwise would have resisted the penetration of capitalist relations of production. Therefore, after the successful anti-imperialist Mau Mau insurrection, an indigenous bourgeoisie inherited a productive base in capitalist agriculture with large units of production and a disciplined state-bureaucracy.[9]

The dependency theorists see Third World plantations and mines as subservient institutions, subject to the whims of consumers and importers in faraway lands and consequently lacking the strength to transform their own societies. The Marxists, on the other hand, see them as capitalist firms, with a labor force working for wages and a class of owners expropriating profits. These capitalist firms may well be capable of growth, and the capitalist class may embark upon other ventures that will fundamentally change the local society. It is possible, of course, that the capitalist class will fail in its historical mission of reproducing capital and leading its society to higher productive standards, but if it does, the fault will lie within itself and not with its foreign puppet masters.

The Marxists have an easier time dealing with the capitalist success stories of the Third World than do the dependency theorists. Throughout the postwar period, the Japanese capitalist system has grown with such vigor that it is no longer part of the Third World. In the 1960's and the 1970's, the giants of Latin America, Brazil and Mexico were particularly successful. From the early 1970's through the early 1980's the oil exporters of the Third World enjoyed striking growth. And in the 1980's and 1990's attention turned to the successes of the Asian NICs: Taiwan, Singapore, South Korea and Hong Kong. The oil exporters may be a special case, but in all of the other countries growth has been led by private firms, in partnership with supportive governments, borrowing technology from abroad and aggressively seeking new markets both inside and outside their borders. Dependency theorists sometimes claim that this growth is doomed to failure in the long run because it is dependent on foreigners, or they concentrate on the new forms of exploitation caused by the growth, the new urban slums and impoverished peasants, for example. The world systems variant of the dependency school explains the growth of these countries by thinking of them as a "semiperiphery," which embodies some features of the core and some features of the periphery, and which consequently is able to enjoy some economic growth and some improvements in standards of living.

The Marxists, in contrast, see the economic success of these countries as validating their view that the capitalist class in Third World countries is sometimes capable of becoming the engine of growth. They acknowledge the human devastation that capitalism often leaves in its wake: the destroyed peasant cultures, the urban slums and the overworked wage laborers. But capitalism is always uneven and unfair, they argue; certainly it was a massively destructive force in Europe, as well as a creative force, and it will show both faces in the Third World as well. The capitalist system is, after all, class warfare.

Marx himself believed that capitalism was a necessary stage in social evolution, for although it was exploitative it was the only mode capable of developing the productive resources of a country. Although he dealt almost exclusively with Europe, he did write a series of articles about India in which he welcomed imperialism as breaking down the structure of feudalism and thereby opening the way for capitalism. Socialism, he believed, would follow upon the self-destruction of the mature capitalist system. As matters actually turned out in the twentieth century, however, none of the mature capitalist societies has collapsed—although there were several close calls in the Great Depression of the 1930's—and the socialist revolutions have all occurred in poor countries. One of the pressing questions for the twentieth century, therefore, has been whether socialism offers a better path for economic and social development than capitalism does.

The great majority of the writers in the dependency school believe that socialism is a more hopeful path. In contrast, the modernizationists look to capitalism and free markets (guided, to be sure, by government planning). The Marxists have a rather ambiguous position. Ultimately, they see capitalism as the enemy, because it exploits the workers. For the present, however, capitalism may be the best choice for many Third World countries, provided that it is a system with strong internal coherence that can develop the country's productive capabilities. For Marxists, socialism is the ultimate goal, but that goal may have to wait until the capitalist engine of growth has done its work. There are, of course, differences of opinion about this among Marxists; many in Latin America look to socialist Cuba as a model, for example.

The rebirth of this classically Marxist perspective coincides, ironically, with the decline of communism in much of the world, beginning in the late 1980's. In the Soviet bloc countries, communist regimes collapsed, while in China and Vietnam, the regimes continued but the economies turned increasingly to market capitalism. How could such a period be a fruitful one for the resurgence of Marxist thinking?

The answer is that Marx himself was a student of capitalism, not a prophet of communism. He had little to say about the structure of a communist society, and leaders of communist movements have found no blueprints in his writings. But he had a great deal to say about the historical development of capitalism, and about the class conflicts inherent in capitalism. Consequently, as capitalism has grown stronger in the late twentieth century, so too have the opportunities for Marxist social analysis.

Limitations of These Approaches

The three principal perspectives on the Third World—modernization, dependency and Marxism—are all valuable. Although very different one from the other, and in many respects contradictory, they all have insights that can help one begin to understand the causes of poverty in the world.

It is helpful to consider a variety of different theories at the same time, rather than just a single view. The truth is that social reality is infinitely complicated, confused and puzzling. It consists, after all, of 5 billion human beings, each one of whom is a thinking, creative person. Society can be thought of as a ball of tangled string: there is no consistent pattern to it, no way of adequately describing its twists and meanderings. Nevertheless, one tries. One way of trying is to take a sharp knife, cut a cross section through the ball and then attempt to describe the surface that has been created. Of course, it is still very difficult to find a pattern in that surface and to describe it in words—but it is easier than the impossible task of analyzing the whole ball of string. Suppose that one can adequately describe the flat, cut surface. The problem remains that different people will choose to cut the ball at any number of different angles, and they will therefore discover different patterns and will come up with different explanations. All of the explanations are "true," but they are also partial and therefore in a way untrue, because they do not comprehend the full complexity of the ball of string.

This is the basic problem in trying to make sense out of the many variations of development theory, the many explanations of why there is so much poverty in a world of riches. All of the variations have useful, accurate insights—and they are all partial. The same could be said of theories that are Freudian, Keynesian, Christian or deconstructionist. The human mind has not reached the elevated point at which there is a single superior school of social science that dominates all others. That being the case, it behooves one to be open to different approaches.

Take, for example, the debate between modernization and dependency theorists about whether the present-day cultures of the Third World are best thought of as traditional or dependent. In reality, the cultures of the world are marvelously varied, and they are both traditional and dependent. At the heart of even the "modern" societies of Europe and North America is found much that is traditional, that has roots going far back before the capitalist epoch. The religious forms of the rich countries—the many variations of Christianity as well as Judaism—have ancient origins and yet are still vital presences for many. They are not disappearing; in fact some forms, such as charismatic and fundamentalist Christianity, are growing stronger as people turn to them to make sense out of constant change and dislocation. Likewise, and to a much greater extent, in the Third World, religions, philosophies, family structures, and attitudes toward fertility and death often have roots that go back centuries and even millennia and certainly deserve to be called traditional. But these traditional values are not by themselves responsible for poverty. The dependency theorists are often correct in seeing poverty as imposed upon the Third World from outside.

Nigerian novelist Buchi Emecheta's wonderful book *The Joys of Motherhood*[10] describes the anguish of a traditional village woman who tries to adapt to the modern world by providing educational opportunities for her eldest son. Modernizationists could read the novel as a case study of their philosophy, seeing the mother drawn out of the traditional world toward the world of modern education, which promises to transform if not her life, then the lives of her children. But that is not quite how the narrative proceeds. The son continues on to ever higher levels of western education and finally disappears into the clouds of an American graduate school, never to be heard from again in his mother's lifetime. She has sacrificed everything for her son's education and is left impoverished by her struggle. The foreign world has taken her principal resource, her son, and given her nothing in return. So the novel can also be read as a case study in dependency.

Shahhat's world is a mélange of the dependent and the traditional. He grows wheat and lentils for export to the markets of Cairo and beyond, and he copes unsuccessfully with the modern agricultural technology of irrigation systems, chemical fertilizers and hybrid strains, all imported from abroad. At the same time, his unquestioned faith remains with Allah, the age-old deity.

What is an almost gentle mixture in Shahhat's life is a devastating conflict in Rigoberta Menchu's. She is exploited in the coastal export plantations, scorned in the capital city and attacked in her village by an army supported by the United States. At the same time, she clings to a traditional culture whose roots go back long before the arrival of white people in Mesoamerica, a culture that gives her the strength to resist the assaults of the dominant world. In the richness of these few lives, one sees the limits of any single social scientific theory.

Why Is Poverty Not Retreating?

There is no end in sight to world poverty. This is so in spite of the extraordinary explosion of science and technology in the last two centuries, and in spite of the nationalist and revolutionary movements that appeared to bring autonomy to Third World people in the twentieth century. The technological and political changes seemed to promise a better life for the majority of the world's people, but that promise has somehow been betrayed. It is difficult to discover why. The three theories have three different approaches to an answer, all of them with some validity.

In comparing the three approaches, one notices first that the modernizationists tend to deny the very phenomenon under discussion. That is to say, the modernizationist view is almost by its nature optimistic. It shows that well-designed policies can lead to progress, and it sees progress at every turn. Most social scientists of the mainstream western variety acknowledge that there is terrible poverty in the Third World, but they see the poverty slowly disappearing over time. The dependency school takes precisely the opposite view. Underdevelopment is inherent in the world order as long as the world is dominated by rich capitalist countries. The Marxists are eclectic: poverty may or may not disappear, depending upon the class structure and strength of each country.

Although the modernizationists are for the most part optimistic, a person seeking explanations of why poverty continues and worsens can find any number of clues in their scholarship. The issue for the modernizationists frequently comes down to policy—policy of governments both in the Third World and in the rich countries. Rural Indians are still desperate, a modernizationist would argue, because the Indian government has neglected agriculture and stressed industry, because it has failed to develop extension programs that reach the villages, because it has not packaged the new agricultural technology to make it accessible to farmers with small holdings, and so forth. Poverty is growing in the Philippines because the government made the wrong choices about development strategy, because it protected markets for local industries that turned out to be inefficient, while it neglected to encourage its export industries. The United States government is culpable because it cut back its foreign aid and failed to direct what aid remained to the countries and projects where the aid would do the most good. These are the sorts of answers that some modernizationists turn to when trying to understand the failure of development.

There is a group of modernizationists on the right wing of the school who blame government policy in a rather different way. Their argument is simply that there is too much policy, that governments of both the rich and the poor countries try to regulate and govern in far too much detail, when what they should do is step back and let the free market take over the task of development. Thus, socialist countries like Cuba have stagnated, they say, because the state has tried to direct the economy through a central planning office, while free-market, capitalist South Korea has thrived because the government has kept its hands off and allowed entrepreneurs to seek profits.

In either case, the modernizationists usually see governments as autonomous bodies, capable of making whatever choices they please. The fact that they make harmful choices about policy is therefore the principal cause of stagnation and poverty, where those phenomena persist.

For both the dependency and the Marxist schools, government policy is far from the central cause of poverty. Writers in both schools are very critical, even scornful, of many government policies. But they do not see governments, of either the rich or the poor countries, as autonomous bodies. The governments of the rich countries are seen as acting in the class interests of the dominant domestic groups. Dependency theorists see most Third World governments as little more than puppets for the capitalists in the rich countries and therefore completely incapable of carrying out policies that could benefit the poor majority at home. The Marxists for the most part reject the idea of foreign control, but they see the governments of Third World countries as acting in the interests of the dominant domestic classes. If governments do not have much autonomy, it is beside the point to criticize them for their policies. One must go a step further to explain why governments act the way they do.

For the dependency theorists, of course, the betrayal of the promise of social change in the Third World lies exactly at the heart of their analysis. The capitalist world system never for a minute held out the hope of real progress to the Third World. It despoiled and impoverished the Third World. The cause of continuing poverty is therefore the failure of the Third World to break its ties with the rich, capitalist countries. For most of the dependency theorists, only full-scale, socialist revolutions will suffice. Without revolutions, in which the mass of the people take control of their societies, the exploitative ties with the capitalist world will remain, and Third World people will be continuously sucked into a life of dependency and poverty.

For the Marxists, on the other hand, the explanation of continued poverty is most often the failure of a dynamic capitalist class to emerge from the social systems of the past. In a Latin American country, for example, the dominant class may be the owners of the great landed estates, people who are content to exploit their tenants and live in luxury off the rents, but who have no commitment to entrepreneurship and to industrial, commercial development. If the landed class controls the government and the military, then the country's policies will result in poverty, not in social change and progress.

Assessment

The dependency school has an insight into the underdevelopment of the Third World that is centrally important, one that is simply missing from the modernization and the Marxist perspectives. For there have been massive changes in the economic structure of almost every area of the Third World over the past several centuries, and these changes in just about every case have come in response to the dynamic of global capitalist economic growth. Most of the population of Latin America—whites, mestizos and blacks—are, after all, the descendants of immigrants from the colonial era. Many areas of the Third World depend upon one or two staple export goods, grown on plantations or produced in mines: bauxite in Jamaica, coffee in Brazil, cocoa in Ghana, copper in Zambia, sugar in Cuba, rubber in Malaysia—the list goes on. Where plantations do not dominate, peasants on small plots produce for the market. The markets for many of these goods are in the rich countries, and the fortunes of the poor rise and fall as the prices of primary products fluctuate in world markets. Capital and technology invade Third World countries from the capitalist core, as do manufactured and sometimes even agricultural goods. Even the population explosion, which threatens to overwhelm some parts of the Third World, was caused for the most part by imported technology—public health, sanitation and medical care—that lowered death rates while leaving birth rates high and unchanged.

So, while there are many remnants of traditional mores still alive in the Third World—cultural, philosophical and economic—the dependency school is correct to see the Third World not as a stagnant, unchanged place but as fundamentally transformed.

It does not follow from this, however, that Third World countries are bereft of autonomy. Many dependency theorists argue that only if Third World countries cut themselves off from their ties to the capitalist world will they regain the internal strength to achieve progressive social change. But this is not true. Cuba and China followed the dependency prescription by pursuing development in the absence of capitalist connections, but Taiwan and South Korea intensified their connections to the international market system, and with some success.

Both routes can be feasible—and, of course, both routes can lead to failure also.

What is most valuable about the dependency school, then, is that it focuses one's attention on the international context of the Third World. Its writers are correct to insist that economic growth is a global phenomenon, the benefits of which have been concentrated unevenly in the fortunate countries. But the dependency school can be seriously misleading. It denies the strength of the capitalist Third World, and most of its adherents hold that socialism is the only road to progress in the Third World.

Dependency theory can all too easily turn into a kind of cultural imperialism of the left. In the hands of dependency theory, all the main actors on the world stage are often seen as coming from the advanced capitalist countries, with the Third World appearing only passive and manipulated. This does an injustice—even when the task at hand is to locate the source of exploitation (as the quotation from an Indian journal at the head of this chapter states). People in the Third World are as capable of inhumanity as are people in the core: it is the Third World that is to be held to account for genocide in Indonesia and Cambodia, for totalitarianism in Japan, for human rights abuses in Argentina and Uganda, for repressive religious fundamentalism in Iran, for military adventurism in Iraq. All of those evils have taken place in the context of world affairs, but it is perverse and ultimately demeaning to argue that the Third World has not generated its own villains.

So too its successes. The world's largest democracy, for all its enormous problems, is India. The world's most creative, state-directed approaches to social and economic change have been in China. The economic success stories of Japan, Hong Kong, Taiwan and South Korea are all the result of the commitment of the people of those societies, not the manipulations of outsiders. The courageous turn to democracy in Latin America in the 1980's was a testament to the strength of the Latin peoples.

The insight to be won from dependency theory is not, therefore, that the people of the Third World are puppets, and not that the source of all initiative for social change lies at the core of the capitalist system. It is not true that Third World countries can progress only if they cut themselves off from the capitalist system through socialist revolutions.

In fact, if it were the case that dependency analysis led inevitably to a prescription for socialist revolution, then recent world events would signal the bankruptcy of dependency analysis. As Eastern Europe jettisoned socialism, as the Soviet Union collapsed as both a socialist economy and a political entity and as it became clear that most of the remaining socialist countries in the Third World could retain their political structure only by totalitarian control over their people, the once proud claims of socialism lay in tatters.

But the usefulness of dependency theory does not lie in its connection to socialism, or in the conclusion that Third World societies lack autonomy. The most important insight of dependency theory is that the social and economic structures of much of the Third World have been created in response to the imperatives of the developing capitalist north. We are not a world of separate nation states, independent of one another; we are one world, completely entangled in one another.

It follows that the development of the Third World is both an international and a national phenomenon. The context within which the Third World exists is an international one; world capitalism and the political relationships between the great powers set the parameters within which the poor of the world must function. But the responses of Third World countries to these outside forces are just as important in determining their fate. It is from this perspective that the modernization and the Marxist schools have more insight, notwithstanding their major differences.

Suggestions for Further Reading

Blomstrom, Magnus, and Björn Hettne. *Development Theory in Transition: The Dependency Debate and Beyond: Third World Responses*. London: Zed Books, 1984.

Chilcote, Ronald H., and Joel C. Edelstein. *Latin America: Capitalist and Socialist Perspectives of Development and Underdevelopment*. Boulder, Colo.: Westview Press, 1958.

Dos Santos, Theotonio. "The Structure of Dependency." *American Economic Review* 60 (May 1970): 231–36.

Foster-Carter, Aidan. "From Rostow to Gunder Frank: Conflicting Paradigms in the Analysis of Underdevelopment." *World Development* 4 (March 1976): 167–80.

Marx, Karl. *Capital: A Critique of Political Economy*. Vol. 1. New York: International Publishers, 1967.

Marx, Karl, and Friedrich Engels. *The Communist Manifesto*. Translated by Paul Sweezy. New York: Monthly Review Press, 1964.

Rostow, Walt W. *The Stages of Economic Growth: A Non-Communist Manifesto*. 2d ed. Cambridge: Cambridge University Press, 1971.

Valenzuela, J. Samuel, and Arturo Valenzuela. "Modernization and Dependency: Alternative Perspectives in the Study of Latin American Underdevelopment." In J. J. Villamil, ed., *Transnational Capitalism and National Development*. Atlantic Highlands, N.J.: Humanities Press, 1979: 31–67.

Notes

1. For an excellent discussion of disputes within the dependency school, see Magnus Blomstrom and Björn Hettne, *Development Theory in Transition: The Dependency Debate and Beyond: Third World Responses* (London: Zed Books, 1984).

2. A.R.M. Lower, "Two Ways of Life: The Primary Antithesis of Canadian History," *Canadian Historical Association Report* (1943), 8.

3. See Paul Bairoch, "International Industrialization Levels from 1750 to 1980," *The Journal of European Economic History* 11 (Fall 1982): 269–333, and Angus Maddison, "A Comparison of Levels of GDP Per Capita in Developed and Developing Countries, 1700–1980" *The Journal of Economic History* 43 (March 1983): 27–41.

4. Walt W. Rostow, *The Stages of Economic Growth: A Non-Communist Manifesto,* 2d ed. (Cambridge: Cambridge University Press, 1971), 7.

5. Ibid., 107.

6. Not to be confused with the "means of production," discussed in the section on modernization. A means of production is a physical thing, like a factory or a worker. A mode of production, as used by Marxists, is a social structure, or a set of relationships between classes.

7. Agustín Cueva, "Problems and Perspectives of Dependency Theory," *Latin American Perspectives* 3 (Fall 1976): 15.

8. Again, see Blomstrom and Hettne for a good presentation of this.

9. Paul M. Lubeck, ed., *The African Bourgeoisie: Capitalist Development in Nigeria, Kenya and the Ivory Coast* (Boulder, Colo.: Lynne Rienner Publishers, 1987), 19.

10. Buchi Emecheta, *The Joys of Motherhood* (New York: George Braziller, Inc., 1979).

CHAPTER FOUR

Imperialism

Our wounds are still too fresh and painful to be
driven from our memory. We have known tiring labor
exacted in exchange for slavery. . . . We have known
ironies, insults, blows which we had to endure morning, noon and night because we were "Negroes."
—Patrice Lumumba[1]

By the old Moulmein Pagoda
Lookin' lazy at the sea
There's a Burma girl a settin'
And I know she thinks o' me
For the wind is in the palm trees
And the temple bells they say
"Come you back you British soldier
Come you back to Mandalay."
—Rudyard Kipling, "Mandalay"

Whatever happens we have got
The Maxim gun and they have not.
—Hilaire Belloc, *The Modern Traveller*

IMPERIALISM SHAPED TODAY'S Third World. Europeans, and
later Americans, spread out over the entire globe, annexing vast areas,
conquering foreign lands and administering millions of nonwhite people. In many areas, imperialism took the form of colonization by white
settler families who displaced the local people, often violently.

Modernizationists seldom pay much attention to imperialism;
implied in their conviction that Third World societies are "traditional"
is the view that imperialism had few lasting effects, and certainly that it
did not transform the Third World in any fundamental way. For Marxists and dependency theorists, however, the history of imperialism is
critical to an understanding of the Third World and its poverty today.
Marxists see imperialism as having shattered old class structures, and
they see the classes and class conflicts of Third World countries today
as having arisen in response to the dislocation of imperialist domination. The dependency theorists go further; as explained in Chapter 3,
they see imperialism and modern day neocolonialism as having created

underdevelopment and poverty in the Third World. Whatever the differences between the latter two approaches, they are surely correct in understanding imperialism as one of the most important movements of our age.

Imperialism let loose the social forces that in turn generated the poverty that is the current common denominator of the Third World. It created the national boundaries of most Third World countries, and it provided their national languages. It was the source of the ideologies that drive many of the political movements of the Third World. It laid out the trade patterns and transportation networks that frame Third World economies; it called forth the plantations and the mines and all of the primary products that the Third World sells abroad. Imperialism destroyed local crafts and manufactures. It pulled millions into urban slums and posed opportunities for new elites to accumulate wealth and power. The imperialists brought with them public health measures that lowered mortality and caused the unprecedented population explosion in the Third World.

The Creation of the European Empires

Any precise dating of European imperialism would be arbitrary; as good a date as any for its onset is 1492, the year Columbus set out on his first voyage of discovery. Not coincidentally, this is also the year the Spanish finally expelled the Moors who had lived for centuries in Spain; prior to 1492, a unified Spanish state capable of supporting trans-Atlantic exploration did not exist. The ending date of formal imperialism came almost five centuries later, in the early 1960's, with the explosion of "new nations" around the globe—the former colonies, taking their seats in world councils. The end of the European empires coincided, again not by chance, with the exhaustion of European strength following two devastating world wars.

For almost 500 years the powers of Europe expanded outward over the globe. The imperialist urge took many forms and rhythms. At times it was marked by the dominance of a single European country, at times by competition among several. It featured massive overseas settlement in some cases, administrative and military control in others and informal economic domination in still others. Its high point came just at the beginning of the twentieth century, when almost every area of what we now think of as the Third World was under the direct authority of an imperial power or was subject to indirect control.

The history of European imperialism falls fairly neatly into three periods: (1) 1492–1776, global expansion; (2) 1776–1870, British dominance and withdrawal of other imperialists; and (3) 1870–1914, the "new imperialism."

1492–1776: Global Expansion

In the first period, imperialism followed the voyages of discovery. In the late Middle Ages, Europe had had some overland contacts with Asia, but most of its communities were isolated. With the discovery of better shipbuilding techniques, the isolation was broken. The late-fifteenth and then the sixteenth and seventeenth centuries were the age of seafaring exploration: of Columbus' journeys across the Atlantic, Vasco da Gama's trip around Africa to India, Magellan's around-the-world voyage, and the Dutch expeditions to the Cape of Good Hope and thence eastward into Asia. The history of the first phase of European imperialism can be traced in the succession of world maps the cartographers drew: largely imaginary at the beginning, and gradually gaining precision over the centuries.

The first great European empire consisted of the Spanish dominions in America, followed quickly by Portuguese colonies. After Columbus came other explorers and then bands of soldiers who took possession of the mainland. Before the might of European weaponry, ancient empires crumbled and were destroyed: the Aztecs by Cortez in Mexico, the Incas by Pizzaro in Peru. The soldiers were followed soon after by the friars, whose sacred mission it was to salvage souls and who succeeded at the expense of wiping out whole cultures. It would be hard to say whether the soldiers or the priests were more destructive. Together, in their search for wealth, hegemony and spiritual conversion they dominated a continent, destroying millions of lives and subjecting the survivors to servitude.

The Spanish forced the native Americans into bondage both in agriculture and in the mines. They established the system of agricultural *encomienda*, under which the natives worked on the Spanish estates for 4 days a week, leaving them 2 for their own subsistence plots. In theory the natives were granted rights analogous to those of semifree serfs in feudal Spanish manors, but it is likely that in most cases these rights were abridged, and that their lives were often taken. When the native Americans proved unable to withstand the rigors of their new situation, their labor was supplemented by African slaves.

It was the discovery of silver in Peru in 1545 that sealed the fate of the Spanish American colonies. The amount of silver ore was staggering, and for decade after decade it was extracted at a fearful human cost and sent back to Spain where it transformed the metropolitan society. Purchases increased, prices rose and commerce prospered, first in the Iberian peninsula and later throughout western Europe, as the riches of the Americas spread. In what was to become a common imperialist experience, however, the native and black miners shared none of the prosperity; their lot was slavery, disease and death.

For the most part, the Spanish did not settle in the Americas; soldiers, administrators and priests were sent out from the homeland, but few women joined them. The unions of the Spanish men with local women spawned a new population—mestizo or mixed blood. Looked down upon by the pureblood Spanish, they nevertheless assumed a position of privilege vis-à-vis the native Americans that lasts until today. Rigoberta Menchu's oppressors in Guatemala are Spanish-speaking mestizos.

The record of destruction of the local people and their societies in South America was exceeded by the British empire in North America. While the Spanish administered South America, British families actually settled in North America, and by the seventeenth century they constituted a population of over a million along the eastern coast of the continent. Farther north, in the valley of the St. Lawrence River, the French settled too, but in much smaller numbers. The British settlers were eventually hemmed in by the French empire along the St. Lawrence, Great Lakes and Mississippi systems, and by the Spanish to the south. In a series of wars the British overcame their competitors and took possession of a continent. In so doing, they almost completely exterminated the native populations, something neither the Spanish nor the French had succeeded in doing. The destruction of the North American Indian was a necessity for the British because of the large number of settlers who flowed in, carving farms out of what once was the hunting ground of the natives. The destruction was so complete that today most of the remnants of native American society that persist are in the barren, desert lands of the United States southwest, which the white man did not covet for agriculture.

The culture and living standards of the United States are founded, therefore, upon the most genocidal imperialism the world has known. It is a fact most Americans would prefer to forget. Americans pride themselves on a certain anti-imperialism, a moral superiority to the British, French and Dutch who held so much of the world in domination. They flatter themselves with revolutionary nostalgia. But the truth is that Americans—at least white Americans—are the beneficiaries of an unparalleled destruction that almost totally eliminated an entire race.

Into the Americas, both North and South, the imperialists brought a new population group: black slaves from Africa. Millions of people were captured in the African interior, traded at the coastal ports and transported in packed, inhuman conditions to the New World. They were set to work on the plantations and mines that produced much of the new wealth, and they bred successive generations of slaves. While Africa had been a source of slaves for centuries, the magnitude of the slave trade exploded after 1700, as the plantations of the New World expanded, producing sugar and cotton for Europe. The islands of the Caribbean—the West Indies—became fabulously productive in the eighteenth century, importing hundreds of thousands of slaves and exporting sugar and molasses to the prosperous new consumers of England and France. The plantation system spread throughout both South and North America, generating huge profits for the colonial traders.

In the first phase of European imperialism, through the eighteenth century, Africa and Asia were incorporated into the world trading network, but they were not as thoroughly settled or as tightly ruled as were the Americas. Slave-trading bases were set up at West African ports, but the European traders seldom ventured inland. The only white settlement in Africa occurred at the southern tip of the continent, where Dutch settlers, eventually adopting the name of "Boers," established farmsteads in the plains spreading out behind the Cape of Good Hope. Christian self-righteousness was the ideology of the Boers, as it had been of the Spanish and the French imperialists in America. But while the French and Spanish had set out with a Catholic mission to convert and rescue native souls, the Boers were equipped with an intolerant Calvinist faith that identified themselves as the saved and the natives they encountered as the damned, the distinction made crystal clear by God in His choice of skin color. The Boers were to prove the most tenacious of the colonialists: even today their subjects have not succeeded in dislodging their descendants, the Afrikaners of South Africa.

The Portuguese explorer Vasco da Gama opened the sea route from Europe to India, around the Cape of Good Hope, in 1498. A lively and profitable oceangoing trade followed. The Portuguese at times terrorized the Indians, killing and mutilating them and destroying their ships and their cities, but they did not rule them or settle on their territory. Their motive was commercial profit. India, the East Indies and other areas of Asia offered a wealth of merchandise for Europe, including both agricultural products and crafts. Indian cottons became prized possessions in European households, as did pottery and rugs. The most valued agricultural products from the east were spices and tea. Asia did not offer much of a market for European products, however. Since the Asians sold but did not buy very much, their treasuries gradually amassed much of the gold and silver that had found its way to Europe from the Americas. A global economy was beginning to form.

The Portuguese were succeeded in Asia by the other imperial powers—by the Dutch, the Swedes, the British, the French and the Danes. Seventeenth- and eighteenth-century trade with Asia was carried out usually by chartered trading companies, not directly by the European rulers. These were not companies as we know them today, but institutions given the authority by their crowns at home to establish order and to rule if necessary, in order to create profitable commercial relations. Eventually, the authority of the great crown companies was replaced by direct military and administrative rule by home govern-ments—but while they lasted, their existence made clear that the motive of imperialism was commercial.

By the middle of the eighteenth century, there was a worldwide imperial system of commerce. Cotton, spices, silk and tea from Asia mingled in European markets with ivory, gold and palm oil from Africa; furs, fish and timber from North America; and cotton, sugar and tobacco from both North and South America. The lucrative trade in enslaved human beings provided cheap labor where it was lacking. The profits accrued in Europe, increasingly in France and Britain, while the Portuguese, Spanish and then Dutch declined in relative power. It was a global network, made possible by the advancing tech-nology of the colonialists.

1776–1870: British Dominance and Withdrawal of Other Imperialists

Scholarly debate rages unchecked over the question of whether to view the century between 1776 and 1870 as a period of imperialist decline or of imperialist expansion. The conventional view, held by students across the ideological spectrum, has been to view it as a period of decline, the consequence being that the resurgence of imperialism after 1870 requires particular new explanations. The American Revolu-tion of 1776 divided the richest jewel of the British Empire from its homeland and led many in Britain to question the cost of maintaining an empire. As the eighteenth century ended and the nineteenth ensued,[2] it seemed to many in Britain that the country's trading com-panies were strong enough to prosper without needing any help from the government. The proponents of "free trade," who adopted the teachings of political economists Adam Smith and David Ricardo, argued that the British would be better off if the government withdrew its controls over trade and commerce. The British gradually disman-tled their system of protective tariffs and loosened their control over their colonies. The remaining settlements in British North America were defended against the United States in the War of 1812, but they were then increasingly granted self-government and left on their own, eventually to become the Dominion of Canada. Prime Minister Disraeli called the colonies, in a famous phrase, "millstones around our necks." The British withdrew from some of the territory they had adminis-tered—for example, the Orange Free State and Transvaal in South Africa—and intended to abandon more.

The contrary view is that the British imperialist thrust ceased not at all in the nineteenth century. If there was perhaps a loosening of administrative rigidity in some areas, it was only because economic dominance and commercial profit could proceed without it. Gallagher and Robinson, writing in 1953, coined the expressive term, "the imperialism of free trade." The concept is particularly apt in Latin America. As the Spanish and Portuguese power receded, and the South American countries became independent around 1820, they traded their formal legal imperial control for an informal, but no less dominating, informal rule by the British. From Mexico south to Argentina, the Latin American economies were structured increasingly to produce primary product exports for the British market—beef, sugar, coffee, gold, silver. The British ruled by the power of the purse, not by military force, but the power of the purse was even stronger, purchasing the allegiance of merchant middle classes.

Even in the middle of the nineteenth century the boundaries of the formal British Empire were expanded in places: there were annexations in Africa, in the Indian subcontinent, in Australia, in New Zealand and in British Columbia. Gallagher and Robinson pointed to conditions in the empire, not in the metropolitan center, as determining whether the formal boundaries of empire were to grow. If political conditions in an area of the empire were sufficiently stable to permit the unimpeded flow of trade, then annexation was an unnecessary expense. "Once entry had been forced into Latin America, China and the Balkans," they wrote, "the task was to encourage stable governments as good investment risks." But if rebellion, anarchy, or the challenge of another imperial power occurred, then the Crown needed to take over. The clue to understanding mid-Victorian imperialism was "trade with informal control if possible; trade with rule when necessary."[3]

The Gallagher and Robinson thesis, that imperialism continued vigorously although informally during the nineteenth century, is doubtless correct when applied solely to Britain. The British never withdrew from empire, and their spectacular economic growth in the nineteenth century gave them the ability to intensify their control over their colonies. But the clue to understanding mid-nineteenth-century imperialism is that it was almost exclusively British; the other countries of Europe, unable to compete with the British, did withdraw from much of their imperial territory. With the final defeat of Napoleon in 1815 the French retired as a world power. The Spanish and Portuguese had been declining. The 1820's saw the revolt of their Latin American colonies, and at the Congress of Verona in 1822 the British, whose ships by then had uncontested rule over the Atlantic Ocean, made it clear that they would not tolerate any further presence of the Spanish and Portuguese in the newly independent South American states. The American Monroe Doctrine of 1823 further excluded European colonies in the Americas. The British were the only world power left, and in the half-century from 1820 to 1870 they dominated the international economy with little threat to their position. They appeared to be indifferent to empire precisely because they were so strong. Beneath the surface their imperial authority was growing, administratively in India and informally but strongly in Latin America.

1870–1914: The "New Imperialism"

If the withdrawal of the British from imperialism in the middle of the nineteenth century was illusory, the withdrawal of the other European powers was quite real. The resurgence of European imperialism in the last quarter of the century was therefore a startling new phenomenon. Dubbed the "New Imperialism," it was quick, explosive and competitive. Besides the British, it involved the French, Belgians, Germans, Italians and Portuguese, as well as the Americans and the Japanese. Between 1878 and 1914 (when the onset of the First World War turned the Europeans' aggressive tendencies against each other), the imperial powers annexed 17 percent of the world's territory, at an average rate of 240,000 square miles a year.[4] The pace of acquisition was extraordinary.

Most dramatic was the scramble for Africa. The French carved out a massive empire stretching from North Africa bordering the Mediterranean Sea, through most of the western bulge of that continent, into central Equatorial Africa and the Congo. The British established control over the Gold Coast, Nigeria and other smaller areas of West Africa, as well as Kenya and Uganda in East Africa. They expanded through Egypt south into the Sudan and also occupied part of Somalia. From their colonies in southern Africa, the British also expanded north into the Rhodesias and Nyasaland. The Portuguese established control over Angola on the west side and Mozambique on the east side of southern Africa. King Leopold II of Belgium formed a private company in 1878, the International Congo Association, that was completely separate from the Belgian government; the association established control over the huge interior area of the Congo. The Germans carved out colonies in South West Africa, Cameroons and Tanganyika. The Italians took control of Libya in North Africa and Eritrea and part of Somaliland in the east.

The ruler of the newly formed German nation, Count Otto von Bismarck, called a conference of the imperialist powers in Berlin in 1885 to establish some order among the wolves in their dismemberment of Africa south of the Sahara desert. Certain rules of conquest were agreed to, and the pace of the imperial acquisitions accelerated. Before 1870 Africa had been the unknown continent; within a few short years it was completely divided into spheres of European influence. The boundaries of the colonies were entirely arbitrary, reflecting only the accidents of military and exploratory expeditions; they bore no relationship to tribal ethnicities, to natural geographic boundaries or to economic realities.

The parceling out of sub-Saharan Africa was the most dramatic event of the New Imperialism, but it was not the only one. Closer to the borders of Europe an imperialist struggle unfolded over the remnants of the great Ottoman, or Turkish, Empire. The multiethnic and religiously tolerant Ottoman Empire stretched from the Balkans through Turkey to the Russian steppes, and thence through Persia, Palestine and Egypt across the southern shore of the Mediterranean to Algeria and Morocco. In the nineteenth century its internal communications weakened, its administration became more rigid and it fell behind the Europeans technologically. As its power ebbed, some of its outlying areas were snatched off by the European imperialists. The Russo-Turkish War of 1877 led to the separation of much of the Balkan peninsula north of Greece from the Ottoman Empire. The Suez Canal was completed in 1869, and to protect it the British occupied Egypt in 1882, an occupation thought to be temporary at the time but which lasted until 1956. The French expanded into North Africa, with colonies in Algeria and Morocco and a protectorate over Tunisia. The weakness of Turkey, and its inability to modernize itself at a pace to keep abreast of its European neighbors, led to continuous struggles for its territories and eventually to the outbreak of the First World War in 1914. The Ottomans joined the losing side of that war and consequently suffered the complete dismemberment of their empire in the postwar peace settlement. Turkey was established as a small republic confined to Asia Minor, while the remaining territories of the empire became mandates under the supervision of the League of Nations: Syria and Lebanon controlled by France, Palestine and Iraq by Britain.

In the Indian subcontinent, the late nineteenth century saw an intensification of British control. The British government had taken over rule from the East India Company in 1858 following the Indian Mutiny, and thereafter British administration stretched with the railway the breadth of India. In 1885, to counter a threat from the French, the British annexed Burma, across the Bay of Bengal from India, and they also established a protectorate in the Malay States. Further east, the French established control over a major portion of Southeast Asia, including Cochin China (later Vietnam) and Laos. The Dutch, long the dominant power in the East Indies, consolidated their control over the vast archipelago that became known as Indonesia.

The interior of China was not occupied during the nineteenth century, but the imperial powers dominated it. In the so-called Opium Wars of 1839–42, the British broke down the Chinese refusal to trade with the imperial powers and forced the Chinese to import opium. Tariffs on other goods fell, and foreigners were given permanent rights in a number of treaty ports. The ruling Manchu dynasty declined in strength throughout the nineteenth century and was militarily defeated by the Japanese in 1894–95. The British, French, Germans and Russians, determined to retain their rights to Chinese trade, were unwilling, however, to permit Japanese hegemony in the area. The United States, which by the late 1890's was an important Pacific military power, announced its Chinese policy of an Open Door in 1898, under which annexation would be disallowed and all of the imperial countries would have trading rights and other legal privileges. What it amounted to was that the Chinese were permitted to keep their own governmental and administrative structure, but that structure was controlled by outside countries in a particularly demeaning way. Not only were all Europeans removed from the jurisdiction of Chinese courts of law, but so were all Chinese who had disputes with Europeans.

In the Americas, the late nineteenth century saw a continuation of British hegemony, and it also saw the growth of U.S. imperialism. By the Monroe Doctrine of 1823, the United States had announced its interest in Latin America and its unwillingness to allow the resumption of European imperialism in the western hemisphere. In the Mexican War of 1845, the United States annexed half of Mexico, the territory stretching from Texas to California. In 1898, the United States went to war with Spain, easily winning and thereby ending Spain's four centuries of American empire. As a consequence of the war, Cuba became independent but under the protection of the United States by virtue of the Platt Amendment. Puerto Rico and the Philippines were annexed directly by the United States. In a separate action, the United States annexed Hawaii in 1898.

The Pacific islands were partitioned among the imperialists in the 1880's and 1890's. The British established rights over parts of New Guinea and over numerous smaller island groups, including the Gilbert and Ellice Islands and the Cook Islands. The Germans also had holdings in New Guinea, along with the Solomons, the Carolines, the Marshalls, Samoa and others. The French possessions included Tahiti and a shared dominion with the British over New Hebrides.

By the early twentieth century almost all of the world was under effective control; the empires were complete. The United States had effected a transition from colony to imperial power, and Japan was beginning to exercise control over adjacent areas on the Asian mainland. The British domains were divided into two parts: areas of white settlement that were achieving independence from the mother country, and areas with predominantly nonwhite populations that were being administered more tightly. Latin America was for the most part nominally independent but under the effective control of British commerce and investment. Sub-Saharan Africa and North Africa were carved into European colonies, as was most of Asia and the Pacific. China, while not completely colonized, was humbled and controlled by the Europeans. It was the high point of European power, the culmination of four centuries of expansion. It seemed destined to continue;

there was hardly a hint that it would not. Any prediction at the time that the European empires would crumble in a few short decades would have seemed bizarre.

The Causes of Imperialism

A great deal of ink has been spilled on the question of why the nations of Europe created empires around the world—and in particular why there was such an orgy of imperialist gluttony at the end of the nineteenth century. In 1902, the British economist J. A. Hobson ascribed the New Imperialism to underconsumption, that is, to the failure of the European masses to buy the goods produced by European industry. As a consequence, the European industrialists had to export their capital abroad in search of new markets—and to secure those capital investments and markets they needed to acquire imperial control. A socialist reformer, Hobson argued that imperialism would be ended if income at home was redistributed from the rich to the poor, so that ordinary people had the resources to buy the capitalists' output.

V. I. Lenin's 1917 tract, *Imperialism, the Highest Stage of Capitalism*, used some of Hobson's analysis, but with a more ominous twist. Lenin believed that mature capitalism necessarily led to rich monopolists on the one hand and to impoverished workers on the other. As Marx had predicted, the capitalist system was about to collapse because the workers could not buy the industrial products. Lenin argued that the export of capital to foreign lands, or imperialism, represented the last, futile attempt of the capitalist system to avoid its demise. Lenin, of course, was not a reformer like Hobson but a revolutionary, and he did not believe that the capitalist-imperialist system was capable of rescuing itself.

The Hobson-Lenin thesis fails ultimately as an explanation of late-nineteenth-century imperialism because, although the Europeans invested heavily abroad, very little of their investments went to the newly acquired colonies; a great deal more of it went to the Americas and to India. In particular, almost none of the European foreign investment went to Africa, where the greatest acquisitions of territory occurred.

A more promising economic explanation of late-nineteenth-century imperialism is the voracious demand of the industrializing countries for raw materials and for food imports from the world's tropical areas. Some have argued that it was their fear of being cut off from their sources of supply that led the imperialist countries to acquire territories. Other writers have explored military strategy as a cause of imperialism, most importantly the need of each European power to establish a worldwide system of naval bases and of military supplies. Gallagher and Robinson, as noted above, pointed to conditions in the colonies themselves: the main motive of imperial expansion was to quell disorder among the natives. The economist Joseph Schumpeter advanced the most anti-economic thesis of all. Imperialism made no sense economically, he argued; as any classical economist could demonstrate, free trade, unfettered by any government controls, was the most profitable. Imperialism therefore represented an atavistic throwback to an earlier, irrational era.

These attempts to explain late-nineteenth-century imperialism are all useful, if partial. Behind them, however, lies the unexpressed assumption that imperialism is an anomaly, that it is unusual for a powerful country to exert political, military, economic and cultural dominance over weaker peoples. If it is unusual, it must be explained by some unique coincidence of forces.

But imperialism is not exceptional at all. To a large extent the history of civilizations is the history of empires. Greeks, Romans, Mongols, the Ming dynasty, Ottoman Turks, Tartars, Aztecs, Incas and countless other peoples established dominance over strangers. At times they conquered nearby lands and eventually incorporated them into their own country. In other cases their empires were far flung and never fully integrated. Even today, the Soviet Union is in effect the Russian empire, albeit a crumbling one. The United States was created as an empire, expanding across a large portion of an entire continent, displacing native Americans and Mexicans and annexing territories in the Atlantic and Pacific oceans.

Empires are the normal way in which political power is exercised, not the exception. A system of independent, autonomous, sovereign nation states, that is to say, the system of world organization that most of us think of as the norm, is actually quite exceptional. It has never really existed before the present. Greek and Roman times knew city states and empires, but not nation states. European nation states were created in the breakup of medieval feudalism over several centuries, and the process of European nation-building was not really completed until just over a century ago, with the unification of Germany and Italy in 1870-71. One should think of Europe as being organized into nation states only for a period of generations, not for time immemorial. In the Third World, it would be a complete anachronism to think of the areas ruled by the imperialists as having been divided into countries prior to their conquest. India was ruled by shifting coalitions of princely hegemonies; Africa was organized predominantly along ethnic, tribal lines without clear geographical boundaries; China was itself an empire. The current nation states of the Third World were created as a consequence of the disintegration of the European empires; they did not predate the empires.

Living in the late twentieth century, one thinks of the nation state as almost a sacred entity, worthy of one's patriotism, with legitimate power to command lives and allegiances. From this perspective, empires—the dominance of one people over another people—seem illegitimate, illegal and in every respect reprehensible. Empires may be reprehensible, because they institutionalize oppression and dominance, but they are not exceptional. It is not just the Third World that has been formed by imperialism: it is the whole world. European culture resulted from the Hellenistic empire, from the Roman Empire and, in the Middle Ages, from the Holy Roman Empire. Canada, the United States, Australia and New Zealand are creatures of the British Empire. Empires have been the dominant force of social change in history and have formed the world's civilizations. Imperialism is the means by which the world was integrated, technology was transferred and adapted and the social organizations within which we live were established.

The fundamental cause of imperialism, then, lies not in the particular structure of late-nineteenth-century capitalism, or in a particular strategic competition, but in the existence of unequal power. Throughout human history, strong powers have dominated the weak. Unequal power can generally be traced to the uneven development of technology. Almost without exception, the imperial centers have been those that have developed the most advanced military technology and productive methods. The Assyrians, the Greeks, the Romans and, in modern times, the Europeans all had access to technology that was superior to that of other peoples. They used this technology to dominate and exploit their neighbors, for their own benefit. Their imperialism was masked with idealism—they persuaded themselves that they had the sacred mission of expanding civilization, or salvation, or economic development, or peace—but what lay at the base of each instance of imperialism was simply the dominance of the weak by the powerful.

The age of European imperialism, the imperialism that created the modern Third World, should be seen therefore as one phase in an unending stream of imperialisms that constitutes world history. It was unique principally in the fact that it was the first imperialism to cover the entire globe. The British Empire was the first to be able to claim that the sun never set upon it. It stretched from Ireland to North America through the Caribbean Sea and Latin America, over much of Africa, the Middle East, the Indian subcontinent, parts of China and islands of the Pacific Ocean both great and small. The Spanish, the Portuguese, the Dutch, the French, the Germans, the Italians and, more lately, the Americans all established geographically dispersed empires as well. What allowed them to dominate the whole globe, as the earlier empires had not, was the tremendous development of science and technology that spurred the growth of capitalism. It was technology that allowed small groups of adventurers, soldiers and settlers to dominate vast millions. Cortez conquered Mexico with only a few hundred men because of the superior weaponry and horsemanship he commanded. Very small numbers of British were able to rule the millions of Indians because their garrisons had modern arms.

Never before the period of European hegemony had the growth of technology been so rapid, and so constant. While previous empires had enjoyed technological advantage, that advantage had been for the most part static, unchanging. Now change became the only constant as the method of scientific experimentation came to be applied to all sectors of human endeavor, including agriculture, crafts, manufacturing, weaponry, shipbuilding, power sources and on and on. An explosion of technology transformed the European world by raising standards of living to undreamed heights and transformed the Third World by allowing imperial control of it. Imperialism in turn fed the growth of the European economies, providing them at various times with plundered gold and silver, with commercial profits for investment in domestic enterprises, with a cheap source of primary products and raw materials and with an outlet for profitable investment. From the very moment that Europe began to cast off the constraints of the stagnant Middle Ages and to develop its economic and technical resources, it began also to dominate the world. This domination created the conditions that exist now in the Third World.

What seems to be the strange history of nineteenth-century imperialism can be understood rather simply. After Napoleon's defeat in 1815 and the independence of the Spanish and Portuguese American colonies around 1820, all the European countries except Britain were in a process of withdrawal from their imperialist adventures. Why did the British continue to expand while their competitors withdrew? The answer is that the industrial revolution began in Britain in the late eighteenth century; by the early and mid-nineteenth century the system of manufacturing in factories, using water and steam power, gave the British an enormous advantage in economic and military strength. No other country could dare to challenge the British. In fact, British strength was so dominant that it could appear in some respects to withdraw from empire, while retaining control over an entire world system of trade.

The New Imperialism of the late-nineteenth century, which involved competition among many countries, followed from the fact that the other countries caught up with Britain technologically. The French, the Germans, the Russians, the Americans, the Japanese—all learned from the British, copying their industrial methods and improving upon them, achieving their own industrial revolutions 50 to 100 years later. By the late-nineteenth century they were on a par with the British. Not until the twentieth century would Britain actually fall behind her competitors, but by 1880 the competitors had reached such strength that Britain could no longer dominate world commerce. As soon as the other European countries became industrialized, and as soon as their strength approached Britain's, they too sought empires. The British, of course, were not about to surrender their preeminence, and so they also were forced to become more aggressive.

The New Imperialism resulted therefore not from some particular feature of mature capitalism, as Hobson and Lenin surmised, but from the emergence onto the world scene of a multitude of industrial powers, jealous of each other and vying for advantage. These countries competed at first overseas in their empires, and later in the catastrophic First World War.

The Culture of Imperialism

The legacy of the European imperialist age is pervasive, extending to every area of culture and economy. No part of that legacy is more permanent or personal than the transformation of language. In most regions of the Third World the common and official language is not a native language at all, but the European language of the imperialist. This is not the case universally, the most notable exceptions being China and the Arab Middle East. China retained its linguistic uniqueness because it was not completely occupied by the imperialists, and also because its own two principal languages, Mandarin and Cantonese, are spoken by such a large number of people. In the Middle East, Arabic was spoken over such a wide area, and had such status, that it could not be displaced. But most other peoples of the Third World were invaded thoroughly by European languages. The common languages of Latin America are Spanish and Portuguese. Although numerous native American languages persist in Latin America, they are spoken in isolated pockets and lack the power to facilitate communication between large numbers of people. Rigoberta Menchu cannot communicate with most of the other people of the Guatemalan Highlands, because they speak twenty-two different ethnic languages. In the Caribbean islands, English and French are spoken along with Spanish. Most Africans speak a European language in addition to an ethnic language, and the European languages are the official languages of the independent countries, be they French, English or Portuguese. The common language of the Indian subcontinent, made up today of India, Pakistan and Bangladesh, is English. Hindi is recognized as an official language of India, but it lacks the universality to unite the country, as English does. Some countries have rejected their colonial languages; the Indonesians no longer use Dutch, and the Vietnamese no longer use French. But the Philippines, incorporated into the fledgling American empire less than a century ago, uses English as a common tongue.

The indigenous languages persist—they are the languages of the local marketplace and of the home—but they do not often function in national communications or in government or official discourse. The European language is often promoted by the central government as a way of overcoming tribal and ethnic divisiveness and of encouraging national unity.

The displacement of native by foreign languages was a consequence of the unequal power of the imperialist confrontation. With very few exceptions, the imperialists refused to learn the local languages and essentially forced the native people to learn theirs.

The imperialist languages do bring the people of the Third World into communication with the ideas and information of the broader world. They allow the novelists, poets, songwriters, scholars, journalists and diplomats of the Third World to address a worldwide audience. But there is a tremendous price to be paid for the abandonment of one's own language.

Languages run as deep as the soul, and they are not, in their most basic functions, translatable. A European or American who has tried to translate Shakespeare into French, or Molière into English, knows that the subtle nuances are lost, transformed into something else. How much greater the shock in moving from Xhosa (a southern African language) into English. Xhosa is the language of the spirits, of the ancestors, of the forests and the plains and of the gods of the rivers. There is no translation into English that can save these concepts as anything other than museum pieces.

Some ideas that are fundamental in Third World cultures cannot be thought in the imperialist's language. Among the Managalase, for example, an ethnic group of 6,000 people in New Guinea, marriage negotiations are extraordinarily delicate occasions, conducted entirely in the rhetoric of allegory and metaphor. Skillful use of the language is required, to avoid open embarrassment of any of the parties and to advance ideas into the public discourse without appearing to have made them directly. If anything goes wrong with the linguistic interactions, the marriage can collapse, and with it political alignments within the community.[5] Without the Managalase language, the marriage negotiations would be impossible.

When the imperialists imposed their languages, therefore, they stole ways of thinking from Third World people and replaced them with their own. By refusing to learn the local languages and to accept them on an equal basis, they planted a sense of psychological and cultural inferiority among their subjects. It was in a way the ultimate imperialism: mind control. The damage continues in the postimperialist age, as the European languages grow stronger and the ethnic languages weaker.

Along with language came the traditions and cultures of the conquerors. The conflict between the imported culture and the native one was long and protracted, and it is not over yet. But the imported culture is on the advance, the local one in retreat. Laura Nader, the University of California social anthropologist, tells the seemingly benign story of the Kaiser Aluminum Company's setting up a plant in the interior of Ghana and providing medical benefits for its employees and their dependents. The workers welcomed the medical benefits and assumed they would be available to all of the members of their extended families, that is to say, dozens, and in some cases even hundreds, of people. Sorry, said the company, its generosity did not extend quite that far, just the *nuclear* family please—the husband, wife and their children. But the nuclear family was not a relevant concept to the people of this ethnic group. So in order to be eligible for medical care, the workers had to make artificial divisions in their families, creating distinctions and privileges where none had existed before. The company was not consciously evil; quite the contrary, in its own eyes it was beneficent, and proud of it. But it was the more powerful of the two cultures, and its effect on the local family structure was catastrophic. There are many examples, of course, in which the imperial power was not so beneficent.

One of the most powerful tools of cultural disruption that the imperialists brought with them was their Christian religion. Christianity, whether of the Catholic or Protestant variant, provided the imperialists with an aura of superiority and a sense of mission. The aura of superiority is not surprising; every religion gives its adherents the conviction that they have the truth. But the sense of mission was particularly harmful. Christianity was not willing to coexist with other faiths; it demanded conversions. The conversion was a highly charged symbolic moment in which the new adherent rejected his sinful, error-filled past and adopted the new dogma. We know that many of the converts to the imperialists' religion went through the ceremony with proverbially crossed fingers, and that Christianity in fact coexisted in many souls with a wide variety of other beliefs. Nevertheless, the basic Christian intolerance of other worldviews meant that converts frequently experienced a massive shift in belief systems.

The traditional religions that the imperialists encountered varied a great deal from culture to culture, but a common thread among most was that they grew organically out of the daily lives of the people. They provided an explanation of the rhythms of ordinary life; in fact, there was frequently no real distinction between the spiritual life and the daily life of work and family. Christianity cut this unity asunder because it was a foreign belief system with foreign symbols and artifacts; its god was the god of the conquerors, not the god of the local soil and the nearby river. Christianity supported in subtle and not so subtle ways the authority of the imperialists; it cloaked their actions in a veil of respectability.

Shortly before his murder by the police, Steven Biko, the leader of South Africa's Black Consciousness movement, discussed the influence of Christianity on his people. His description could apply to many other areas of the Third World:

> We as blacks cannot forget the fact that Christianity in Africa is tied up with the entire colonial process. This meant that Christians came here with a form of culture which they called Christian but which in effect was Western, and which expressed itself as an imperial culture as far as Africa was concerned. Here the missionaries did not make the proper distinctions. This important matter can easily be illustrated by relatively small things. Take the question of dress, for example. When an African became Christian, as a rule he or she was expected to drop traditional garb and dress like a Westerner. The same with many customs dear to blacks, which they were expected to drop for supposed "Christian" reasons while in effect they were only in conflict with certain Western mores. . . . Black theology does not challenge Christianity itself but its Western package, in order to discover what the Christian faith means for our continent.[6]

Even when the Christian missionaries failed to convert the heathens, they often succeeded in disrupting their societies, by sowing seeds of mistrust in their own belief systems and by introducing alien ideas. In *Arrow of God*, the Nigerian novelist Chinua Achebe weaves a rich tale of how a Christian mission confounded the villagers' beliefs in their local gods. Ezeulu, the priest of the paramount god Ulu, has the responsibility each year of calling the harvest festival, the Feast of the New Yam. He knows when to call it, because at each new moon during the year he has eaten one of thirteen sacred yams that have been stored from the previous festival—when all of the yams are eaten it is time for the new festival and the harvest. This year, however, Ezeulu has been imprisoned by the British colonial authorities for more than a month and has consequently missed eating a sacred yam at two new moons. He refuses to call the festival until the yams are eaten. This refusal, which he regards as an act of obedience to Ulu, threatens to throw the village into chaos, since the yams that have been planted will rot in the ground if they are not harvested on time. The missionary, Goodcountry, provides a "solution" to the village's problem by having the Christian church sponsor a harvest festival. Goodcountry assures the villagers that if they take part in the Christian festival and harvest their crops, his god will protect them against the wrath of Ulu. He thereby succeeds in separating the village from its traditional priest and its traditional god. Achebe closes his novel with these sentences:

> The Christian harvest . . . saw more people than even Goodcountry could have dreamed. In his extremity many an Umuaro man had sent his son with a yam or two to offer to the new religion and to

bring back the promised immunity. Thereafter any yam that was harvested in the man's fields was harvested in the name of the son.[7]

Christianity provided a moral cloak that could mask the destruction wrought by the imperialists. Massacres were justified in Latin America on the grounds that they led to the advancement of the Christian faith. In the California missions, Spanish padres held native Americans in virtual slavery, while apparently persuading themselves that they were saving their souls. In China in the nineteenth century Christian missionaries encouraged the addiction of millions of people to the opium that was imported by the British.

Not all of the effects of Christianity in the Third World were negative; in fact the balance of gains and losses is complex. Note that Steven Biko's statement quoted above does not condemn Christianity per se, but rather the association between Christianity and western imperialism. The Christian churches with their messages of redemption have provided a tool to many Third World groups in their struggles for self-determination. In South Africa, where almost all African organizations were banned until recently by the white government, the Protestant churches and their leaders stood out as centers of black resistance. In Latin America, the local Catholic clergy with their "liberation theology" inspire hope and resistance among the poor. But the losses, and the costs, have been staggering.

The Europeans brought with them not only their religion, but their secular ideologies, too. The early Spanish, Portuguese, Dutch and French colonizers carried with them a belief in autocracy, monarchy, even the divine right of kings. It was an ideology that oppressed the common people at home, and that oppressed the colonial natives even more heavily. But by the nineteenth and early twentieth centuries, the reigning European ideologies had liberalized. It is one of the marvelous ironies of imperialism that it brought to the Third World the very ideas that would eventually liberate it—the ideas of freedom, equality, democracy, socialism and revolution. Social movements in the Third World took these European ideas, adopted and melded them sometimes with indigenous belief systems, and used them in the struggle against imperialist control.

The story of Indian independence illustrates the use of British ideology, combined with Indian beliefs, to defeat the British. The great Indian nationalist and spiritual leader, Mohandas Gandhi, was trained in London as a lawyer and became thoroughly committed to the doctrines of English common law that bestow unchallengeable rights of legal equality on all subjects of the Crown. After leaving England, he discovered that British imperial practice deviated from the common law when he experienced severe racial discrimination against Indians in the Union of South Africa. In response to racism and in order to secure the *British* right of equality, he developed the attitudes and techniques of nonviolent resistance. He later used this system to lead the movement for Indian independence. The rights he was asserting were a part of British doctrine, not Indian. Indian society, with its rigid caste system rooted in Hindu scripture, certainly did not recognize the equality of all people. The Gandhian nonviolent resistance movement had a base in Indian culture, but Gandhi was deeply influenced also by the writings of the American philosopher Henry David Thoreau. Gandhi combined these initially foreign ideas with his own religion, Hinduism, and that of his brothers and sisters in India, Islam, to fashion a compelling social movement that eventually drove the British from India and captured the imagination and allegiance of people throughout the world. The story of Gandhi is a particularly apt one for illustrating the interconnectedness of the world, for in leading the more recent revolution in race relations in the United States, the Reverend Martin Luther King, Jr., turned to the example of Gandhi, using Indian ideas that in turn had their antecedents in London and in Massachusetts. Imperialism opened the Third World to the liberating ideas that would eventually bring about its defeat.

Liberalism was not the only ideological export of the imperialists. Socialism and Marxism found their way to the colonies in short order, too. Ho Chi Minh, the future leader of the Vietnamese communist revolution, developed his ideas in the working class cafés of Paris' Left Bank and from the insurrectionary French journals published in the years after the First World War. He traveled to Moscow in the early years of the Russian revolution, soaking up the ideas of Marx and Lenin. The movement that he led for decades in Southeast Asia was a mixture of classic Marxism with traditional Vietnamese patriotism.

China's revolutionary leader Mao Tse-tung did not travel to an imperialist center, but he steeped himself in the communist ideology emanating from Europe. The successful communist revolution he led was based on Marxist principles, although he adapted them broadly to the Chinese reality. Most importantly, what was a doctrine of urban, working-class revolution in Russia became the practice of rural, peasant revolution in China. But if Chinese communism had its own tints, it was, first of all, communism, the doctrine of Karl Marx, a German scholar.

Almost all of the social movements of the Third World have had this character: adapting ideas from the center of Europe to the local conditions. In recent years the most significant exception to this rule has been the Iranian revolution of the Ayatollah Khomeini, based solidly in fundamentalist Islamic doctrine and rejecting any hint of European ideology. So also the genocidal extremism of the Khmer Rouge movement in Cambodia represented a radical turning away from foreign doctrines. Still, the exceptionalism of these cases shows all the more clearly how, in most instances, the Third World has adapted the ideas of its oppressors.

The Foundations of Third World Poverty

In the economic sphere, the legacy of imperialism is central. The dependency theorists are correct in insisting that imperialism formed the economic structures of the Third World, which even today leave the vast majority of the human race in desperately poor conditions.

An earlier section argued that the existence of European imperialism can be explained primarily by unequal power, that is, by the military, technological and economic strength of the Europeans in contrast to the relative weakness of what became the Third World. The fact that the late-nineteenth-century European economies had a particular capitalist structure is much less important than Hobson, Lenin and their followers claimed. Imperialism would have occurred anyway, as long as European technology was dominant, even if the European societies had had a different sort of noncapitalist structure.

When we turn to the other side of the story, however, to the effects of imperialism upon the economies and societies of Asia, the Middle East, Africa and Latin America, then the fact that the imperialists were capitalist is centrally important. The essence of capitalism is alienation. The factors of production—land, labor and capital—are treated in a capitalist system as commodities, to be bought or sold. They are not part of a person's birthright. In many peasant societies, in contrast, the factors of production are inherently connected as part of an integrated system. A person is born to a village society and automatically cultivates land passed down from one generation to the next, using the product to sustain the family. These peasants, although usually exploited by a landowning or ruling class, are nonetheless secure in knowing their place in the world. The advent of imperialism broke this world apart, creating labor forces that worked for wages on other people's projects, and land that could be bought and sold. Imperialism converted the peasants of the Third World into separate components of the capitalist system, components whose survival depended upon the vagaries of global markets over which they had no control.

Before the arrival of the imperialists, the majority of the people of the Third World were involved in producing food for their own use—as hunters and gatherers in some regions, but for the most part as cultivators of the soil. They typically produced some surplus food, over and above their own needs, which was used to support a ruling group, but this was usually a small portion of their production. For the most part, they produced what they needed to survive. Imperialism changed this picture. It did not totally displace subsistence production, of course, because people still had to eat; on top of subsistence production, however, the imperialists imposed the production of primary export commodities—agricultural goods and minerals from the colonies that were intended for use in the metropolitan centers. The colonies were turned into a vast production system for sugar, cacao, tobacco, wheat, cotton, meat, fish, jute, coffee, coconuts, rubber, wool, palm oil, rice, bananas, ground nuts, indigo, tin, gold, silver, bauxite, copper and many more products.

As Europe developed its manufacturing industries in the nineteenth century, and as its own peasants were drawn off the land and into its unspeakable cities, it required new sources of primary agricultural commodities—both to feed the urban labor force and to provide raw materials for the factories. It was no coincidence, then, that colonial export production intensified at the same time that capitalist industrial production was growing in Europe; the colonial exports were required for the growth of industry at the imperial centers.

Imperialism produced a world of economic specialization: manufacturing in the core of Europe and agricultural and mining production in the periphery of the Third World. The doctrines of free trade and comparative advantage, noted in Chapter 3, provided an intellectual justification for this specialization. Free trade and economic specialization were to the advantage of every country, taught classical economist David Ricardo, even if some countries were more efficient in the production of *every* good, and some countries less efficient. What mattered was relative efficiency, or comparative advantage. A poor colonial economy might be less efficient in the production of crops than Britain was, but provided that its disadvantage in crops was less serious than its disadvantage in manufacturing, both it and Britain would be better off if it specialized in agricultural production, shipping its surplus crops off as exports to Britain and importing British manufactures. It was a lovely theory, promising benefits from international trade to all participants.

One of the lasting puzzles of economic history is to assess whether this Ricardian theory of comparative advantage really worked. One fact is clear; as Ricardo and his followers posed the theory it is far too narrow. It is easy, and even trivial, to grant the main conclusion of the Ricardians, that at any given time a country will do better by specializing in those goods for which it has a comparative advantage. The more difficult question is whether that specialization will be to the benefit of a poor country in the long run. In fact, the economic case to be made against imperialism is that the specialization of the colonies in primary production impoverished them in the long run, by making their economies incapable of sustained economic development.

The case against comparative advantage, and against the world division of production brought about by the imperialists, is not entirely easy to make, because there are obvious counterexamples. Canada is the best of the counterexamples. From the sixteenth century through to the twentieth, Canada fit precisely into the imperialist economic mode: it produced primary products for export to Europe, and it imported European manufactured goods. On the basis of those primary exports it was successful; it developed into one of the richest countries in the world, with a standard of living higher than most European countries. Canada developed its economy to a high level by exploiting a series of primary exports, or "staples." In the sixteenth century the French discovered the rich fisheries off the coast of Newfoundland. Their successors ventured inland, eventually across the entire continent, in search of beaver furs, which were processed into felt hats for European consumers. The fur trade was succeeded by timber, and then by the greatest staple export of all, wheat. In the twentieth century, wheat was supplemented by minerals. Immigrants flocked to the new land to develop each staple export as it came along. The income they generated was used both to raise their standard of living and to reinvest in productive activities designed for local use. In Canada, primary exports became the engine of sustained economic growth. A national manufacturing sector grew up behind the staples to meet the needs of the local settlers, and in this way Canada developed a technologically advanced, productive modern economy.

To cite the Canadian example is to show, however, how exceptional it was, for the export industries established in most of the rest of the colonial world did not lead automatically to self-sustaining economic growth for the local population. Far more often they led to poverty, to destitution on the land and to urbanization without hope. Even in Argentina, which for many decades resembled Canada, and by as late as the 1920's had a higher standard of living based upon its beef export industry, stagnation eventually set in.

The best answer to the question of why the concentration on colonial agricultural export production led to stagnation in the Third World instead of to prosperity as in Canada lies in the fact that the exports transformed the social structures of the Third World (but not of Canada) in such a way as to render genuine economic development less likely. The heart of social transformation in the Third World was the fact that the local labor force, or the land, or both, had to be wrested, often forcibly, from their existing uses. The problem of forcibly changing the use of local labor and land did not arise in Canada, because in that colony the native population was either exterminated or shunted off to reservations, leaving behind them lands that for the most part had never been tilled. But in the Third World, the local populations generally stayed and were in possession of the land.

The colonialists in the Third World often confronted intensive labor shortages. Frequently the local people did not constitute the sort of labor force that capitalist enterprises required; they were not willing to give up their subsistence pursuits and work for wages—at least not for the low wages normally offered by the white man. In some cases forced labor of the local people resulted in many deaths—for example, in the mines and plantations of the Spanish empire in Latin America. The slave trade was the first answer to this problem—millions of Africans were shipped to the western hemisphere—until it was effectively shut down towards the beginning of the nineteenth century. As the nineteenth century progressed, however, the need for colonial labor only increased, so other expedients were developed. Indentured service, or the labor contract, became common; it was a system by which a person made the commitment to work in a foreign land for a period of years in return for a guaranteed wage and a return passage home. Indentured Indians, Chinese and other Asians were shipped long distances to work in semifree conditions in the imperialist plantations. Many did not return to their homelands, and their descendants today create ethnic heterogeneity in many areas of the Third World.

In addition to importing labor, the Europeans devised ways of forcing the local people to work for them. In Indonesia the Dutch established the "culture system," a kind of throwback to European medieval feudalism, by which native people were required to devote a certain portion of their land and labor to the production of export products, these to take the place of taxes. A common technique in Africa and elsewhere was to impose a hut tax or a head tax. These were taxes that had to be paid in the imperialist's currency by each person. But the peasants did not earn or use this currency in their villages. So in order to pay the tax they had to earn the currency, and in order to earn the currency they had to work as laborers for the white man. The head tax led to the pernicious colonial theory of the "backward-bending supply curve of labor": the lower the wage rate the longer the natives would work, since their goal was to earn a certain fixed amount in order to be able to pay the hut tax. It was a system of forced labor, pure and simple. Frequently taxes did not induce sufficient work, however, and they were supplemented by more direct means: the compulsion of labor by military force. The use of armed force by King Leopold of Belgium in the Congo to create a labor force was particularly notorious.

The formation of a capitalist labor force, an army of labor working for wages, has never been an easy process. European historians, from Marx onward, have documented the terror, bloodshed and misery imposed as European feudal peasants were forced off the land to which they had common-law rights and into the filthy cities and deadly early factories. In the colonies the goal was somewhat different—to move the peasants from subsistence village life into commercial agriculture—but the process was often equally devastating. At least in Europe the descendants of the displaced peasants have eventually come to enjoy rising incomes; for most people in the Third World there has been no payoff to speak of so far.

If the accumulation of a labor force was a problem, the amassing of land to be used by capitalist enterprises for export crops was often even more difficult. Most of the land was, of course, already occupied. The Europeans were faced with the need either to expel the local people from the most fertile land, or to persuade them to grow export crops in their villages. Expulsion was often the order of the day. In some parts of southern and East Africa, settlers carved out farms reminiscent of European commercial farms. The Boers at the Cape, and later in the Orange Free State and the Transvaal, and the English settlers in the highlands of Kenya worked cattle ranches and wheat farms, hiring African labor in limited numbers to help them. The land distribution in southern and East Africa became unbelievably skewed, with the Europeans, a small proportion of the population, owning the great majority of the land and the Africans crowded into small areas with inferior soil.

Far more common were the large plantations, in Africa and Asia owned and overseen by Europeans and worked exclusively by natives. In the nominally independent countries of nineteenth-century Latin America, the plantation owners (or *hacendados*) were generally local people, but of pure Spanish or Portuguese descendence, while the peons were of native or mixed race. Plantations were created for rubber in Malaya, for rice in Vietnam, for tea in India, for coffee in the Belgian Congo, for bananas in Honduras, for sugar in Cuba, for cocoa in the Gold Coast and for many other crops throughout the colonies. Landholding patterns became incredibly unequal; it was common in many areas of the Third World for a scant 1 or 2 percent of the landowners to control at least half of the arable land. The land available for peasant use was reduced proportionately and, of course, many of the peasants, having lost their land, had to work as wage laborers, usually for very low wages, on the great plantations.

Export crops were often grown by village peasants along with their subsistence crops. It was the essence of the Dutch "culture system" in Java, for example, to require this kind of dual agriculture by the peasants. The system was not confined to Indonesia. Cotton and rice were grown by Egyptian peasants, wheat in India, palm oil in the Congo, ground nuts in French West Africa. It was common, in fact, for the same crop to be grown by both plantations and independent peasants in the same area. Malayan rubber, for example, was grown both on large-scale plantations and in small scattered plots.

The imperialist world economy, and the insatiable demand of European industrialization for food and raw materials, therefore transformed the agricultural sectors of the Third World, where the great majority of the populations were located. Imperialism forced millions of people to migrate, it separated masses of people from the land and recreated them as wage laborers and it brought village-based, peasant agriculture into world markets.

In assessing this tremendous impact, it is helpful to return to the comparison of the Third World with Canada, since Canada parlayed a succession of primary exports into steady economic growth and one of the world's highest standards of living. Why did the concentration on primary exports not pay similar dividends in the Third World? It is a puzzle. Some of the answers that have been given to it over the years seem not very satisfying. Raúl Prebisch and some other Latin American economists argued that the problem was declining terms of trade—essentially that the prices of primary products were falling in world markets to such an extent that, even though Third World countries were selling more and more, they were earning less and less and could afford fewer imports of manufactured goods. The argument is valid for some primary exports and for some countries, over some time periods, but recent scholarship has shown conclusively that as a general explanation for the continuing poverty of the Third World it collapses. Certainly it cannot be a general explanation for the poverty of primary exporters, for if it were, Canada would be poverty stricken as well.

Another line of argument has been that the imperialists and their successors sent the profits that they earned back to their homelands, rather than reinvesting those profits in local enterprises. Modern imperialism and neocolonialism are seen through these lenses as a way of looting the Third World, just as surely as the sixteenth-century Spaniards looted the gold and silver of the Americas. This argument has more to it, since there certainly were enormous transfers of funds from the colonial areas back to Britain and the other colonial powers. It is not really satisfactory, though, as an explanation of continuing poverty, since profits were repatriated from Canada, too, and since even after subtracting the repatriated profits, considerable new wealth stayed in the colonies as a consequence of the export activities.

A more promising explanation is F. S. Weaver's, who argues that the export industries created new wealth and that the wealth reinforced whatever social structure was already existing in the colony. In Canada, the British settlers who populated most of the country outside the province of Quebec were entrepreneurial capitalists to begin with. There was no question of transforming them from feudal or subsistence peasants—they were capitalists from the day they entered the country, in the sense that they were committed to the market, to buying and selling, to producing for export and not for their own use. The income they earned was reinvested in the expansion of their small-scale enterprises, including family farms.

But in the colonies of what is now the Third World, conditions were very different. The relationship that the imperialists had to the natives, and that the *hacendados* had to the peons, was one of oppression. So, when the ruling classes in the Third World accumulated wealth through the export of primary products, they used that wealth and the power that went along with it to intensify the oppression of the local people and thereby to reinforce their own status. Imperialism reinforced the conditions that were already there. Profits were used to expand plantations, but for the local people this simply meant being part of a larger labor force, separate from their ancestral homes and working for minimal wages. Peasant-based export agriculture in theory might have been more beneficial to the local people, but in practice there were severe limits to the expansion of peasant agriculture, because the people stuck to their subsistence farming techniques; consequently, sufficient wealth seldom flowed to the villages to allow them really to escape from their poverty.

One could imagine conditions, therefore, under which agricultural and mineral exports could have led to the prosperity of the Third World—if the local people had not been oppressed, if they had been able to benefit from their own work, if they had been allowed the freedom to be creative and inventive. But these were not the conditions of the European empires.

An enormous system of worldwide trade in primary commodities grew up; it was a system that depended upon impoverished labor forces, in many cases pulled unceremoniously away from their villages and cultures. Income was earned in the colonies from these export industries, but it was not earned by the working people who might have been able to use it creatively to improve their lives. It was earned by upper and middle classes, who used it to increase their consumption and to secure their control over the poor.

By contrast, the primary export producers in Canada—the fur traders, the lumberjacks, the small farmers and the miners—slowly accumulated wealth and increased their demands for manufactured goods that could be produced locally. Over time an integrated economy was developed, with primary exports and manufacturing both growing and supporting each other. In the Third World, since most of the new income was kept from the workers, people could not afford manufactured products. The Latin American "structuralist" school has been particularly successful in showing how the local income generated by imperialist trade went into the hands of an increasingly well-off minority of the population, who turned to European imports to satisfy their demands for sophisticated consumer goods. No mass market for simple manufactured goods ever arose, and so local manufacturing could not get a start.

As the colonialists concentrated upon single export crops, they often impaired the ability of the local people to grow their own food, and even destroyed the ecosystems that permitted the growth of food. Sehdev Kumar demonstrates how French taxation policies in West

Africa forced peasants to devote ever increasing areas to the cultivation of ground nuts. This forced food production out into areas that had previously been used for grazing, and the nomads of the area were therefore compelled to graze their animals on smaller areas of land. The overgrazing resulted eventually in desertification, and with it the cycles of starvation that have come in the twentieth century to the Sahel region. Similar stories can be told in many areas of the Third World. In the short run it may have been advantageous for West Africa to concentrate on ground nut exports, as the Ricardian theory of comparative advantage would prescribe. But the income went into the hands of an elite, not the laboring people, and in the long run the very ecosystem that permits people to survive was damaged.

If imperialism harmed the self-sufficiency of Third World agriculture, it absolutely devastated its manufacturing. Before the age of imperialism, the Third World had not enjoyed industrial production such as exists currently in the developed countries. Factory production is a result of the European industrial revolution. But most Third World areas did have thriving craft sectors, producing textiles, pottery, household utensils and the like. These were systematically destroyed by the imperialists, not at the muzzle of a gun but as a consequence of marketplace competition. The European industrial revolution spewed out manufactured goods that were much cheaper, and often of higher quality, than the colonies' crafts. The imperialists had no motive to protect the local crafts; on the contrary, they had every incentive to open up local markets to European exports. Imperialism led therefore to the collapse of manufacturing and craft production in the Third World.

Table 4.1 Per Capita Levels of Industrialization (U.K. in 1900 = 100)

	1750	1800	1830	1860	1880	1900	1913
Developed							
Countries	8	8	11	16	24	35	55
U.K.	10	16	25	64	87	100	115
France	9	9	12	20	28	39	59
Germany	8	8	9	15	25	52	85
U.S.	4	9	14	21	38	69	126
Canada	-	5	6	7	10	24	46
Third World	7	6	6	4	3	2	2
China	8	6	6	4	3	2	2
India	7	6	6	3	2	1	2

Source: Bairoch, Paul, "International Industrialization Levels from 1750 to 1980," *Journal of European Economic History* 11 (Fall 1982): 294.

The Swiss economic historian Paul Bairoch has constructed some remarkable statistical tables showing how the European industrial revolution and imperialism went hand in hand with the destruction of the craft sector in much of the Third World. Table 4.1 contains index numbers of industrial output per person in different countries in different years. The average level of industrial output per person in Britain in 1900 is set at 100, and all of the other numbers are shown relative to that level. As an example, in 1860, the United States' level of industrial output per person was 21 percent of the United Kingdom's level in 1900.

Table 4.1 shows that among the developed countries, Britain established a lead in industrialization in the nineteenth century, which diminished but did not disappear by the eve of the First World War. Most dramatically, it shows the near disappearance of industrial, or craft, output in the Third World over the same period. Note that in 1750, just before the beginning of the British industrial revolution, Third World industrial output per person was almost as high as Britain's, and substantially higher than in the American Thirteen Colonies. But over the nineteenth century, Third World industrialization declined, so that by 1900 it was just 2 percent of the British level.

Bairoch has compiled a wealth of additional data making the same point in different ways. He shows, for example, that between 1830 and 1900, total industrial output of the Third World fell almost in half. In 1750, the Third World produced 73 percent of the world's manufactured goods, in 1913 only 7 percent.

It is clear that the effect of imperialism on Third World manufacturing and crafts was catastrophic. This is another example of the limited relevance of the theory of comparative advantage. In the nineteenth century, the Europeans were at a comparative advantage, and the Third World at a comparative disadvantage, in the production of manufactured goods; the Ricardians would consequently argue that the result—the concentration of manufacturing in Europe and its disappearance in the Third World—was for the best. Manufacturing production all but disappeared from the Third World, but that is not a reason to worry, teaches the theory, because consumers in the Third World were able to buy cheaper and better goods from the Europeans.

True enough, in the short run. But the long-run effects were hardly advantageous to the Third World, because an entire class of independent craftspeople disappeared. They were for the most part people with highly developed skills who were used to making business decisions on their own, and many of them were to some extent entrepreneurial. They might very well have been able to adapt the new European technologies to their own needs, and as a consequence have led the way to the economic development of their societies. But they were wiped out. Almost the entire Indian textile industry was eliminated because of the import of cheap cotton goods from Britain.

The economic effects of European imperialism were therefore mas-

sive. Millions of people were pulled away from their accustomed pursuits to work in capitalist and export enterprises. Almost all were kept
at low, subsistence incomes, without opportunity to share the benefits
obtained from export production. Land that had been tilled for centuries for subsistence food crops was expropriated for the growth of
export crops. In the countryside, single-crop agriculture brought with
it ecological deterioration. Manufacturing and crafts disappeared, and
as a consequence the economies of many Third World areas became
much more specialized and concentrated.

The Population Explosion

One of the most pervasive and transforming effects of imperialism was
the population explosion in the Third World, which began just at the
end of the imperialist era, in the period between the two world wars of
the twentieth century. Population growth is determined almost exclusively by the gap between birth rates and death rates. For example, a
country like Mexico, which has an annual crude birth rate of about 28
per thousand people, and a crude death rate of 6 per thousand, has a
population growth rate of 22 per thousand, or 2.2 percent a year. This
may not seem like a high rate, but a population growing at 2.2 percent
a year will double in just 32 years, quadruple in 64 years, and so forth.[8]
Nigeria, with a birth rate of 47 and a death rate of 15, and consequently an annual growth rate of 3.2 percent, will double in size in 22 years
and quadruple in 44 years, if these rates are sustained.

Prior to the twentieth century, both birth rates and death rates were
very high in the Third World. Both were often about 40 or 45 per thousand, and net population growth was therefore zero or at least very
small. Death rates were high because of low subsistence standards of
living, because of pervasive infectious disease and because of the
absence of medical care. Birth rates had to be high to maintain the
population. Consequently, cultural practices developed over the ages
that encouraged large families. A typical experience of a mother in the
Third World would be to bear perhaps eight children, of whom five
might die before maturity—and perhaps one or two sons might survive
to provide for her in her old age.

High fertility and mortality existed in pre-industrialized Europe too.
When economic growth occurred in Europe and people's incomes
started to increase, health conditions improved, death rates fell and
the population began to grow. This growth spurt was relatively short
lived, however, because by the twentieth century, most Europeans (and
Americans) had voluntarily reduced their fertility, having decided that
they preferred small families. The evidence seems to indicate that in
most communities of the developed world, rising standards of living
led to reductions in the number of children, even before mechanical

means of contraception were available.

In the Third World there have been remarkable reductions in death rates in the twentieth century—for example from 40 or 45 per thousand people each year to 13 per thousand in India, 7 in China, 13 in Ghana, 7 in Colombia. These improvements in mortality were not set off by rising standards of living in the Third World. To the contrary, they began while the great majority of Third World people were desperately poor and under colonial subjection. Death rates fell largely because the imperialists imported cheap public health technologies, including the spraying of malarial swamps with insecticides, the use of vaccinations and later the introduction of antibiotics.

One cannot complain about the successes of colonial public health measures in saving lives. But it is critical to see that this mortality improvement occurred without any change in the standards of living of the people. In Europe and North America, increased longevity had been an integral part of a long process of social change; in the Third World, increased longevity was bestowed from outside the social system.

In Europe and North America, the social change that improved health conditions and caused death rates to fall eventually led to the reduction of birth rates as well. In the Third World, on the other hand, there was very little of the sort of changes in standards of living and cultural norms that might have persuaded people to lower their family size. The great majority of people have remained poor and continue to see children as material and spiritual assets—the more the better. Children can be put to work at a young age to help increase family income. If they survive, they can provide security for their parents in their old age. The cultural and religious practices of most Third World societies, developed over countless generations in support of high fertility, have been left unchallenged. Girls commonly marry at puberty, and their value in the eyes of their families and frequently themselves is determined by their success in childbearing.

The necessary result of the quickly declining death rates, combined with the sustained high level of childbearing, was a population explosion unprecedented in human history, with populations doubling each generation. This population growth occurred at the same time that land in the Third World was being removed from subsistence cultivation and used increasingly for the production of export crops. More people, less land: the consequences are not hard to see. In the postcolonial decades, since the 1960's, birth rates have begun to decline in a number of Third World countries, but nowhere are they approaching the low death rates.

It is sometimes argued that to focus on the population explosion as a cause of Third World poverty is to "blame the victim," to hold Third World peoples at fault. But this view is incorrect. The population explosion is a consequence of European imperialism. The imperialists imported cheap public health measures that lowered death rates—without at the same time undertaking the much more difficult task of economic development that might have led people with rising incomes to choose to lower birth rates. The result is population growth that has persisted long past the colonial age, threatening to overwhelm the Third World's best efforts at social change.

The Legacy of Imperialism

A quick survey of the age of European imperialism easily dispels the notion, therefore, that the Third World societies of today are essentially traditional, or untouched, as many in the modernization school picture them. They were transformed by five centuries of imperialism, and today they are almost as different from their former cultures as modern-day North America and Europe are from medieval feudalism. They are still poor, it is true, and they still have vestiges of traditional culture, certainly more than exist in the world's rich countries. But the languages, the political structures, the demography and the economic systems that mark today's Third World are to a large extent the result of unequal, oppressive relationships with the European empires.

Some of the motivations of the imperialists were altruistic. Many of the people on the spot—the soldiers, the administrators and the farmers—saw themselves as aiding the local people. The missionaries saw themselves as saving them. Rudyard Kipling, the bard of British imperialism, wrote without irony in 1899:

> Take up the White Man's burden—
> Send out the best ye breed—
> Go bind your sons to exile,
> To serve your captives' need;
> To wait in heavy harness,
> On fluttered folk and wild—
> Your new-caught sullen peoples,
> Half devil and half child.

As discussed in Chapter 3, Karl Marx and many of his followers argued that imperialism was frequently a progressive force, breaking down rigid social structures and opening societies to capitalist development, which was a necessary step on the road to socialism and prosperity. There is a grain of truth in this view—for some imperialist ventures, at some times. Imperialism brought railways and roads, it brought new technology, and for some it brought educational opportunities. But for most people in the Third World it brought oppression and poverty.

The empires were central to the expanding capitalism of Europe. They were needed for their wealth and for their primary products.

Without the empires, European economic growth might never have occurred or, if it had, it might have been restricted and much less impressive. Imperialism was not just an add-on; it did not occur in a "fit of absence of mind," as some thought at the time. It was an integral component of world capitalist development.

Imperialism was one of the major formative movements of the modern age. It brought with it incredible cultural destruction, economic impoverishment, death and even genocide. It opened the world to new ideas, new technologies and new opportunities. It created the world we live in, be we rich or poor.

Suggestions for Further Reading

Eldridge, C. C. *Victorian Imperialism.* London: Hodder and Stoughton, 1978.

Fieldhouse, D. K. *Colonialism, 1870–1945, An Introduction.* London: Weidenfeld and Nicolson, 1981.

Galeano, Eduardo. *Open Veins of Latin America: Five Centuries of the Pillage of a Continent.* New York: Monthly Review Press, 1973.

Gallagher, J. A., and R. E. Robinson. "The Imperialism of Free Trade." *Economic History Review* second series 6(1953): 1–15.

Rhodes, Robert I., ed. *Imperialism and Underdevelopment: A Reader.* New York: Monthly Review Press, 1970.

Notes

1. Cited in Alan P. Merriam, *Congo: Background of Conflict* (Chicago: University of Chicago Press, 1960), 352.

2. As an undergraduate history major at Queen's University in Canada, one of the last vestiges of the ideology of the British Empire, I was enthralled by a statement of my most dignified professor, a gaunt Englishman in flowing black robes who lectured to the class in slow cadences. "The eighteenth century is a vital link," he said, "between the seventeenth century and the, er, nineteenth century."

3. J. A. Gallagher and R. E. Robinson, "The Imperialism of Free Trade," *Economic History Review* second series 6 (1953): 9, 13.

4. C. C. Eldridge, *Victorian Imperialism* (London: Hodder and Stoughton, 1978), 122.

5. This case is reported by William H. McKellin and cited in Howard Rheingold, *They Have a Word for It* (Los Angeles: Jeremy P. Tarcher, Inc., 1988).

6. From Biko's writings collected in Donald Woods, *Biko,* 2d ed. (New York: Henry Holt and Company, 1987), 117.

7. Chinua Achebe, *Arrow of God* (New York: Doubleday and Company, 1969), 261–62.

8. The number of years to double is found by dividing the population growth rate, in percent, into 70. Thus, a population growing at 1 percent a year doubles in 70 years, and a population growing at 2 percent doubles in 35 years, etc.

CHAPTER FIVE

Nationalism and Revolution

Revolt is the only way out of the colonial situation, and
the colonized realizes it sooner or later. His condition
is absolute, and cries out for an absolute solution; a
break and not a compromise. . . . For the colonial
condition cannot be adjusted to; like an iron collar it
can only be broken.
— Albert Memmi, *The Colonizer
and the Colonized*

Political power grows out of the barrel of a gun.
— Mao Tse-tung

I, personally, would wait, if need be, for ages rather
than seek to attain the freedom of my country
through bloody means. . . . The world is sick unto
death of blood-spilling. The world is seeking a way
out, and I flatter myself with the belief that perhaps it
will be the privilege of the ancient land of India to
show the way out to the hungering world.
— Mohandas K. Gandhi

I have not become the King's First Minister in order to
preside over the liquidation of the British Empire.
— Sir Winston Churchill

THE NINETEENTH CENTURY was the age of imperialism in the
Third World, the twentieth century the age of nationalism. Rebels and
patriots fought back against the white imperialists, driving them from
their lands and creating new nations in the wake of their departure.

Nationalism represented resistance to outside rulers, pride in one's
own identity and a program for political self-determination. The
nationalist movement was successful; by the second half of the century,
almost all of the areas of the Third World that had been colonized by
the Europeans achieved independence. At the United Nations, the
great majority of the delegates to the General Assembly were representatives of the newly emergent nations of Asia, the Middle East and
Africa, along with Latin America. But it turned out that the demise of
the European empires and the success of the nationalist program did

not solve the economic and social problems of the Third World; as the twentieth century is drawing to a close, those problems remain as acute as ever.

The Origins of Third World Nationalism

The nationalism of the twentieth century was for the most part a new response in the Third World; it was a response specifically to the experience of being controlled by the European imperialists. With few exceptions, the people of the Third World had not been organized into nations prior to the arrival of the colonialists, and their loyalties had not been nationalist. In Africa and the Americas, people's identities had been to their ethnic and tribal groups, often to their village or their extended family. Most of Asia had been organized for centuries into a shifting series of empires, dynasties and bureaucracies. The concept of the nation state was not a relevant one. But the imperialists were themselves nation states, and they created administrative structures that resembled nations—so when the people of the Third World fought back against their oppressors, they did so in the name of the nation, not in the name of the village, the family, the tribe or the dynasty.

The fact that imperialism engendered nationalism is an indicator of how profound the imperialist experience was in most areas of the Third World. Imperialism severely damaged, distorted, even destroyed the social structures it encountered; when the imperialists finally retreated, those traditional societies could not be brought back to life and recreated by the Third World rebels. Imperialism forced the Third World irrevocably into the dominant world system, a system of nations. Furthermore, imperialism challenged the identities of Third World peoples, their sense of self-worth and dignity. The imperialists generally treated the people they encountered as inferiors, as niggers, gooks and wogs. In response, the people of the Third World needed to affirm their own value and importance, and they did so in large measure by asserting their nationality.

In many areas of the Third World, the nationalist movements began about the turn of the twentieth century. There had been resistance movements earlier, but they had not coalesced around the idea of the nation. For example, the Indian Mutiny of 1857 was a serious enough threat to lead the British to terminate the rule of the East India Company and replace it with the direct authority of the Crown, but the rebels did not conceive of themselves as representing a unified Indian nation. Their grievances had to do with threats to their religious practices and their customs, not with the denial of nationhood. In 1885, however, the principal Indian nationalist organization was founded, the Indian National Congress. While the Congress was open to all factions of Indian society, it was dominated by Hindus, and in response to it the All-India Muslim League was founded in 1906. Both organizations were nationalist, calling for an end to British rule and the establishment of a new country or countries in its place. Their nationalism was complicated by their religious identities; in fact, the eventual inability of the two organizations to resolve the contradiction between a nationalist vision of the future and a sectarian vision led to the partition of Pakistan from India at the time of independence in 1948. But in spite of their sectarian problems, both the Congress and the Muslim League were nationalist organizations, working for the replacement of imperialism by an independent nation state. In many other areas of the imperial world, nationalist organizations began to appear at about the same time.

It is important to distinguish the nationalist program in the Third World from the revolutionary program. Nationalism occurred almost everywhere but revolution only in pockets. The distinction is that the nationalists sought political rights for all of the colonized people; they deemphasized class conflicts among their own people and stressed instead their common oppression by the imperialists. Revolutionaries, in contrast, sought the restructuring of their societies. At his trial in South Africa in 1963, the leader of the African National Congress (ANC), Nelson Mandela, summed up the distinction:

> The ANC's chief goal was for the African people to win unity and full political rights. The Communist party's main aim, on the other hand, was to remove the capitalists and to replace them with a working-class government. The Communist party sought to emphasize class distinctions while the ANC sought to harmonize them. This is a vital distinction.[1]

The strength of nationalism was that it was an ideology capable of uniting an oppressed people, of drawing them together in opposition to their common enemy, the imperialist oppressor. In preindependence India, when the British talked of the difficulties the Indians would have resolving their ethnic and religious differences in an independent country, the leaders of both the Congress and the Muslim League replied in accord that while this might be true, it was no business of the British. The British needed to leave, and following their departure the Indians would settle their own problems in their own ways, without outside interference. It was the one proposition upon which all Indians could agree.

But if national unity was the strength of the nationalist program, it was also its weakness. Nationalist movements in the Third World were willing to focus upon the struggle against the common enemy, but most were unwilling to deal with the ways in which oppression was exercised within the nation. This latter kind of emphasis would have torn apart the unity that was the movement's great strength, so in most cases it was avoided.

In some areas of the Third World, however, nationalism took on a revolutionary cast. Most importantly, in China the struggle against foreign domination (and in particular against the Japanese occupation) merged into a communist revolution that completely overturned the class structures and social relationships of the Chinese people. Similarly, in Vietnam, North Korea, Cuba, Nicaragua and Iran, nationalist movements against a foreign oppressor joined forces with revolutionary movements against local classes. One should bear in mind, however, that the revolutionary movements in the Third World were nationalist as well as revolutionary. They drew strength from the patriotism of their people. Ho Chi Minh's Vietminh movement overthrew landlord and bourgeois classes in its successful revolution in North Vietnam, but it also defended itself fiercely against excessive control by the Chinese communists.

Marx, and after him Lenin and the Russian revolutionaries, had thought that nationalism was a particular manifestation of capitalism. Nationalist identity, they thought, was fostered by capitalists as a way of blinding the workers to their true interest. They had expected that national divisions would wither away as the communist revolution spread throughout the world and revealed that the real conflicts between people were not in terms of their nationality or their race, but in terms of their class. But this did not occur in the twentieth century, and after the failure of international communism to achieve a worldwide revolution, the Soviet communists themselves became more and more identified with the aspirations of the Russian nation. Recently, communism itself appears to be in danger of collapse, as the Soviet Union divides into many separate nations. So too in the Third World, all of the revolutions were intensely nationalist. Mao Tse-tung was first and foremost a Chinese leader, Fidel Castro a Cuban, Gamel Abdel Nasser an Egyptian.

The success of the nationalist movements in the Third World was inevitable, or at least very likely, in the long run. The indigenous people simply cared too much about their own dignity and oppression to allow imperialism to continue generation after generation. The speed with which the independence of the Third World nations was won in the middle of the twentieth century was, however, breathtaking. At the end of the Second World War, the European powers confidently resumed control over their colonies. Within just a couple of years, however, China was convulsed in a revolution, and India was granted her independence. Although these were the two largest countries of the Third World, they were thought at the time to be exceptions. Even in the 1950's, almost no contemporary observers expected the independence of the African nations to come within their lifetimes. And yet by the early 1960's almost the entire continent of Africa was under the control of its own people.

In retrospect, one can see that the timing of the successful movements for national independence was not accidental. The European empires would have collapsed eventually because of the strength of the nationalist movements, but they actually collapsed so suddenly because of the weakness of the Europeans themselves. The nations of Europe subjected themselves to two devastating world wars in the first half of the century. The First World War (1914–18) took a toll of life never before seen in human conflict. Scarcely had the Europeans begun to rebuild their societies and economies when they were hit by the worst economic disaster since the industrial revolution, the Great Depression of the 1930's. Unemployment skyrocketed, plants were left idle and lives were ruined. The depression was finally defeated only by the coming of the Second World War (1939–45), a war that was even more destructive of lives and productive capacity than the First. The continent that had emerged into the twentieth century with such verve, power and confidence found itself at mid-century in tatters.

The Europeans did not understand at the end of the Second World War how exhausted they were. They could see quickly enough that the United States was taking over their accustomed role of world leader and that a bipolar world conflict between the United States and the Soviet Union was emerging, a conflict in which their own role was secondary. Those changes in the world were easy to see, if distressing to the Europeans. But what remained hidden for a time was that Europe had lost both the morale and the economic strength to rule its colonial empires.

The French in particular were recalcitrant. Faced with a nationalist uprising in Vietnam, they engaged in a long war, with the support of the United States, finally conceding defeat only after their spectacular military loss at Dien Bien Phu in 1954. In Algeria they hung on even longer, eventually abandoning the settlers and the army only in 1961. The British were somewhat more peaceful about their withdrawal from empire, but equally unaware that their moment of imperial glory was gone forever. Although Prime Minister Sir Winston Churchill pontificated that he would not preside over the liquidation of the British Empire, that is exactly what he and his successors did. Even in the mid-1950's in Africa, the British and French colonialists were saying that independence would take generations, since the Africans were not yet ready to assume control of their own countries. Ready or not, they did assume control, in a few short years before and after 1960.

So, the nationalist movements in the Third World originated as responses to the European imperialists, and they succeeded because of the weakness of the imperialists. Without exception, they promised both dignity and also material progress to their oppressed peoples.

With some exceptions, they failed to deliver on their promises.

The Indian Subcontinent

The first significant area of the Third World to achieve its independence after the Second World War was India, in 1947. At the end, the British left under amicable terms, having agreed upon independence in return for the participation of Indians in the military effort of the Second World War. But the struggles in the previous decades were anything but friendly.

The British had ruled India directly since the Mutiny of 1857, and in the twentieth century they faced increasing resistance from nationalist groups, in particular from the Congress party and the Muslim League. The great leader of the Indian independence movement was the ascetic, spiritual teacher Mohandas Gandhi, who had developed his techniques of nonviolent resistance in South Africa and had then returned to India in 1919.

Gandhi worked within the Congress party—in fact he was president of the Congress from 1925 to 1934—but he was not a politician in the conventional sense. He was a man of the spirit who taught by example. In her 1938 novel *Kanthapura*, the Indian writer Raja Rao showed how Gandhi was incorporated into the pantheon of spiritual leaders, how his teachings were connected to the deepest traditions of the people. The storyteller weaves this legend for the villagers, in which the sage Valmiki addresses the supreme god Brahma:

> "You have forgotten us so long that men have come from across the seas and the oceans to trample on our wisdom and to spit on virtue itself. They have come to bind us and to whip us, to make our women die milkless and our men die ignorant. O Brahma, deign to send us one of your gods so that he may incarnate himself on earth and bring back light and plenty to your enslaved daughter." . . . "O sage," pronounced Brahma, "is it greater for you to ask or for me to say Yea? Siva himself will forthwith go and incarnate himself on the earth and free my beloved daughter from her enforced slavery." . . .
> And lo, when the Sage was still partaking of the pleasures Brahma offered him in hospitality, there was born in a family in Gujerat a son such as the world has never beheld! Hardly was he in the cradle than he began to lisp the language of wisdom. You remember how Krishna, when he was but a babe of four, had begun to fight against demons and had killed the serpent Kali. So too our Mohandas began to fight against the enemies of the country. And as he grew up, and after he was duly shaven for the hair ceremony, he began to go out into the villages and assemble people and talk to them, and his voice was so pure, his forehead so brilliant with wisdom, that men followed him, more and more men followed him as they did Krishna the flute-player; and so he goes from village to village to slay the serpent of the foreign rule. Fight, says he, but harm no soul. Love all, says he, Hindu,

Mohammedan, Christian or Pariah, for all are equal before God. Don't be attached to riches, says he, for riches create passions, and passions create attachment, and attachment hides the face of truth. . . . He is a saint, the Mahatma, a wise man and a soft man, and a saint. You know how he fasts and prays. And even his enemies fall at his feet.[2]

Gandhian nonviolence, called *Satyagraha*, has been mistaken sometimes as a passive strategy, but it was not. It was an active means of focusing the world's attention upon the violence and injustice of the oppressor. It was a means of changing the oppressor's acts by shaming him and calling his good sense into question. When Gandhi's followers were attacked savagely by the British, they suffered without fighting back; and by bearing witness in this way they put the British into an untenable ethical position. Had the struggle been one of military force, imperialism in India might have lasted much longer, because the British had almost a monopoly of armaments. But Gandhi succeeded in turning the battle into one of conscience, and on that basis he and the Indians were successful.

The strategy of nonviolent resistance raised many questions in India, as it did later in other areas of the world—for example, in the southern part of the United States in the civil rights movement of the 1960's. It was attacked by militants as being a strategy of cowardice. It was attacked by socialists as evading the central issue of class structure. But it drew worldwide sympathy to the cause of anti-imperialist nationalism in the way no other strategy could have.

Gandhian nonviolence succeeded in eroding the moral position of the British and driving them out of India. It was not successful, however, in solving the communal problems of the Indians. The Muslim League, under the leadership of Mohammed Ali Jinnah, refused to accept the position of being an ethnic minority within an independent India dominated by Hindus. Gandhi fought for the idea of a nonsectarian state, where all religious groups (and, within the Hindu population, all castes), would have the same rights and would be treated with equality. Throughout the 1930's and 1940's, while the Indians were uniting in their negotiations with and struggles against the British, however, they were failing to achieve a consensus about the structure of postindependence India. In 1947, as independence came, the new country collapsed into two parts: India, with a heavy majority of Hindus; and Pakistan, which was almost exclusively Moslem. Because of the geographical location of most Moslems, it was necessary to establish two sections of the Islamic state, East and West Pakistan, which were separated by 1,000 miles of Indian territory. As the two new nations were formed, there was a massive movement of population—of Moslems out of India and of Hindus out of Pakistan. The entire subcontinent exploded in an orgy of violence. With the normal social constraints lifted, the frustrations of each religious group with the other were unleashed, and the slaughter was horrifying. Gandhi tried desperately to stop the violence by fasting almost to death, and he may have had some positive impact, but he could not control it. Then just a year after independence, Gandhi himself fell victim to the subcontinent's hatred, assassinated by a Hindu extremist.

The nationalist movement of India therefore came to its conclusion in an incredibly contradictory manner. Indian independence was the greatest triumph of nonviolent direct action the world has seen, and yet the moment of independence was a moment of unprecedented violence. The Gandhian spirit was one of the reconciliation of all peoples, and yet the polity of the subcontinent solidified into sectarian blocs.

Postindependence India and Pakistan have struggled with this confused legacy. India became the world's largest democracy, with contending political parties vying in elections that have been for the most part quite free. At the same time, however, the prime ministership of India was handed down in succession to three generations of the same family (Jawaharlal Nehru, his daughter Indira Gandhi and her son Rajiv Gandhi) in a dynastic fashion. And while the official policy of India is nonsectarian, still communal violence rises to the forefront often, not only between Moslems and Hindus, but also between Sikhs and Hindus, and between Hindu castes. Mohandas Gandhi, Indira Gandhi and Rajiv Gandhi all fell victim to assassins.

The basis of Pakistan has been quite different; it is an explicitly Moslem state (Pakistan in Urdu means "land of the pure"). Yet, religious commitment could not unify the two sections of the country. East Pakistan, more crowded and poorer than West Pakistan, declared independence in 1971 under the name of Bangladesh and with Indian help defeated a West Pakistani army at the cost of great loss of life. Bangladesh's independence brought with it another tremendous flow of refugees, this time millions of Hindus crossing from Bangladesh into the Indian state of West Bengal. Democracy has been much more precarious in Pakistan and Bangladesh than in India; for most of the period of independence the regimes of both nations have been military.

The three countries—India, Pakistan and Bangladesh—now constitute about 20 percent of the world's population and continue to share widespread poverty. None of their successive governments has been able to address the plight of the poor in any consistent way. While there have been some areas of progress, the living standards of their people are still among the lowest in the world.

China

While the peoples of the British Empire in India were struggling to forge three independent republics, the other great population group of Asia, the Chinese, were embarked on a very different sort of struggle towards nationhood. China was never part of a western empire, but its ports, commerce, administration and legal system were controlled by the European imperial powers from the middle of the nineteenth century. In the twentieth century, the Chinese went through a series of revolutions that made them masters in their own nation. The first revolution occurred in 1911, when the Manchu dynasty, which had presided over the humiliation of China by the foreigners, was deposed and replaced by a westernized military regime. This regime was in turn challenged, almost from the beginning of its rule, by the Kuomintang, or Nationalist party, led by one of China's great revolutionary figures, Sun Yat-sen. Sun Yat-sen propounded a vision of the Chinese nation that was new; China in his eyes was not just a shifting series of alliances under an emperor, but a unified state to which the millions of Chinese could and should show allegiance. It was critical to his strategy to terminate the imperialist control that still existed over China. Neither the new regime in Beijing nor the western powers were prepared to accede to this program, and consequently a long civil war broke out.

Sun Yat-sen died in 1925 and was succeeded in the leadership of the Kuomintang by General Chiang Kai-shek. Chiang achieved considerable success in the 1920's, exerting military control over most of the country and persuading the western powers to relinquish most of their extraterritorial rights. The seeds of disaster for the Kuomintang were sown, however, in 1927, when Chiang broke with the party's left wing, the communists. Threatened by the growing strength of the communists, Chiang purged them from the party and expelled the Russians who had been providing support and advice. In the years that followed, Chiang suppressed other groups within the Kuomintang that were challenging his leadership. Within 10 years of taking over the party, he had converted it from the broad, democratic, nationalist ideals of Sun Yat-sen into an authoritarian, primarily military organization.

The communists, one of whose leaders was Mao Tse-tung, organized among the peasants in the southeastern region of China and developed their military capacity. The Kuomintang attacked and dislodged the communists, who in turn responded in 1934–35 by undertaking a 6,000-mile trek, later called the Long March, through the west and into the north of the country. The Long March began with 90,000 people, only half of whom survived. Along the march the communists deepened their roots among the peasants and established tremendous popular appeal. The civil war resumed with the communists in a much stronger position. It was interrupted, however, by the Japanese invasion of northern China; the communists persuaded the Kuomintang to join forces with them to defend China from the Japanese. The alliance, although precarious, lasted for most of the Second World War.

With the defeat of Japan at the end of the Second World War, the

Chinese civil war resumed in earnest, this time with the United States in full support of Chiang's Kuomintang armies. But the Kuomintang by now had lost almost all vestige of popular support; Chiang had become indistinguishable from a long line of traditional Chinese warlords. The communists steadily gained ground, eventually driving the Kuomintang forces from the mainland to the island province of Taiwan and declaring the People's Republic of China in October 1949.

The Chinese was the world's second great communist revolution, following the Russian Revolution of 1917. In the eyes of United States policymakers in the years following the Second World War, there was little difference between the two. The world appeared to be divided into two camps, with the Russians and the Chinese together representing the principal threat to the "free world." This perception was heightened by the outbreak of the Korean War in 1949, with the communist North Koreans, supported by the Chinese, fighting against the South Koreans, who were supported by the Americans. But it was a naive view. The Chinese revolution was very different from the Russian, and the two regimes eventually became antagonistic.

Even the theories of communism espoused by the Russians and the Chinese were different. For the Russian revolutionaries, schooled in classical Marxism, the urban workers were the revolutionary class, while the peasants were "prerevolutionary," or possibly even antirevolutionary. The Russian Revolution, from its very inception, had an antirural cast (and in consequence has always had a relatively unproductive agricultural sector). But the Chinese communist movement was a peasant revolution. Mao's followers had their roots among the peasantry; their most popular programs were land reform and the destruction of the landlord class. It was the Kuomintang that controlled the cities—so the Chinese Revolution was in large measure the revolt of the peasants against the urban dwellers.

Although the ideology of communism was internationalist, in the end both the Chinese and the Russian revolutions developed into deeply rooted nationalist movements. Particularly in the Chinese case, the communist revolution actually created the nation. Sun Yat-sen's ideal had been a nationalist one, but his vision of national unity had been betrayed by his successor, Chiang Kai-shek. So it was left to the victorious communists to develop a program for the Chinese nation as a whole.

Chinese communism departed from the nationalist movements of many other areas of the Third World, however, in that it was also profoundly revolutionary. That is, there was no attempt to reconcile all of the various classes and interests in the country. The purpose of the Chinese Revolution was to overthrow and destroy the oppressing classes, and it did. In particular, the hated landlords were eliminated as a class, as were independent commercial people. The history of China since the revolution is an extraordinary tale of a politicized society, driven at all levels, from the national to the local, by strong and shifting ideologies. There have been both leftward movements and rightward reactions. The full apparatus of totalitarianism was developed, with hundreds of thousands, perhaps even millions, of arrests and deaths. But side by side with the police state repression was the mobilization of intensive social pressure, to raise the consciousness of the people and direct them toward constructive social action.

After the victory of the Chinese Revolution in 1949, two further social convulsions were promoted by the communist leaders themselves. From 1958 to 1961, the country went through the deeply disruptive Great Leap Forward, when rural communities were organized into large communes and heavy industry was dispersed in small-scale units into the countryside. The changes brought about during the Great Leap Forward were so disruptive that production fell drastically, and with it living standards. In the respite that followed in the early 1960's, some private enterprise was allowed and production levels recovered. But then in 1966 an even greater disruption began—the Great Proletarian Cultural Revolution, a movement begun by the aging Mao and destined to last for almost a decade. The new generation of Chinese, too young to have experienced the original revolution, were called upon to create their own revolution. This they did, with remarkable thoroughness. Politics ruled above all; people with technical expertise were suspected of being insufficiently true to Maoist doctrine. Tremendous numbers of people were dismissed from their positions and purged. Many skilled people were sent to the countryside for rehabilitation. Universities were closed. The handbook of the Cultural Revolution was Mao's "Little Red Book," a collection of his sayings. The Little Red Book was studied assiduously by workers in their factories and their communes, as the guide to correct action.

Following Mao's death in 1976, a new group of leaders took power, wresting control from the Maoist leaders whom they dubbed the "gang of four." They led modern China far from the ideas of the revolution's founder, deemphasizing politics as an organizing principle and stressing competition, expertise and markets. They opened the country to foreign technology, foreign investment and foreign ideas. After decades of social and economic instability, the Chinese people responded actively to these opportunities; they raised both agricultural and industrial production and began to enjoy some improvements in their living standards.

The new Chinese leaders were not prepared to relax their totalitarian political domination, however. The Communist party continued to control political life, providing privileges for its members and denying opportunities for dissent and opposition. In contrast, in the late 1980's, the Soviet Union, led by Premier Gorbachev, was experimenting with *glasnost,* that is to say, openness and democracy. These ideas spread to

China but were suppressed. When Chinese students who were inspired by Gorbachev demonstrated for democracy in the spring of 1989, they were shot down in the streets, imprisoned and executed. In the years that followed, political control by the party did not relax, although the economy continued to move toward decentralization, markets, individual entrepreneurship and capitalism.

It seems, therefore, that the Chinese Revolution is at odds with its own people. The revolution was fought to rescue the masses from oppression. Almost all independent Chinese voices that can be heard in the west claim, however, that the revolutionary state has become the oppressor, and that the Chinese people are still subject to tyranny.

Vietnam

Vietnam was the site of one of the Third World's bitterest and most protracted nationalist struggles for independence. Lying to the south of China, Vietnam has suffered centuries of foreign invasion and occupation, most often from the Chinese. As a consequence, there is actually a long tradition of resistance in Vietnam; Vietnamese nationalism is not just a reaction to recent European imperialism. In the twentieth century, however, the Vietnamese did engage in successive wars against foreigners, first against France and then the United States.

From the late-eighteenth century to the late-nineteenth, French explorers, adventurers, soldiers and missionaries traveled throughout the area they called Indochina, an area that consisted of the present-day countries of Laos, Cambodia and Vietnam. They asserted control where they could, often by use of military force, but their control was uneven and sporadic. After a century of forays, however, the French finally established control over the entire region in 1883, as part of the much wider expansion of European imperialism at the end of the nineteenth century. In 1887, they created the Indochinese Union, consisting of the four areas of Cambodia, Cochin China, Annam and Tonkin (the latter three corresponding to modern-day Vietnam), and in 1893 they added Laos to the Union. They established a colonial export economy based mostly on rice and rubber. In so doing they expropriated a great deal of the land for use by French owners, and they also facilitated the concentration of much of the land in the hands of a small number of local people. Indochina became a most profitable component of the French overseas empire. French control over the area was brutal when necessary; however, it never succeeded fully in eliminating local resistance.

The leader of Vietnamese resistance in the twentieth century was one of the most remarkable figures to come out the Third World: the revolutionary, nationalist, Communist Ho Chi Minh. Ho was born in central Vietnam in 1890, just as the French were establishing administrative control over the region; he died in 1969, at the height of the conflict that was both a civil war and a struggle against U.S. imperial control.

Ho actually spent a great deal of his life outside Vietnam. After a fairly conventional education, he left his country at the age of 21 as a cabin boy on a French freighter, and he was not to return for 30 full years. He spent his young adulthood in the west—in the United States, where he lived as a laborer in Brooklyn, in Britain where he worked in the kitchen of an elegant London hotel and then for 6 very formative years in Paris. In Paris, the capital of his country's oppressor, he imbued himself deeply in French culture, reading widely, joining in discussion groups and writing. He also made contact with and was influenced by French socialist and communist groups. At the end of the First World War, he tried to influence Woodrow Wilson at the Peace Conference of Versailles to include Vietnam in his vision of self-determination, but without success. He had very little success with the French socialists, either, as he tried to persuade them to embrace the cause of independence for Vietnam. He discovered that they were as nationalist as they were socialist, and had no interest in calling for the dismemberment of the French empire. In the intellectual ferment that spread throughout Europe after the success of the Russian Bolshevik revolution in 1917, Ho gradually shifted his allegiances from the moderate socialists to the revolutionary communists. But he did so out of a motivation that was nationalist; he thought that the Russian Communist party had the capacity to promote a worldwide revolution that would lead to the liberation of Vietnam. He later said, "It was patriotism and not Communism that originally inspired me."[3]

In the 1920's and 1930's, Ho traveled throughout the world, including Russia and China, as a revolutionary intellectual. Nowhere did he have a secure home, certainly not in China after the Kuomintang broke with the communist party. He finally returned to Vietnam in secret, in 1941 at the age of 51, to join with compatriots in the struggle against the Japanese. The Japanese had invaded Vietnam from China in 1940, driving out the French and imposing a reign of terror much more fierce than even the French had contemplated. Along with Vo Nguyen Giap and Pham Van Dong, he formed a nationalist party, called the Vietminh, which was to lead the country through 34 unbroken years of military struggle.

With the end of the Second World War in 1945 and the defeat of Japan, there was a moment of hope for Ho and the Vietminh that independence might be attained. Ho declared Vietnamese independence, quoting liberally from the United States Declaration of Independence, which he admired, and hoping for support from the Americans. But the British and the French, who were in occupation of the country at the end of the war, had no interest in Vietnamese independence. In particular, the French were committed to the reestablishment of their empire throughout Indochina. There were negotiations in Paris, but they collapsed, and the Vietminh consequently began engaging the French militarily in 1946. Although the Americans professed an anti-colonial ideology, they ended up by supporting the French. In fact, by the time the French were finally defeated in 1954, the United States had given them more military aid for their Indochinese battles than they had given them economic aid for the rebuilding of their economy after the Second World War. The Americans were persuaded to support the French against the Vietnamese because of the emergence of the cold war immediately after the Second World War, and then the hot war in Korea in 1949. The Americans were coming to see themselves as locked in a deathly struggle for survival of their way of life against the Russian communists. Other communists, in China, Vietnam and North Korea, were seen as dupes and fellow travelers of the Russians. What might have been viewed as a local conflict was transformed, in the eyes of the Americans, into a geopolitical struggle for the survival of the free world—and the Americans, as the world's strongest country in the postwar era, believed themselves to have no alternative but to support their French colleagues. It was a disastrous decision, for both the Vietnamese and the Americans.

The war between the French and the Vietnamese culminated in the decisive battle of Dien Bien Phu in 1954, in which the forces commanded by General Vo Nguyen Giap defeated their enemy and made the continued presence of the French in Vietnam untenable. An international conference in Geneva followed, at which the independence of all of French Indochina, that is, Laos, Cambodia and Vietnam, was recognized. There was a catch, however. Vietnam was to be divided at the seventeenth parallel of latitude into two parts: North and South Vietnam—the North with its capital in Hanoi to be governed by the communists under Ho Chi Minh, and the South with its capital in Saigon to be governed by an anticommunist, western-backed group. Under the terms of the Geneva agreement this division was to be temporary and was to be ended when countrywide elections were held in 2 years. The Vietminh agreed to the division, because it had no doubt that it would prevail in an election. What it had won on the battlefield, however, it lost at the conference table. In 1956 the South Vietnamese regime refused to schedule the elections, and in this decision it was supported by the United States, which saw this strategy as a way of containing the global advancement of communism.

Deeply dismayed, Ho set about to continue the military struggle for the unification and independence of Vietnam. A guerrilla movement, the Viet Cong, was established in the south. In 1960, the National Liberation Front, a revolutionary political arm or government in hiding, was established for South Vietnam. The National Liberation Front, the Viet Cong and the regular army of North Vietnam were remarkable for their integration of women at all levels. As the communists increased their pressure against the South, the United States responded by increasing its support of the southern regime. Under President Eisenhower, several hundred military advisers were sent, some of whom lost their lives in skirmishes, and both military and economic aid were increased. Under President Kennedy, support grew and South Vietnam increasingly became a client of the United States. In fact, the United States began to control who was in power in the South; it was implicated, for example, in the assassination of President Ngo Dinh Diem in 1963.

It was under President Johnson that the United States committed itself irrevocably to a full-scale war in Vietnam. The only official authorization for the war was a congressional resolution passed during a moment of national hysteria following a military engagement involving American ships in the Gulf of Tonkin. Journalists were later able to prove that the Gulf of Tonkin incident had been consciously provoked by the United States in order to manipulate the Congress. The military effort that ensued was major, with the number of American troops in Vietnam rising to a peak of 543,000 in 1969. The war pitted conventional armed power against a guerrilla foe who was able to melt into the local population. The United States and its South Vietnamese ally never succeeded in securing the allegiance of the villagers, in winning their "hearts and minds," as the phrase went, and in the end their effort was doomed.

Because of his failure to bring the war to a successful conclusion, President Johnson declined to run for reelection in 1968, and he was replaced in 1969 by Richard Nixon. Nixon was as committed to victory as Johnson had been, but after years of failing to achieve a breakthrough, and facing increasing opposition to the war at home, he finally brought American involvement to an end. In 1973, most of the American troops pulled out, leaving the pursuit of the war to the South Vietnamese army. It was unequal to the task, and in 1975 the northern armies marched into Saigon, renamed Ho Chi Minh City, as the last remaining American diplomats fled ignominiously by helicopter from the roof of the American embassy.

The Vietnam War left devastation in its wake. In the United States it was responsible for the disaffection of a generation of young people from the government, and for the abandonment of the once promising War on Poverty at home. More than 57,000 Americans died, and returning veterans found themselves both scorned and ignored for years by many of their compatriots. It was the first war lost by the United States,[4] and while such a chastening experience may ultimately have been constructive, it left severe scars on the self-confidence of the nation. The war brought the morality of the country into question. Millions of people, particularly the youth, could not understand what possible interest the United States had in opposing what they regarded as the legitimate aspirations for independence of the Vietnamese people.

In Vietnam, the consequences were much more severe. The loss of human life over the 34 years of warfare was staggering, probably in the neighborhood of 2 million. The economic dislocation was enormous, too; once the ricebowl of Southeast Asia, a major exporter of food, Vietnam became a food importer, unable to meet its own most basic needs. The scores that were settled in South Vietnam after the northern victory were not pretty. Hundreds of thousands of people regarded by the victors as collaborators were deprived of their property, and many were sent to punitive "reeducation" camps. Many people attempted to escape from the new regime—and the world became numbed to the stories of the boat people, some of whom were robbed, maimed, raped and killed by pirates as they left the country. Meanwhile, rather than devote its energies to the peaceful reconstruction of the country, the Vietnamese leaders continued their military involvement by invading and administering Cambodia. (At the time of the North Vietnamese victory, Cambodia was going through its own excruciating hell, in which close to 2 million of its own people were killed in a genocidal orgy of purification by its Khmer Rouge faction).

Ho Chi Minh had been a man of enormous principle and vision. His successors, doubtless conditioned by more than a generation of warfare, turned out to be people of narrow views, unable to bring to their people the benefits of peace and independence. At the beginning of the 1990's, there was some indication that a new group of Vietnamese leaders, having withdrawn from Cambodia, were willing to turn their attention to the reconstruction of the country and the welfare of their own people. Like the Chinese rulers to their north, however, they were not willing to loosen their authoritarian political control.[5] For almost half a century, therefore, the Vietnamese revolution and independence movement had brought little but tragedy to the country.

Algeria

Algeria in North Africa was the scene of another of the Third World's bitter struggles for nationalist self-determination by a colonized people. The Algerian war of independence against France was fought from 1954 until 1961. Algeria had been a territory of France since 1840, when a French army had chased out the last remaining representatives of the Ottoman Empire and systematically conquered the country. France extended control to neighboring Morocco and Tunisia as well, but only in the form of "protectorates," allowing the local governments to remain. France's relationship to Algeria was quite different. Incorporated directly as part of the French state, Algeria had representation in the French legislature. Most importantly, France encouraged the settlement of a white population in Algeria in the nineteenth century.

Only half of the settlers were actually French—the other half were poor southern Europeans from other countries, primarily Spain and Italy. Within a couple of generations, however, they had been molded together into a cohesive group, fervid in their patriotism toward France and in their distrust of the Arabs. By the time the war of independence broke out, there were 1 million French settlers in Algeria, most of whose families had been there for many generations, and about 9 million Arabs.

The white settlers owned most of the fertile land, much of which was used for the production of wine grapes. The process by which the settlers had gained ownership of the land was only partially through the use of military force. The French regime had actually introduced into Algeria the concept of land ownership. Under the Ottoman Empire, different tribal groups had different sorts of use rights over the land, but they did not own it. That is to say, the people who tilled the land did not have the authority to transfer or sell it, except in quite rare circumstances. When the French introduced the foreign concept of ownership, it became possible for the settlers to acquire legal title to the land and to expropriate it from the people who had used it for centuries.

The coming of the Europeans therefore transformed the Arab population from a state of self-sufficiency into a new state of impoverishment. People who had once worked their own land were reduced to the status of wage laborers, in a country where labor was plentiful and therefore poorly paid. Land that had once produced food to feed the local population now produced wine to delight the palates of the metropolitan French. There were several revolts in the nineteenth century to protest this state of affairs, but they failed, and there were no revolts in the first half of the twentieth century.

Pressure for change was building, however. Hundreds of thousands of Algerians migrated to France for jobs; while there they were exposed to the liberating ideas that were the legacy of the French Revolution. At home, the Algerian people were turning increasingly to Islam, as a belief system that reinforced their identity and provided a form of at least symbolic resistance. The French failed to grasp the meaning of these developments, in large measure because they were used to dealing with the small minority of Algerians who did own land, wielded some authority and professed allegiance to the French. This layer of bourgeois Algerians served effectively to mask the growing disaffection of the majority of the people.

The fate of Algeria was sealed by events external to it. The Second World War saw the defeat of France, and although the free French resisted and ultimately triumphed, the tragedy of the war sapped both their physical strength and their morale. For the Algerians, the spectacle of a defeated France gave hope that the colonizer was not all-powerful. Algerians served in the French army during the war, gaining experience and self-confidence. In the immediate postwar years, their leaders argued for concessions but were unsuccessful. The contradictions of colonial rule were becoming untenable.

The French refusal to grant concessions was based on two enormous realities. First, Algeria was the only French colony where there was significant French settlement. The mother country was willing to grant independence to her other colonies in North and West Africa, but she was not willing to abandon the white settlers to Arab rule. Second, after World War II the French army had been in continuous action in Indochina, where it had ultimately been humiliated by its former subjects. Upon losing the battle of Dien Bien Phu in 1954, the French army retreated from Vietnam, and it was determined never to suffer another like defeat. In Algeria, then, the French army took upon itself an aggressive role that was quite extraordinary for a western democratic country, insofar as the army was to a large extent independent of its own national government.

The Algerian revolt broke out in 1954 in the mountainous eastern regions of the country. It spread 2 years later to the cities, in particular to the Casbah section of Algiers. It was a war of rural guerrilla action and urban terrorism by the Algerians, opposed by massive police and military action by the French. Both sides used torture as a weapon in their struggles. The French engaged in massive forced movements of population to uproot support for the rebels.

From a military point of view, the French were successful. They destroyed the urban resistance in 1957 and largely succeeded in suppressing the rural movements. The Algerians were forced to develop a military capacity outside the borders of Algeria, mostly in Tunisia, while their internal forces were decimated. But the Algerian military forces, although defeated in the field, had done their damage politically. The French government and people were losing the willpower for continuous military engagements. They were more interested in rebuilding France economically and joining in the postwar European prosperity.

The settlers and the army found themselves therefore fighting a rearguard action on the political front. Their commitment to a French Algeria brought about the downfall of the French government in 1958 and the ascendancy of wartime hero General Charles de Gaulle as president, but even this could not save them. Within 2 years, de Gaulle had decided to abandon Algeria, in return for the promise of peace. The settlers turned in rage against the French government, aided and abetted by the army. The fury against de Gaulle, whom they had thought to be their savior, was fierce. The president survived an assassination attempt, and most of the army in Algeria mutinied in 1961. But the mutiny was put down, and the settlers were abandoned. Algeria became an independent country in 1961, although it remained closely tied to France for aid and technology. Most of the settlers were forced out.

The ideologies lying behind the Algerian war of independence were varied and complex. There was a resurgence of religious commitment, and there were strains of socialism, even communism. But what united the Algerians was nationalism, a love of their country, a grim determination to recover the lands and the dignity of which they had been robbed.

At independence, Algeria was left destitute as the French pulled out. By one estimate, there were fewer than a dozen trained typists in the country, for example, and the prospect of running a bureaucracy seemed hopeless. But the Algerians persevered, and with some luck and with quite a lot of support from France, they developed a sustainable economy and raised the people's standard of living fairly regularly in the decades after independence. Algeria took the leadership in organizing the Group of Seventy-Seven, a coalition of Third World countries that struggled for a "New International Economic Order" in the 1970's. Perhaps the Algerian successes can best be seen through Marxist lenses: whatever its other effects, the more than a century of French colonialism had so pulverized the traditional forms of social organization in agriculture that after independence the population could be mobilized fairly efficiently for economic development.

All is not smooth in Algeria, however. In 1988, there were large-scale urban riots that were suppressed ruthlessly by the army, with a loss of life running probably into the thousands. The rioters had both economic and social grievances against the one-party state. On the economic side, they protested rising food prices and the unavailability of housing and government services. On the political side, the target was corruption. One of their slogans was, "Ali Baba oui, les quarantes voleurs non" (Ali Baba yes, the forty thieves no).

So, Algeria is as positive a story as there is about the aftermath of a revolutionary, nationalist independence movement in the Third World. It is not without its very serious problems, however.[6]

Moslem and Jewish Nationalism
and the Dilemma of the Middle East

The Algerian revolution was connected to the nationalist reawakening of the entire Arab world. The Arabic-speaking regions of North Africa and the Middle East had been a part of the sprawling Ottoman Empire, which collapsed slowly in the nineteenth century as it was confronted by the European empires. The French, British and Italians established colonies or protectorates over the entire Arab world in the twentieth century, and then relinquished control to independent nation states. More than twenty countries emerged, sharing between them the Moslem faith and the Arabic tongue.

For the most part, the new Arab states were governed as autocracies;

while there were sometimes elections, there were seldom legitimate opposition movements. The people gradually developed national identities, although these always had to compete with supranational identities—of being Moslem and Arab. It has seemed curious, both to outside observers and to Arabs, that so many countries existed, since the cultures were so similar. In fact, many Arabs reject the idea of separate countries and proclaim instead an "Arab nation." There have been numerous attempts to break down the national boundaries and form larger and more powerful nations, but they have always foundered, sometimes on the competitive ambitions of the countries' rulers, sometimes on real cultural differences.

What aroused Arab nationalism more than anything was the creation of a Jewish state, Israel, in Palestine. The conflict between Jew and Arab has persisted now for decades and shows no signs of abating. Although foreign control over the Arab states is a phenomenon of the past, Arabs still tend to view the state of Israel as an imperialist vestige, a dagger aimed at their heart.

Inspired by the ideology of Zionism, European Jews had been migrating to Palestine, the Holy Land, since the late-nineteenth century, when the area was still administered by the Ottoman Turks. The British took control of Palestine during the First World War and administered it as a League of Nations mandate after 1922. They were largely responsible for the conflict that ensued, for they promised the area twice during the First World War: to the Arabs and also, by the 1917 Balfour Declaration, to the Zionists as a "Jewish homeland." In the 1920's and 1930's, the British tried to restrict Jewish immigration, in order to preserve the ascendancy of Arabs in the region, but the immigration continued as Jews fled an increasingly dangerous Europe. With the Second World War came the Holocaust, the murder of the 6 million and the destruction of European Jewry. Survivors fled to Palestine in increasing numbers both during and after the war, seeking a homeland in which they could be safe from virulent anti-Semitism. The British were hardly encouraging, but neither did they prevent the ingathering. They attempted to work out an agreement between the Arabs and the Jews, and when that failed, they turned the problem over to the United Nations. In 1947, the UN voted for a geographical partition of the area, and on the basis of that vote the British withdrew in 1948. But the UN vote hardly resolved matters. As the British withdrew, the Jews pronounced the founding of the republic of Israel—and the Arab armies invaded. By the end of the war, the Israelis had doubled the territory voted them by the UN, and half a million Palestinian refugees had fled the country.

Four more Arab-Israeli wars were fought, in 1956, 1967, 1973 and 1982. The 1956 war occurred when the British withdrew from the Suez Canal Zone and President Nasser of Egypt moved to nationalize the canal and exclude Israeli shipping from it. The Egyptians prevailed when the United States refused to support the intervention of Britain, France and Israel. In 1967, there was a quick 6-day war when the Egyptians closed the Gulf of Aquaba; along with their refusal to let the Israelis use the Suez Canal, this would have cut off all Israeli commerce to the east, and the Israelis retaliated. They scored a striking victory, taking over the West Bank of the Jordan River and the eastern part of Jerusalem from Jordan, the Golan Heights from Syria, and the Gaza Strip and the Sinai peninsula from Egypt. Their geographical expansion brought another million Arabs under Israeli rule. While the Israelis did not incorporate the new areas directly into their state, they did encourage a number of Jewish settlements in the occupied territories, with the consequence that the return of the land to Arab authority would be much more difficult in the future. On the Jewish holy day of Yom Kippur in 1973, the Egyptian and Syrian armies attacked Israel. While the fighting was much lengthier than in 1967, again the Israelis prevailed, reoccupying the Golan Heights and crossing to the west bank of the Suez Canal. It was at the time of the 1973 war that the Arab countries instituted a boycott of oil sales to the United States—to punish it for its support of Israel—and then a few months later converted the boycott into a substantial increase in the price of oil.

After the 1973 war, President Anwar Sadat of Egypt made peace with Israel, to the consternation of the other Arab countries. Sadat visited Jerusalem and Israeli president Menachem Begin visited Cairo, following which the two leaders signed the Camp David Accords in Washington in 1979, to signify the end of 30 years of hostility. Israel agreed to withdraw from the Sinai, while Egypt agreed to recognize Israel and to permit Israeli shipping through the Suez Canal.

The 1982 war occurred when Israel invaded Lebanon, to close down refugee camps from which the Palestine Liberation Organization (PLO) had been attacking Israel, and to try to create some sort of orderly and friendly government in a country that had collapsed into anarchy. The Lebanese conflict proved to be too much for even the Israelis, and they eventually withdrew without accomplishing their objectives.

In the 1991 Persian Gulf war, Israel was attacked by Iraqi missiles but did not retaliate.

Throughout their existence as a state, therefore, the Israelis have never known the peace they had hoped they would find when fleeing the anti-Semitism of Europe. They have developed into a military state, with enormous weapons capability and a reputation for swift, precise action. That reputation was damaged in the 1982 incursion into Lebanon, when they permitted a Lebanese Christian militia to massacre civilian residents of a PLO refugee camp. It was further damaged in the *intifada*, the uprising of Arab youth that began in the late 1980's in Israel. The army proved unable to suppress the attacks but responded at times with brutality. Still, Israel has developed one of the world's strongest arsenals and has greater military capability than all of its neighbors combined.

Arrayed against Israel is the confusing coalition of Arab nationalists. At the heart of the resistance is the Palestinian people, represented in effect by the PLO. Palestinian refugees have lived for more than a generation now in the countries surrounding Israel. They have never been absorbed into the host countries, and their bitterness has grown. Since the 1967 war, more than a million of the Palestinians have actually been ruled by the Israelis, on the West Bank and the Gaza Strip. The Palestinians are on the whole a well-educated, sophisticated and articulate people, whose determination to secure a homeland for themselves has only grown in intensity.

The Arab countries surrounding Israel have all opposed the Jewish state, but have seldom been able to join forces in a coherent way to achieve their ends. The Egyptians led several wars against the Israelis, but then made peace so that their resources could be used to advance the welfare of their own people and not be squandered in war. The Syrians, under a militant left-wing government, have maintained their hostility against Israel and are particularly committed to the return of their territory on the Golan Heights, but they have refused to allow the PLO on their territory because of the threat that it represents to their regime. King Hussein of Jordan, too, has been reluctant to allow the PLO much of a foothold lest it destabilize his rule. In 1988, he abandoned responsibility for the Palestinians living in the Israeli-occupied territories. Iraq has been continuously hostile to Israel and used the occasion of the Persian Gulf war to launch missiles against it, without much effect. The Lebanese were the least aggressive of Israel's neighbors until their country collapsed as an administrative unit in 1975; since then Lebanon has been the scene of almost continuous warfare and jockeying for power.

The problem of Israel and the Palestinians has become so complex as to be almost beyond solution. Israel seems incapable of defining the direction in which it even wants to proceed. It cannot at the same time retain the occupied territories on the West Bank and the Gaza Strip, which are predominantly Arab in population, and be a Jewish state, and be a democracy. If it is a democracy, allowing each person a vote, and if it continues to hold the occupied territories, then it will eventually cease to have a Jewish majority. But if it is not a democracy, and continues to deny the rights of political participation to its Arab residents, then it will lose the idealism that is so necessary to its sense of itself and to the support that it needs from abroad.

It seems inescapable that there must be a negotiated settlement between Israel and the Palestinians. In the early 1990's, multilateral negotiations began among the Israelis, the Palestinians and the neighboring Arab countries, sponsored initially by the United States and the then-Soviet Union. The Labor Party, which formed the new Israeli government, seemed open to the possibility of ceding land for a Palestinian "state" that would have at least some of the attributes of sovereignty, provided that this concession would lead to a plausible peace treaty. The negotiations have been fraught with obstacles, however, and at least in the first two years of meetings, little has been accomplished.

One cannot know the course Arab nationalism would have taken had the struggle against Israel not become so central. As matters turned out, a great deal of resources and energy were directed toward the conflict that might otherwise have been used to improve living conditions.

The Islamic world extends beyond the Arab states—to black Africa in the south and to Turkey, Iran, Afghanistan, Pakistan and beyond. Throughout this entire vast region of the Third World, the end of imperialism brought with it powerful new forces of social change—an upsurge of pride and nationalism and innumerable clashes between social and religious groups. Western technology was widely adopted, accompanied in the case of some of the Moslem countries by an unprecedented accumulation of wealth as a result of increasing petroleum prices. Nowhere were these tensions experienced more acutely than in Iran.

Iran has a long history of foreign domination and of resistance to that domination. After the Second World War, the Shah of Iran, supported by Britain and the United States, overthrew a reform parliament that was threatening to nationalize the country's oil industry, and thereafter ruled autocratically with the endorsement of the west. He supported the modernization of the country and the introduction of new business enterprises, as well as the growth of a westernized middle class. He also was ruthlessly dictatorial, however, ruling with the support of a brutal secret police and making massive use of torture and execution.

The opposition to the Shah's regime was motivated in part by revulsion at his use of state terror, but more fundamentally by resistance to the westernization of popular culture. The Moslem fundamentalism that eventually engulfed Iran in the revolution of 1978 was growing throughout the Islamic world; it is a movement that rejects all western influences, including western technology, individual democratic rights, and the equality of women. In Iran, riots and strikes led to the overthrow of the Shah and the assumption of power by a clerical hierarchy, led by the fierce figure of the Ayatollah Khomeini. Almost in a moment, the trappings of western culture disappeared from Iranian life. Women covered their heads with the veil and were restricted from public life. Alcohol, western dress for women, mixed bathing, the western press, western music and many other forms of foreign culture were banned. Justice was administered by stern Islamic courts. Much of the fury of the revolution was directed against the United States, which had supported the Shah and which was seen to be the embodiment of evil. The new regime soon found itself in an 8-year war with its Arab neighbor Iraq, a war marked by the slogans of righteousness and the seemingly endless slaughter of the young.

Iran's nightmare could well be repeated elsewhere. The nationalist resentment of imperialism and pride in one's cultural identity that have occurred throughout the Third World were combined in Iran with a furious rejection of western ideas and faith in the Islamic scriptures to produce an intolerant, terrifying regime bent on the destruction of foreign elements and willing to sacrifice vast numbers of its own people.

Sub-Saharan Africa

Independence came to most of sub-Saharan Africa in a dazzling moment: a few short years just before and after 1960 that were anticipated by virtually no one. Africa had been partitioned almost overnight in the late-nineteenth century, and independence came to the continent in an even more compressed period of years. Prior to 1957, only Liberia and Ethiopia were independent countries, but after 1964 almost all of Africa except the southern region was composed of autonomous states. By 1990, even southern Africa, with the exception of the Republic of South Africa, was governed by its black majorities.

The first African country to attain its independence, in 1957, was the Gold Coast, which took on the name of an ancient African kingdom, Ghana. Thereafter, as the colonialists realized that the nationalist movements could not be defeated permanently, they made haste to withdraw from most of their possessions.

There were some exceptions. White settlers were loath to give up political control to the Africans, and so the struggles for independence in Kenya, and later in Zimbabwe (formerly Southern Rhodesia), were more protracted and difficult than they were in the areas that had simply been administered by the imperialists, without settlement. In addition, the most backward of the European imperial powers, Portugal, was untouched by the arguments for independence that swayed the other imperialists, and it held on to its two principal territories, Angola and Mozambique, until 1975.

Nowhere has the promise of independence been more cruelly betrayed than in Africa. In most countries, any semblance of democracy has disappeared, and one-party states are the norm. Many countries are controlled by a military faction. Some of the world's worst human rights abuses occurred in Uganda, principally but not exclusively under the regime of Idi Amin. The continent's most creative social programs, in Tanzania under the leadership of Julius Nyerere, did little to rescue that country from underdevelopment. The economic giant of black Africa, Nigeria, prospered in the 1970's during the world oil boom, but then collapsed in the 1980's as a consequence of the oil bust. Hundreds of thousands of people have starved in the vast deserts. There has been no sustained economic growth, and taken as a whole the continent is scarcely better off, perhaps worse, than it was at independence.

The greatest tragedy of Africa was for decades in the Republic of South Africa, where a white minority society became entrenched and successfully resisted whatever nationalist movements were arrayed against it. Only in the 1990's did there appear any prospects at all for peaceful, democratic change.

Dutch settlers arrived at the Cape of Good Hope as early as 1652. Sternly Protestant, they mixed over the years with other Protestant settlers, most notably the French Huguenots, to form a people who eventually called themselves Afrikaners. Afrikaner mythology includes the claim that the whites preceded black Africans into the southern tip of the continent, but this position cannot be reconciled with the fact that the Dutch settlers fought wars against African tribes and enslaved Africans on their farms. In 1814, the British annexed the colony as part of the settlement of the Napoleonic Wars. Eventually, the Afrikaners escaped what they regarded as oppressive British rule in their "Great Trek" to the interior, establishing the two independent republics of the Orange Free State and Transvaal. However, when diamonds were discovered in the Orange Free State and gold in Transvaal at the end of the nineteenth century, the British moved to annex the two republics. The Afrikaners, now called in some contexts Boers, resisted and the Boer War (1899–1902) resulted. The British won the Boer War but lost the peace. Following the war, the British granted full independence in 1910 to the Union of South Africa. All whites, both Boer and British, were given the vote; the Africans, the Indians and the mixed-race "coloreds" were given no consideration at all. Over the course of the twentieth century, the right-wing, religiously fundamentalist Afrikaners gradually gained power over the somewhat (but not remarkably) more liberal British.

Throughout the twentieth century in South Africa, black nationalist movements attempted to challenge the minority rule of the whites, but the principal result was to produce a long chain of martyrs and to entrench even further the white minority. The Afrikaner Nationalist party came to power in 1948 and erected the structure of *apartheid,* or separateness of the races. The doctrine of apartheid is based upon the pretense that the races live separately in South Africa, that the blacks are actually foreigners in the country. In fact, the races have never been separate. Even most of the early Afrikaner farms used black labor, and today's advanced industrial economy is completely dependent upon the labor of Africans. The wealth of the white minority depends upon the exploitation of black labor in the gold mines and in the factories; it is impossible for the two races to be "apart." Nevertheless, apartheid became the system of control that allowed the exploitation to continue. Independent "homelands" were established (in barren areas), and the black population was given "citizenship" in these homelands, the result being that the black labor force in the Republic could be treated as an alien population, without civil or political rights.

One of the first leaders of the South African resistance was Mohandas Gandhi, who developed his nonviolent philosophy while working among South Africa's Indian population. Generations of black leaders fought the white oppression; some of the great names of recent history are Robert Sobukwe, Steven Biko, Archbishop Desmond Tutu and Nelson Mandela. As the nationalist movements grew stronger, and as the world community paid increasing attention to the worst remaining case of colonial oppression, the Afrikaner tribe seemed to turn increasingly inward, developing its economic strength and its military arsenal, regimes around the world. The South African government today has nuclear weapons.

Although the military power of the government remains unassailable, its commitment to white supremacy appears to have collapsed. In the early 1990's, it embarked upon a new course that seemed bound to lead to black majority government. In 1990 it released Nelson Mandela, the country's most famous political prisoner, rescinded many apartheid laws, granted legitimacy to outlawed nationalist movements and began negotiations with representatives of those movements on a new constitution. The target date for the country's first non-racial election was 1994. The process of bargaining for constitutional change has been set back by violence, but it seems unlikely that the evolution of democracy can be forestalled.

Latin America

The history of Latin America in the twentieth century has been different from that of Asia, Africa and the Middle East, because almost all of Latin America was independent—in fact had been independent since about 1820. The Spanish and Portuguese had withdrawn from their American empires just after the Napoleonic Wars, and they had not been permitted to return. The independence of the new Latin American states was guaranteed on the one hand by the British, whose navies controlled the Atlantic and who refused to allow the former colonialists to return, and on the other hand by the United States, whose Monroe Doctrine had asserted the freedom of the Americas from European control. But the legal independence of the Latin American countries did not imply true autonomy. In the nineteenth century, the British established strong trading relationships with most of the Latin American countries. To ensure the stability of their trade and also of their investments, the British established commercial alliances with the ruling groups in most of the countries, and those groups in turn kept the peace at home so that the economic connections with the outside world could continue to prosper.

In the twentieth century, the British role in Latin America was gradually taken over by the United States, as the former's relative power in the world faded and the latter's increased. The Americans maintained alliances with the ruling groups, which in turn promoted tranquillity in the local markets. The role of the United States was not always predictable; although the Americans preferred to exercise their hegemony by peaceful, economic means, they were much less reluctant than the British had been to resolve conflicts by the use of armed force. From the Mexican War of 1846, when the United States annexed half of the territory of Mexico (securing Texas, which had previously asserted its independence, and acquiring what became the states of New Mexico, Arizona, Colorado, Utah, Nevada and California), to the invasions of Grenada and Panama, the support of the Contras in Nicaragua, and the backing of the military government in El Salvador, the United States has regularly been willing to make use of its military capability in Central and South America. But the United States did not establish formal colonies in Latin America. Even when the United States separated Cuba from Spanish control in the war of 1898, it did not take Spain's place—rather it allowed a nominally independent Cuba under American tutelage. In sum, Latin America was subjected to informal, neocolonial domination by the United States, but never to formal colonial control.

As a consequence, the social struggles within Latin America have had a quite different cast from those in the rest of the Third World. The struggles have been for the most part internal wars, in which some factions within each country have sought to defeat their own ruling classes. Of course, the United States has seldom been far from the minds of Latin American rebels in the twentieth century, since in most cases the ruling elites have been supported by the United States. The United States has consistently supplied arms and economic assistance to right-wing regimes in Latin America. But the relationship between social movements and United States domination has been an indirect one.

Many of these themes are illustrated by the history of the Mexican Revolution, which took place between 1910 and 1920. The proximate target of the Mexican Revolution was the regime of General Porfirio

Díaz, who had ruled the country since 1875. Díaz was a successful national entrepreneur, who brought into the country huge amounts of British and American capital to develop the country's resources. A railway network was built across the country, mines were opened up and manufacturing industries were established. But the Mexican peasants, both Indian and mestizo, lost access to the land they had tilled for generations. The hacienda system of huge commercial landholdings was reducing the peasantry to the status of semifree peonage. The peasant rebellion was led by Emiliano Zapata in the south-central region of the country and by Pancho Villa in the north. Its rallying cry was "Land and Liberty." The peasant rebellions were successful militarily; they drove Porfirio Díaz from his seat of power, and they occupied the capital of Mexico City. But they had no political strategy or program and therefore were not able to maintain control of the country. Control passed on through many hands in the second decade of the century, and the cause of the peasants gradually slipped from center place. A constitution was adopted in 1917, expropriating the oil fields from their United States investors and calling for the redistribution of land to the peasants. Little land reform was actually accomplished, however, until the presidential term of Lázaro Cárdenas in the 1930's.

Had Mexico actually been colonized by Britain or the United States, the goal of the revolution would have been clearer—to expel the colonizer and establish an independent nation acting on behalf of all of its people. But since the neocolonial power, the United States, was in the background, the goals of the revolution were less obvious. It was not a war of independence. Neither was it a definitive class war, as the Russian Revolution in 1917 was to be. In some ways it was the last of the pre-twentieth-century revolutions, closest in spirit to the French Revolution of a century and a half before—a revolution fought against a ruler perceived to be oppressive, and on behalf of rather abstract principles of liberty, but without a vision of completely restructuring the social system of the country. The revolution is certainly the most important event in Mexican history. Yet, despite some land reform, the peasantry is still largely excluded from land ownership, and the distribution of income is very unevenly skewed. From the time of the revolution, Mexico was for all practical purposes a one-party state, with politics controlled from the top down. The 1988 election may have represented the beginning of a multiparty democracy, but it is too early to be certain. The Mexican Revolution changed some things, but not as much as the official myths would have it.

The protagonist of Carlos Fuentes' great novel *The Death of Artemio Cruz* was born to poverty in central Mexico in 1889. He fought in the revolution and was captured. While in captivity, he managed to escape execution through the betrayal of a fellow prisoner, a young lawyer who was the son of a rich landowner, or *hacendado*. After the revolution he insinuated himself into the good graces of the lawyer's father, married the lawyer's sister and eventually took over the hacienda. A life of increasing power and manipulation followed, in which Cruz scorned any form of reciprocal love and instead chose to pursue authority and wealth. He colluded with U.S. investors, exploiting them for his own benefit while opening doors to Mexican resources for them to exploit on their part. That is, he acted as the privileged go-between for the neocolonialists, just as Porfirio Díaz and his associates had before the revolution. It is a novel of the betrayal of the revolution, a plaintive, compelling reflection on the fact that the revolution changed the names and faces of the exploiters, but not the exploitation.

Still, the Mexican Revolution was important; more than any other event it created the national myths by which Mexicans of today define themselves. Harriet de Onis wrote:

> During the nineteenth century the literature and art of Mexico were, for the most part, refined, sophisticated, very European. But out of the Revolution there came a new art, centering about "the underdogs"—mestizos, Indians—their problems, their aspirations, represented by the painting of artists like Diego Rivera, Orozco, Siqueiros, and the literature of the Revolution and post Revolution. . . . At the same time the mother lode of the folk revealed itself in the songs and ballads in which the people wrote their own history of the Revolution, celebrating its heroes, narrating its triumphs and vicissitudes. When the Revolution was over, Mexico had become fused into a homogeneous whole.[7]

Mexicans have an acute sense of their nationality, of their culture and of being both an oppressed and a revolutionary people. Living next to the colossus of the north, they can never forget their vulnerability. "Alas poor Mexico," Porfirio Díaz may have said, "so far from God, so close to the United States." The revolution, no matter how thoroughly its aims of land and liberty for the peasants have been betrayed, remains the moment of national pride.

To the south of Mexico, in the small Central American country of Nicaragua, the Sandinista revolution of 1979 fought for over a decade for its survival. In 1990, it lost in a free election to a coalition of opposition parties.

Nicaragua's was a classic revolution in the sense that it was fought on behalf of the poor people of the country against an oppressive ruling class and its military arm, the National Guard. It received aid from the Soviet Union, and consequently the United States government tried to portray it as a beachhead for Soviet expansionism in the western hemisphere. But the preponderance of the evidence is that it was a profoundly nationalist movement and, as such, refused to be put into a subordinate role by the Soviets. It was certainly an anti-American revolution, hardly surprising in view of the decades of American occupation of the country and the unwavering support of successive U.S. governments for the dictators who ruled Nicaragua during most of the twentieth century. It was a Christian revolution, based upon the religious faith of the people and the liberation theology of many of the clergy.

United States involvement in Nicaragua began early in the twentieth century; President William Howard Taft sent military forces in 1909 to depose a nationalist movement under Liberal Nicaraguan president José Santos Zelaya. Nationalist rebellion continued, and the United States sent Marines into the country in 1912, to "restore order," that is to say, to ensure the stability of a friendly Conservative government.

The Marines stayed in Nicaragua from 1912 to 1933, with one temporary withdrawal in 1925–26. During this period of occupation, the United States armed and trained the Nicaraguan National Guard, expecting it to be a military force that would create conservative stability in the country and support American interests. During the U.S. occupation, a guerrilla force under the leadership of Augusto César Sandino achieved considerable success, organizing peasants and workers and harassing the government troops.

When the Marines left in 1933, power was gradually transferred to Anastasio Somoza García, the commander of the National Guard. One of his first acts was to execute Sandino, in spite of a promise he had made to protect his life. Somoza and his two sons maintained personal, dictatorial rule in Nicaragua for over 40 years, until they were finally driven out by the revolution in 1979. Anastasio Somoza was assassinated in 1956. His son Luis Somoza became president until 1963. After a short period of rule by puppets, Luis' brother Anastasio became president in 1967.

The Somoza family ruled by the force of military power. They had no concern for the welfare of the Nicaraguan people; their style of government could best be described as ruling by looting. They amassed extraordinary wealth while living conditions worsened throughout the country.

Up until their last few years, the Somozas enjoyed the enthusiastic support of successive U.S. governments. The family was skilled at maintaining this support; they were all educated in the United States, fluent in the American idiom and able to manipulate their benefactors with ease. They were responsive to changing currents in American thought. When President Kennedy instituted the Alliance for Progress, for example, Luis Somoza adopted some of the trappings of democracy. But when the Kennedy era was over, Anastasio Somoza made little attempt to hide his personal and brutal control. In his last years, Anastasio Somoza did manage to lose the support of President Carter's government, over the issue of human rights abuses.

The Sandinista insurgency began in 1961 and gradually gained strength over the following two decades. By the mid-1970's, the revolutionaries were able to make raids in the capital city of Managua and, on one occasion, to hold hostages and to bargain with the government over their release. During the 1970's, the greed and brutality of the Somoza government became more overt. Following the catastrophic earthquake in Managua in 1972, Somoza and his followers absconded with most of the foreign funds that were donated for relief and reconstruction, leaving the city essentially destroyed until the Sandinistas took over. The National Guard's campaign against the Sandinistas was marked by exceptional brutality.

The event that triggered the final War of Liberation was the government's murder, in January 1978, of the editor of the newspaper *La Prensa*, Pedro Joaquín Chamorro. The Sandinista army engaged the National Guard and finally forced Somoza out of the country in July 1979, when the United States offered refuge. The conflict cost 50,000 deaths, or 2 percent of the Nicaraguan population.[8]

The Sandinista revolutionaries, led by President Daniel Ortega, were engaged in continuous warfare after 1981. The opposition Contras received financial support from the United States, and their leadership was selected and trained by the Americans. While the Contras harassed and attacked the new government and its forces, they did not have any permanent successes; they were not able to exert secure control over any areas of the country. Nevertheless, they were strong enough to divert the resources of the new government away from the urgent tasks of economic development. The United States Congress grew increasingly weary of supporting the Contras, however, and in 1988 declined to authorize additional funding. Meanwhile, a peace plan was devised by the Central American countries, under the leadership of Costa Rican president Oscar Arias Sánchez (and with the opposition of the U.S. government, which seemed to prefer a military solution).

The controversies surrounding the Nicaraguan revolution were extraordinary. The right-wing American opponents of the revolution portrayed it as dictatorial and under the thumb of the Soviets. Nicaragua, in fact, became one of the two or three chief foreign policy obsessions of President Reagan. The opening sentences of one of his speeches on the subject, in 1985, were:

> The Sandinista dictatorship has taken absolute control of the government and the armed forces. It is a communist dictatorship. It has done what communist dictatorships do: created a repressive state security and secret police organization assisted by Soviet, East German, and Cuban advisers; harassed, and in many cases expunged, the

The Nationalist Identity

There were many more nationalist and revolutionary movements in the Third World in the twentieth century. They varied tremendously, from gentle to violent. One feature they all shared, however, was a concern for identity. Imperialism had shorn away the dignity of Third World peoples; nationalism was at least in part a yearning to recover it. Nowhere was the issue of identity more important than in black Africa, where the imperialist experience had been particularly tragic. Especially in West Africa, centuries of the slave trade had ravaged the indigenous communities. Large migrations had shattered cultural roots. The Africans had been a people to be exploited, or if not exploited, excluded. Throughout the twentieth century, therefore, African nationalist movements and the cultural expressions that accompanied them have been filled with assertions of identity and self-worth, of "negritude" and "black consciousness."

Particularly notable was the movement for negritude that accompanied the nationalism of French West Africa, an insistence that blackness was beautiful, was soulful, was creative and expressive. Treated though it was by the imperialists as a mark of shame and slavery, blackness was in truth a badge of pride. One of the leaders of the negritude movement was the Senegalese poet Léopold Sédar Senghor, a man who embodied the ambiguities of the colonial age. Senghor was educated in France and honored in French literary societies. He fought in the French army in the Second World War and then became a deputy, representing Dakar, West Africa, in the French Assembly. In 1960, he led his nation to independence and became its first president. Deeply connected to French culture and at home in the salons of Paris, he nevertheless was acutely aware of race. Although he wrote in French, his images were black:

> Femme nue, femme noire
> Vêtue de ta couleur qui est vie, de ta forme qui est beauté![11]
>
> Woman nude, woman black
> Clad in your color which is life, in your shape which is beauty!

In Senghor's poetry, negritude was a proud proclamation, but it was not an angry one. Senghor made his peace with the French; he was almost one of them. His own experience mirrors that of most of the territories of French West Africa. When the territories became independent in 1960, all of them but one, Guinea, chose to remain in an association with France, hoping to benefit from foreign aid and technology, while at the same time developing a more equal relationship political opposition; and rendered the democratic freedoms of speech, press, and assembly punishable by officially sanctioned harassment and imprisonment or death.

But the communists are not unopposed. They are facing great resistance from the people of Nicaragua, resistance from the patriots who fight for freedom and their unarmed allies from the prodemocracy movement.[9]

Supporters of the revolution saw it in quite different terms, as one of the most hopeful movements for the poor and oppressed ever to come out of Latin America. In contrast to the Chilean communist government of 1970–73 under President Salvador Allende, it was capable of defending itself militarily. In contrast to the Cuban revolution, it was willing to permit at least some diversity of opinion and some opposition groups. The revolution's supporters contended that whatever attacks there were on peaceful opposition groups were the unfortunate consequence of the country's being at war. President Ortega made clear statements about the regime's intention to support plurality:

> We're struggling to establish a regime that is of a democratic and pluralistic nature. . . . We seek pluralism in the sense that even though the Nicaraguan revolution is a very profound process, it does give room for participation by diverse groups. The revolution has established a framework within which different political, economic, and social forces can be active, can move about.[10]

Ortega made good on this pledge, permitting free, multiparty elections in 1990. In a stunning reversal, however, Nicaraguans rejected the Sandinistas in that election, choosing instead a coalition under the leadership of Violeta Chamorro, widow of the assassinated editor. The 11 years of Sandinista rule had brought almost universal suffering and a declining standard of living as the economy had descended into shambles. Chamorro's support apparently came from people who believed she could end the warfare and restore friendly relations with the United States, thereby bringing a semblance of normality to the country.

She did succeed in ending the warfare. Friendly relations with the United States were more difficult to achieve, however. At home, Chamorro did her best to balance competing interests by permitting the Sandinistas to retain considerable power in the new regime. She allowed the army to remain under the leadership of Sandinista commanders, and she permitted Sandinistas to retain property they had appropriated. The U.S. government became increasingly skeptical of this strategy, and greatly reduced its support of the Chamorro government. The internal affairs of this tiny country continued to be buffeted, therefore, by the global agenda of the United States, much as they had been throughout the century.

with the former colonialist. Independence as a nation was necessary because the people could not remain subject, but the independence came amicably. Negritude was a philosophy of moderation.

As such, negritude earned the scorn of Africans whose struggles were harder and whose emotions were more bitter. The angriest, most piercing cry, not only in Africa but in all of the Third World, came from the pen of Frantz Fanon. Fanon was born in 1925 in the French colony of Martinique in the West Indies. He studied in France and became a psychiatrist. During the Algerian war of independence in the late 1950's, he practiced medicine in an Algerian hospital and became an ally of the Algerian rebels. He wrote extensively about the psychology of the colonial relationship; his last and greatest book, *The Wretched of the Earth*, was written in a frenzied rush in 1961, as he was simultaneously working in the war effort and dying of cancer. Fanon, more than any other writer, expressed the rage of the Third World against the imperialists, and he deeply influenced a generation of nationalists, both in Africa and further afield.

Fanon wrote from the context of the settler colonies, the colonies like Algeria in which Europeans had expropriated the land and established their own farms. It was in these colonies that the anticolonialist struggles were the most bitter. The native people regarded the land they had lost as sacred and life-sustaining, while the European settlers were completely committed to their new homes and absolutely unwilling to give them up. Each page, each sentence of Fanon's work screams with outrage:

> Every time Western values are mentioned they produce in the native a sort of stiffening or muscular lockjaw. During the period of decolonization, the native's reason is appealed to. He is offered definite values, he is told frequently that decolonization need not mean regression, and that he must put his trust in qualities which are well-tried, solid, and highly esteemed. But it so happens that when the native hears a speech about Western culture he pulls out his knife. . . . In the colonial context the settler only ends his work of breaking in the native when the latter admits loudly and intelligibly the supremacy of the white man's values. In the period of decolonization, the colonized masses mock at these very values, insult them, and vomit them up.[12]

Rather than recoil from violence, Fanon relished it; after generations of suffering from colonial violence, the people of the Third World could recover their wholeness by striking back:

> For the native, life can only spring up again out of the rotting corpse of the settler. . . . For the colonized people this violence, because it constitutes their only work, invests their characters with positive and creative qualities. The practice of violence binds them together as a whole, since each individual forms a violent link in the

great chain, a part of the great organism of violence which has surged upward in reaction to the settler's violence in the beginning. . . . Violence is a cleansing force. It frees the native from his inferiority complex and from his despair and inaction; it makes him fearless and restores his self-respect.[13]

In later chapters of his book, Fanon withdrew somewhat from the glorification of violence, but not from his anger. The imperialists had tried to pluck out the humanity of the natives, and now that they were leaving they were establishing a native middle class to do their work for them. It was up to the people, the masses, the peasants to rise up and reassert their right to their own destiny. Fanon expressed the urgency and the fury of Third World peoples who had been subjugated.

Senghor's negritude and Fanon's anger were combined in the 1970's in the Black Consciousness movement led by Steven Biko in South Africa. Biko was a student leader who expressed the growing aspirations of his age group. Although Biko and the young South African blacks venerated the leaders of the previous generation, they approached their struggle against apartheid with a new urgency. The white minority had oppressed the black majority not only in physical and material terms, but in terms of their own self-image. South African blacks were a defeated people, Biko argued, and it was time for them to reassert their own worth. He and his colleagues refused any longer to work with white liberals in the student movement, because they needed to proclaim their own pride and leadership. The journalist Donald Woods has collected some of Biko's writings from his student days:

One should not waste time here dealing with manifestations of material want of the black people. A vast literature has been written on this problem. Possibly a little should be said about spiritual poverty. What makes the black man fail to tick? Is he convinced of his own accord of his inabilities? Does he lack in his genetic makeup that rare quality that makes a man willing to die for the realization of his aspirations? Or is he simply a defeated person? The answer to this is not a clearcut one. It is, however, nearer to the last suggestion than anything else. The logic behind white domination is to prepare the black man for the subservient role in this country. . . .

All in all the black man has become a shell, a shadow of man, completely defeated, drowning in his own misery, a slave, an ox bearing the yoke of oppression with sheepish timidity. . . .

The first step therefore is to make the black man come to himself; to pump back life into his empty shell; to infuse him with pride and dignity, to remind him of his complicity in the crime of allowing himself to be misused and therefore letting evil reign supreme in the country of his birth. This is what we mean by an inward-looking process. This is the definition of "Black Consciousness."[14]

The concern with pride, identity and race was strongest in Africa, but it was evident throughout the colonized world. Everywhere whites imposed their rule they evoked a fierce counterresponse. On each continent, the colonized asserted their worth.

The Legacy of Nationalism

The expectations created by the nationalist movements were enormous. Millions of people in the Third World had come to see the imperialists as responsible for their miseries, and they consequently expected their burdens to be lightened with independence, with the victory of the revolution. Not only would the people expel their colonial exploiters, they would assert the dignity of the nation. In place of exploitation, they would achieve sustenance for those who had suffered. In place of deceit and manipulation, they would find idealism, trust and policies carefully designed to repair the damage. With the victory of the independence movements and the revolutions there was an outpouring of enthusiasm. In country after country, the joy could be tasted; the future seemed rich with possibility. In the revolutionary countries the task eagerly picked up was nothing less than creating a new humanity. Previously, people's personalities had been deformed by their oppressive circumstances; the new generation would be raised in a spirit of pride and cooperation.

There is no story more common in human history than the betrayal of the promises inherent in a revolution. The French Revolution, fought to free the people from their masters, degenerated into the Reign of Terror. The Russian Revolution culminated in a police state, purges and the Gulag. Both permanently changed their countries —indeed the world—by destroying the old order and releasing remarkable new social forces; it is hard to imagine the modern world without the French and Russian revolutions. But the legacy of both was far more ambiguous and tortured than the participants ever imagined. What seemed at the time to be a clear-cut victory for humanity turned out to bring advances for some and disaster for others, while replacing one system of power with another.

So too with the Third World nationalist movements. We are still too close to their initial moment of victory to assess their long-term impact completely accurately, but there is no doubt that they share the ambiguities of the French and Russian revolutions. They permanently ended the age of global European imperialism and thereby fundamentally altered the face of the world. But they did not reverse the misery suffered by Third World peoples, and in some cases they added to it. Independence and revolution brought no easy solutions to the many fundamental problems facing the Third World.

The economic problems all remained. After independence as

before, many of the economies of the Third World were dominated by export crops that faced uncertain markets and that depended upon cheap labor in order to remain competitive in world markets. Independence hardly changed this situation at all, except that foreign faces were often replaced by local ones in positions of control.

Particularly hard to bear, however, were political developments in the Third World that represented a betrayal of the nationalist movements. As local people took over power, it turned out that they often had all the capacity for exploiting their compatriots that the imperialists had exhibited.

The creative literature of the revolutionary and nationalist movements often shows that even at the times of the armed struggles themselves, some of the perceptive participants could see the seeds of betrayal. One of the most remarkable predictions came from Fanon's pen at the height of the Algerian revolution. At the beginning of *The Wretched of the Earth,* he celebrated the uprising of the native, but by the middle of the book he showed how that uprising would be betrayed. In a prescient chapter entitled "The Pitfalls of National Consciousness," he wrote that the imperialists would be replaced by a national middle class that would lack even the abilities that the former oppressors had had:

> This traditional weakness . . . is the result of the intellectual laziness of the national middle class, of its spiritual penury, and of the profoundly cosmopolitan mold that its mind is set in. . . . The national middle class which takes over power at the end of the colonial regime is an underdeveloped middle class. It has practically no economic power, and in any case it is in no way commensurate with the bourgeoisie of the mother country which it hopes to replace. . . . The national bourgeoisie of underdeveloped countries is not engaged in production, nor in invention, nor building, nor labor. . . . Its innermost vocation seems to be to keep in the running and to be part of the racket. . . . To them, nationalization quite simply means the transfer into native hands of those unfair advantages which are a legacy of the colonial period.[15]

From a different angle, novelist Mariano Azuela foresaw the betrayal of the Mexican Revolution because the fighters themselves had such an uncertain grasp of their own goals. Azuela, a doctor, joined Pancho Villa's army and took part in military actions, but he then withdrew to El Paso, Texas, when Villa was defeated. In El Paso in 1915, he wrote what has become one of the major novels of the revolution, *Los de abajo,* or *The Underdogs.* It is an unromantic portrait of a band of revolutionary Indians and mestizos, drawn together by their hatred of the landlords and the *federales,* but without any clear program. The only character with a coherent revolutionary ideology is Azuela's fictional counterpart, the doctor Luis Cervantes, who abandons his compatriots at the critical moment to establish a business in El Paso. But the peasants have only the ideology of continued fighting:

> Villa? Obregón? Carranza?" says one. "What's the difference? I
> love the revolution like a volcano in eruption; I love the volcano
> because it's a volcano, the revolution because it's the revolution!
> What do I care about the stones left above or below after the cata-
> clysm? What are they to me?

The wife of the protagonist, an Indian, Demetrio Macias, asks him:

> "Why do you keep on fighting, Demetrio?"
> Demetrio frowned deeply. Picking up a stone absentmindedly, he
> threw it to the bottom of the canyon. Then he stared pensively into
> the abyss, watching the arch of its flight.
> "Look at that stone; how it keeps on going."[16]

As early as 1915, Azuela could see the middle class revolutionaries
trampling over the backs of the poor, and the poor dissipating their
military and moral strength in anomie and confusion.

One of the most perceptive chroniclers of the betrayal of the nationalist movements has been the Nigerian Chinua Achebe. In his novel *A
Man of the People,* the young, university-educated idealist Odili reflects
on the process that has brought the corrupt nationalist politician Chief
Nanga to power:

> A man who has just come in from the rain and dried his body and
> put on dry clothes is more reluctant to go out again than another
> who has been indoors all the time. The trouble with our new
> nation—as I saw it then lying on that bed—was that none of us had
> been indoors long enough to be able to say "To hell with it." We had
> all been in the rain together until yesterday. Then a handful of
> us—the smart and the lucky and hardly ever the best—had scrambled
> for the one shelter our former rulers left, and had taken it over and
> barricaded themselves in. And from within they sought to persuade
> the rest through numerous loudspeakers, that the first phase of the
> struggle had been won and that the next phase—the extension of our
> house—was even more important and called for new and original tac-
> tics; it required that all argument should cease and the whole people
> speak with one voice and that any more dissent and argument outside
> the door of the shelter would subvert and bring down the whole
> house.[17]

In country after country, the ideals of the peoples' movements were
abandoned by the leaders. Democracy faltered as one-party states and
military regimes stifled dissent and violated human rights. Not everywhere, but in many places.

So the legacy of the nationalist and revolutionary movements in the
Third World is unclear. They were victorious. They ended the empires,
created nations where none had existed, tripled the number of inde-

pendent countries and asserted the autonomy of the world's majorities. They made Third World people responsible for Third World problems. They changed the colors on the globe. But they did not end exploitation; they reframed it. At the core of their inability to realize the promises embodied in their movements was the intractibility of the economy. With a few exceptions, the new regimes could not bring about economic development, nor alleviate poverty.

Suggestions for Further Reading

Fanon, Frantz. *The Wretched of the Earth.* Translated by Constance Farrington. New York: Grove Press, 1968.

Gandhi, Mohandas K. *An Autobiography: The Story of My Experiments with Truth.* Boston: Beacon Press, 1957.

Lacouture, Jean. *Ho Chi Minh: A Political Biography.* New York: Random House, 1968.

Memmi, Albert. *The Colonizer and the Colonized.* Boston: Beacon Press, 1965.

Wolf, Eric R. *Peasant Wars of the Twentieth Century.* New York: Harper and Row, 1969.

Notes

1. Donald Woods, *Biko,* 2d ed. (New York: Henry Holt and Company, 1987), 28.

2. Raja Rao, *Kanthapura* (London: George Allen and Unwin, 1938), 11–12.

3. Stanley Karnow, *Vietnam: A History* (New York: The Viking Press, 1983), 122.

4. With the exception of the U.S. Civil War (1861–65), which half of the country lost.

5. "The Slow Road to *Doi Moi,*" *The Economist* (July 29, 1989): 19–22.

6. I am grateful to my colleague Edmund Burke for some of the information about modern Algerian history.

7. From the foreword to Mariano Azuela, *The Underdogs: A Novel of the Mexican Revolution,* translated by E. Munguia, Jr. (New York: New American Library, 1962).

8. Thomas W. Walker, *Nicaragua: The First Five Years* (New York: Praeger Publishers, 1985), 22.

9. Quoted in Peter Rosset and John Vandermeer, *Nicaragua: Unfinished Revolution: The New Nicaragua Reader* (New York: Grove Press, 1986), 10.

10. Ibid., 5.

11. Léopold Sédar Senghor, *Chants d'Ombre* (Paris: Editions du Seuil, 1956), 21.

12. Frantz Fanon, *The Wretched of the Earth,* translated by Constance Farrington (New York: Grove Press, 1968), 43.

13. Ibid., 93–94.

14. In *Biko,* 130–31 (see note 1).

15. Fanon, 149–52.

16. Mariano Azuela, *The Underdogs: A Novel of the Mexican Revolution,* translated by E. Munguia, Jr. (New York: New American Library, 1962), 136, 147.

17. Chinua Achebe, *A Man of the People* (New York: Doubleday and Company, 1969), 34–35.

CHAPTER SIX

Economic Development

The division of labor among nations is that some specialize in winning and others in losing.
                    —Eduardo Galeano, *Open Veins of Latin America*

The Heads of State . . . are convinced that nothing
short of a complete restructuring of international economic relations through the establishment of the New
International Economic Order will place developing
countries in a position to achieve an acceptable level
of development.
                    —Economic Declaration of the Fifth Summit
                         Conference of the Non-Aligned
                         Governments, Sri Lanka, 1976[1]

The task, then, for the governments of the developing
countries is to reorient their development policies in
order to attack directly the personal poverty of the
most deprived 40 per cent of their populations.
                    —Robert S. McNamara, address to the Board
                         of Governors, the World Bank, 1972

The field of economics is very complex and very
boring.
                    —Daniel Ortega, former president of Nicaragua

THE NATIONALIST MOVEMENTS won independence for the
Third World, transforming the international political order. The age of
imperialism is largely over. The majority of the world's population are
now represented by the majority of the world's independent governments. There are 179 sovereign members of the United Nations, most
of them Third World countries that a few decades ago were European
colonies. Politically the world has changed completely—but economically, not a great deal.

With independence achieved, the principal concern in the Third
World has been the economy. At the top of almost every country's priority list has been economic development, by which it means increases
in production, income, standards of living and education. Some
improvements have occurred, but the breakthroughs have been scarce

and the disappointments many. Most people still live in the conditions of poverty that they have known throughout this century.

There have been some successes. Four Asian countries, two of them very small (Hong Kong[2] and Singapore) and two of them moderately large (Taiwan and South Korea), have achieved rapid growth in production over several decades and have become influential participants in international markets. They have even managed to spread some of the benefits of their growth among the poor. Some other countries have enjoyed spurts of rapid growth, which were impressive while they lasted—for example, Brazil from the mid-1950's through the mid-1970's. The oil-exporting countries of the Third World—most of the Middle Eastern countries as well as Venezuela, Mexico, Nigeria and Indonesia—had a tremendous decade of prosperity from 1973 to 1983, before slipping back to a more stagnant state. Some countries have remarkable achievements to their credit in some sectors; for example, the Chinese and the Cubans have brought basic literacy, health care and employment security to almost all of their people. In most of the other Third World countries (with the exception of those in Africa), there have been some modest improvements in productivity and national income.

But on the whole, for the majority of people living in the Third World, the economic condition is dismal, and the future unpromising. Most people are still desperately poor, with little prospect of escaping from their poverty. As Chapter 2 showed, theirs is for the most part not the traditional low-income life of ancient villages, a way of life supported by the tribal deities and the ancestors. For most people of the Third World, that traditional way of life has been uprooted—by colonialism, by urbanization, by commercialization and by population growth. The modern poverty of the Third World is a new phenomenon, but it does not appear to be transitory.

The history of economic development since the time of independence has been a history of false promises. A series of what seemed at the time to be easy answers have appeared, keys that once turned would unlock the door to riches. They have not. One by one, the fashionable answers proved wanting—in some cases because they ignored the reality of a much-too-complex world, in other cases because they were abandoned by the people who should have been responsible for their success. The false answers included nationalism and independence alone, socialism and government planning, savings and capital investment, investment in human capital, industrial growth and a shift away from agriculture, population control, a basic human needs approach to development, a hike in oil prices and the New International Economic Order. The story of the false paths is revealing; it helps to explain why people in the Third World feel such confusion and bitterness about economic development. In the decade of the

1990's, the overwhelming economic reality that many Third World countries have to face is a crushing debt burden, along with growing uncertainty about what the feasible path of economic development could possibly be in the future.

Political Independence

To say that nationalism and independence were false paths is not to deny that they were necessary for economic progress, for they surely were; it is to deny, however, that political autonomy was a sufficient condition, for it was not.

Before independence, the imperialists paid little if any attention to the economic well-being of the local people. The colonial powers had economic interests in the Third World, of course. They were looking for cheap raw material exports to support industrialization at home, and they also expected the colonies to generate enough income to the public till to cover the costs of their administration.

But these interests had nothing to do with improving the lot of the local people. In fact, the economic attractiveness of the colonies lay largely in the fact that labor was cheap, that is, that standards of living were marginal. The imperialists certainly had no incentive to improve average living conditions. When administrators thought at all about the welfare of the colonized peoples, it was almost always in terms of peace, order and efficient government. In the opinion of the imperialists, colonial administration was justified for establishing a rule of law, suppressing local conflicts, breaking down customs thought to be uncivilized and establishing communications between different areas. Hardly any of the rulers conceived that these changes could, or should, bring about significant improvements in the incomes of the local people. Not until the independence movements began to be successful after the Second World War was the subject of economic development in the Third World taken at all seriously.

As Chapter 5 explained, a spirit of euphoria accompanied the independence of the Indian subcontinent, of sub-Saharan Africa and of the other countries of the Third World that threw off their colonial yokes in the years following the Second World War, even of the tiny Pacific islands. Independence was a mark of pride, a sign of equality in the world, and it was also taken as a portent of a better life ahead. Almost without exception, the nationalists and their followers believed that by casting off the oppressive hand of the colonialists, and taking control of their own economic destiny, they could vanquish the exploitation that was responsible for their poverty. To be an independent nation seemed synonymous with economic progress.

It turned out not to be so. Independence brought with it no automatic release of the powers of economic progress. Certainly, colonial exploitation was responsible in part for the poverty of the new nations, but that exploitation did not end with independence; it continued in a neocolonial guise.

The leaders of the new nations—the Nehrus and the Nkrumahs— might have understood this better had they paid closer attention to the example of the Latin Americans. Almost all of the Latin American countries had been independent, after all, for more than a century, since about 1820. Some of them, most notably Argentina, had actually enjoyed periods of prosperity. But in the post–World War II period they were all poor, or at least the vast majority of their people were. In Latin America, neocolonial exploitation was reinforced by domestic exploitation, with small groups of landholders, military leaders and urban commercial families wresting wealth from the cities and the countryside, often leaving their fellow citizens destitute. In Nicaragua, for example, by the end of their rule, the Somoza family owned fully one-quarter of the country's land, and either owned or controlled the country's most profitable industries, including public transportation, the meat industry and prostitution. The Latin American example showed that independence might create opportunities for a local oligarchy to replace the colonialists and advance at the expense of their brethren, but this was not the promise that had led millions to dance in the streets throughout Asia and Africa as independence was proclaimed.

Independence was a precondition of economic prosperity, because it removed the imperialists from direct authority over the Third World. But of itself it did not lead to significant economic change, since it changed very few of the conditions that created the poverty. It did not change the fact that most people pursued agriculture with primitive technology, or produced low-priced commodities for export to the (former) colonial centers, or were crowded into urban slums. Frantz Fanon's predictions proved chillingly accurate in many countries: the nationalist leaders settled simply for independence, for replacing foreign exploiters, but they lacked the vision and ability to replace the exploitative system. For those who thought independence would bring automatic improvements, the subsequent decades were devastating.

Socialism and Government Planning

A large part of the promise of independence was thought to be that the governments of the new nations would be able to intervene forcefully in the economic and social structures of their countries, changing their direction, casting aside the elements that were exploitative and stagnant and replacing them with a new order that addressed the needs of the people. To assert the people's control over the economy, some countries turned to socialism, to a social revolution that was intended to replace greedy capitalist classes with public ownership of the means of production. Other countries were more moderate in their approach, but even the countries that intended to retain a capitalist framework with private enterprise invariably saw government planning at the center of a national commitment to economic development.

From the beginning, even in the 1940's, the nationalist leaders in Asia and Africa—and even to a certain extent in Latin America—had a commitment to some version of government direction of the economy. A purely free-market approach to economic development was dismissed as being hopelessly weak and impotent. Students of economic development argued that the free market, that is to say, individual companies and consumers operating without any constraints imposed by the government, might have worked for Britain in the middle of the nineteenth century, but it had never been sufficient since that time. France, Germany, Russia, the United States, Canada and the other developed countries that followed Britain had all made strategic use of the power of the government, for example, by erecting tariff barriers to protect infant industries. The developed countries might argue for free trade and free markets today, but the industrialization of the United States had followed closely after the passing of the Morrill tariff in 1861, and the industrialization of Canada closely after the National Policy tariff of 1879. The now developed countries had shown no hesitancy in the nineteenth century in using their governments to promote economic development. In the twentieth century, the challenges facing Third World economies were much greater than those of a century before, and so the role of government was thought to be even more crucial.

In the first few decades after independence, almost all observers of Third World economies believed that if governments did not intervene to alter the path of economic growth, then the world's poor countries would just continue the way they were currently going. In a free-market system, producers make goods for which the market demand is strongest—and the strongest market demand was coming from the rich countries with their insatiable need for cheap primary commodities. So the free market was pushing the Third World deeper and deeper into a swamp. Unless governments intervened to change the pattern of production, most economists argued, the populations of the Third World would become increasingly trapped in low-wage primary export activities, in unproductive subsistence agriculture and in urban slums. There was no hope along that path, they thought.

The common wisdom was that the Third World needed to develop its manufacturing and service sectors to complement its mining and agriculture. True economic development required complex economies, with different types of production and a wide variety of occupations, so that there could be mutually reinforcing interchange and commerce between different activities. A complex economy needed help from the government if it was to get started. If a Third World economy were left unprotected against the market, its manufacturing sector could never compete with the cheap imports from the developed countries. Manufacturing needed tariff barriers against import competition, and it probably also needed subsidies, licenses, loans at low interest rates and many other forms of government support.

Economists in the mainstream, modernization school took the lead in this way of thinking. Although their ultimate faith rested with private enterprise, they believed that Third World economies needed a plan, an overall blueprint prepared by the government to show the expected path of growth. So in the decades after independence, economic plans proliferated throughout the Third World. Many of them showed in great detail the growth that was expected in each sector and the government policies that were needed to ensure that growth.

The basic assumption behind these plans was that Third World economies needed a "big push." Slow incremental development was doomed to failure. Planners in universities throughout the world, in international agencies and in Third World governments agreed that a sharp break with the past was essential. The big push needed to be an integrated effort, one that included the entire economy. It would not be possible, for example, to start an automotive industry on its own, because the inputs, skills and markets were all lacking. But if at the same time as auto production was being started there was an increase in technical education, engineering, steel production, electronics and rubber on the input side, and highway construction and trucking firms on the output side, then an auto industry could be successful. The only way to have all these activities proceed together and at the proper pace was to have them planned by the government. It was not always necessary to have the government own and operate the new companies, but it was necessary for the government to give the right signals and subsidies to ensure that privately owned companies would undertake the activities. This sort of planning strategy was the orthodoxy, even among the most conservative of Third World governments.

Among observers of the development process in the rich countries were a few cautionary dissents to this consensus, as early as the 1950's. Not all of the modernizationists favored government planning. The conservative British economist P. T. Bauer argued strenuously for a free-market approach to economic development, saying that individual entrepreneurs, risking their futures in pursuit of profits, were the most effective possible force for economic development. Government planners, he felt, would invariably make the wrong choices, because they had nothing to lose. Rare was the government bureaucrat who risked being fired for having chosen to subsidize an unsuccessful company. In the United States, Albert O. Hirschman, a student of Latin American economies, argued for unbalanced, unplanned growth. To take the previous example, a typical Third World country lacked the managerial resources to plan successfully all of the myriad components of automotive development. It would be better, said Hirschman, to proceed without integrated planning, to allow bottlenecks to emerge, and then to trust that someone would find it profitable to break the bottleneck by providing either the input or the market that was needed.

These dissenting views titillated the academics in the developed countries, but they had very little influence among the politicians and bureaucrats of the Third World. The predominant opinion in the Third World was that the unconstrained private sector was incapable of producing real economic progress and was actually responsible for many of the problems of the new nations.

The debate within the Third World was rather different. It was between those who favored government economic planning in partnership with private sector capitalism, versus socialists, communists and revolutionaries who wanted to replace the private sector altogether. The former were influenced by the modernizationist approach to social change, the latter by dependency and Marxist theory. The goal among the latter was to change the national class structure, to eliminate the upper, property-owning classes that had used their privilege to exploit the ordinary people. There was no possibility of partnership with the privileged classes, they thought, since the interests of those classes were utterly at odds with those of the majority. In China, Burma, North Korea, Cuba and other revolutionary socialist countries, the path to progress was to replace private with public enterprises, controlled by the government and operated for the benefit of the people.

The socialists argued that if private enterprise dominated the economy, the government could plan all it wanted, but it would lack the authority to implement the plan. Even more fundamentally, if private enterprise dominated the economy, then rich capitalists would dominate the government, and the government for its part would have no interest in planning on behalf of the majority of the people. So private corporations should be expropriated, and the government acting on behalf of the people as a whole should own and operate industries— this, after all, was the Soviet model that seemed such a beacon.

The socialists believed that the market should not be relied upon to give signals to enterprises about what to produce. In a market system, only people with high incomes had any influence; firms concentrated on producing goods for the rich, who could pay high prices for them. Decisions about what to produce should be made instead by a centralized public planning office that would take as its highest priority the needs of the majority. In other words, a socialist government's economic plan would not be just a statement of hopes and wishes; it would be a document of actual instructions, made on behalf of the people as a whole.

The two giants of Asia have exemplified these two approaches to economic planning. India, while socialist in ideology, has remained stubbornly capitalist in fact. The United States, the world's archcapitalist country, actually has a greater proportion of government-controlled economic activity than does India. Not coincidentally, the strongest Third World contributors to the modernization school of social science have come from India. Although India has published a series of 5-year plans showing in considerable detail the expansion that is expected in each region and sector, the main initiative in the economy has remained in private hands. The plans served mainly to delay and disrupt economic development.

In revolutionary communist China, on the other hand, the guesswork was taken out of the planning process. A centralized planning office in Beijing set overall goals for the entire economy, and a series of regional planning offices was responsible for their implementation. Since the manufacturing plants were owned publicly, the planning offices were in a position to issue instructions and to set quantitative goals for each plant. Plant managers were given bonuses for meeting or exceeding the production goals that were set for them.

While there was heated debate for decades between proponents of these two models, the Indian and the Chinese, virtually no one in the Third World thought that government direction of the economy might be part of the problem. Remarkably in the 1980's, however, the consensus in favor of government control collapsed. There was a worldwide retreat from central planning, and even from socialism. The "monetarist" economists, who favored free-market solutions to almost every problem, found themselves with new respect.

One reason for the retreat from planning was that the most successful examples of Third World economic growth in the 1980's were ones in which the role of the government was distinctly reduced.

The startling news of the 1980's was the success of four proudly capitalist countries in Asia: Taiwan, Hong Kong, Singapore and South Korea, the "newly industrializing countries," or NICs. Each achieved rapid economic growth through an aggressive strategy of export promotion—not the traditional primary commodity exports, but new manufactured exports. Manufacturing in each country began with textiles, but then moved on to products embodying higher technology, including electronics and automobiles. The initiative for this growth came from the private sector, from individual entrepreneurs. The governments were not passive in these four countries. They directed resources, licenses and finances where they were most needed. But rather than control the economy and plan all of the interrelationships in it, the governments concentrated on creating an economic environment in which private firms could thrive.

Not only did capitalism without a controlling government plan lead to fast overall economic growth in these four countries, it led to at least some benefits for the poor. There is still poverty in the NICs, as there is throughout Asia, but there has been a sharp improvement in the amount and share of income going to the poorest.

At the same time as these relatively small capitalist countries were successful, the world's two largest communist countries, the People's Republic of China and the Soviet Union, essentially abandoned socialism as an economic system.

After the death of Chairman Mao in 1976, the Chinese under Deng Xiaoping set out on a rightward path, leaving behind much of the central planning and the collective ideology that marked the first decades of the revolution. This new direction represented a reaction against the excesses of Mao's Great Proletarian Cultural Revolution, which lasted from 1965 to 1975. Mao had feared that the Chinese were forgetting the revolutionary struggles that were their legacy, and that they were allowing class distinctions to reemerge. So the Cultural Revolution reasserted the primacy of ideology, planning and political orthodoxy. Expertise was shunned, many people with skills were thrown out of work, schools and universities were closed down and the economy ground to a halt, all in the name of a rejuvenation of revolutionary fervor.

The reaction against the Cultural Revolution after Mao's death was profound. The Chinese reasserted their traditional respect for learning. They rehabilitated most of the people who had been disgraced in the previous decade, recalling them from the menial tasks and prisons to which they had been consigned, and restoring their jobs. Private enterprise was introduced into both the farming sector and industry. Farmers were encouraged to cultivate individual plots of land and were allowed to profit individually from their productivity. Urban markets flourished, with the prices of many goods set by the forces of supply and demand, not centrally by a planning agency. The Chinese solicited foreign investment, and looked for export opportunities.

The changes in the Chinese economy occurred gradually, first in one sector, then in another. They were guided by the Communist Party, which retained rigid political control of the country. But for the most part, socialism was abandoned in the economy.

The Soviet Union's retreat from economic centralization was more precipitous. It began later, and culminated in the complete collapse of the country as a political entity. The Soviets had enjoyed remarkable successes in the twentieth century in heavy industry and military technology, but they did not do nearly as well at improving the quality of life of their citizens. Premier Gorbachev and the reformers he gathered around him became convinced that the heavy hand of the Communist Party bureaucracy was responsible for much of this stagnation. They called for *glasnost*—openness and free discussion—and for *perestroika*, a restructuring of the economy to make more use of the market. The Soviet encouragement of glasnost was the opposite of the Chinese policy of suppressing free expression.

As it turned out, glasnost could not be contained by the Soviet rulers. Once people could express their views openly, they rejected the entire apparatus of the Soviet state and its empire. First the satellite countries of Eastern Europe were released from Soviet control, then the constituent republics of the Soviet Union exerted their independence from Russia. A short-lived coup against Gorbachev in the summer of 1991 failed, but in surmounting the coup Gorbachev put himself in the control of Russian nationalists and democrats, led by Premier Boris Yeltsin. The Russians administered the final death blows to the Soviet Union before the year was out, with the resulting independent republics aligning themselves in a loose confederation.

The collapse of the Soviet Union brought with it the collapse of centralized economic planning and socialism. It did not, however, bring with it a well-articulated market system. The economies of the former Soviet Union descended into a certain chaos, with sharp cuts in production, rampant inflation and serious threats of starvation. Here and there, entrepreneurs emerged with new products and more efficient ways of doing things; most of the economy, however, was trapped in a downward spiral. What in China was a gradual evolution towards the market, directed by the strong hand of a centralized party, was in Russia a quick abandonment of the failed socialist economic system, with no clear vision of what was to replace it. Accompanying the economic chaos was political chaos, as people who were loyal to the old Communist vision, or to Gorbachev's version of reform, struggled against Yeltsin's presidency.

The changes in China and in the Soviet Union had a major influence throughout the Third World. In many countries it was no longer taken for granted that the interests of private enterprise were necessarily at odds with the common good, or that the interests of government bureaucrats were necessarily congruent with it. The Third World did not warmly and universally embrace capitalism. Rather, it questioned old truths. Centralized decisionmaking, public ownership and comprehensive economic planning did not deliver the goods as they were expected to, so they were reconsidered. One of the fixed principles of economic development strategy was found wanting, but it is not yet certain what will take its place.

The United States government has warmly supported the shift towards the market and away from central planning. This shift fits well with American notions of freedom, as well as with the interests of American companies doing business in the Third World. The Americans have not followed through with serious support, however. While preaching the virtues of the market, they have done little, for example, to relieve the debt burdens of Latin American countries that have moved towards freer economies.

Savings, Foreign Aid and Capital Formation

In the 1940's, 1950's and well into the 1960's, most people believed that the clue to economic development was capital formation. That is, low-income countries needed massive new investments in factories, in equipment, in agriculture, in transportation and in communications, in order to raise the productivity of their labor forces. Economists believed that countries were poor because their people were working with primitive equipment. A worker with a shovel will make only slow progress in building a road; a worker with a huge earth mover powered by an diesel engine will make much faster progress. Economists thought that economic development depended upon an increase in capital investment in the Third World, a rapid substitution of mechanized earth movers for shovels.

That capital formation was the key to growth was the lesson of economic theory at that time; it was also the apparent lesson of postwar European reconstruction. After the Second World War, the European economies were in shambles. A few years later they were back on their feet again, with the help of American foreign aid through the Marshall Plan, which provided funds for rebuilding the factories.

In the 1950's, politicians, bureaucrats and academics alike thought that this European experience could guide Third World development. With international cooperation, generous foreign aid and some government planning, European productivity had bounced back. The common wisdom was that the same sort of concerted effort could set the Third World on a path of self-sustained economic growth and rescue the millions of non-Europeans from their poverty. Third World countries simply needed to construct capital goods—factories and machines—and their problems would be solved.

To buy the capital goods, the poor countries needed investment funds. The funds could come from two sources, foreign or domestic, and each bears some discussion.

Resources for investment could come into the Third World from abroad in a variety of ways. The most obvious, following the example of the Marshall Plan, was foreign aid. After decades now of experience with foreign aid, we have grown accustomed to rather cynical analyses of its uses, understanding as we do how foreign economic aid is often indistinguishable from foreign military aid, and how both are frequently used in support of geopolitical aims that have little connection with a humanitarian purpose. Still, the basic justification for foreign aid, and some of the actual practice, is that it should be used in support of economic development. Aid comes to the Third World from individual governments among the developed countries, and it also comes from multilateral international organizations, such as United Nations agencies, the World Bank and regional development banks. Some aid is in the form of grants, while other aid is in the form of loans at subsidized interest rates that are lower than the Third World countries would have to pay if they borrowed from commercial banks.

Some foreign aid should properly be called "relief," because it is used directly to feed the hungry or to supply the basic needs of the poorest. While this kind of aid has saved lives, relief is not the real point of foreign aid. The objective is to provide Third World countries with the resources to increase their capital—to finance projects, to build factories, to construct irrigation networks, to process fertilizers, and so on. The hope is that foreign aid will be used in such a way as to increase the country's productivity, so that in the future, relief-type aid will not be needed.

A second foreign source of capital is the private sector, providing loans and investments to the Third World. This source of capital has become even more controversial than foreign aid. There are two ways in which private foreign capital enters a Third World country—as equity capital or as loans. What equity means is that foreign investors buy an asset in the Third World—a company, for example, or a factory. The investors may actually build the asset. They may own the asset completely on their own or jointly with a local partner. In either case, the foreign investors own a piece of the Third World economy, that is, they have equity capital. The flow of equity capital into the Third World has led to the controversy over the role of multinational corporations.

Much of the equity investing is done by enormous international companies, the biggest in the world, that own operations in dozens of countries. They frequently tower over the countries in which they operate. The Aluminum Company of America (Alcoa), for example, has worldwide sales greater than the entire gross national product of Jamaica, the country in which it mines most of its bauxite. The multinational corporations provide capital and technology to poor Third World countries. The criticism of them is that they tend to dominate and distort the countries in which they operate, imposing their own standards and displacing the local ones. They are sometimes so rich and powerful as to be able to secure favors for themselves that are not available to local companies. When they send the profits they have earned back to their home countries, they may actually drain capital out of the Third World.

The alternative way for private foreign capital to come into the Third World is in the form of loans. In this case, the ownership of the companies stays in the Third World country. The disadvantage is that a loan is a fixed obligation. No matter how well or how poorly the borrower does, it is still faced with the obligation of making regular payments back to the lender, at fixed contractual rates of interest.

During the 1960's and 1970's, when multinational corporations were spreading quickly throughout the Third World, critics were vehement in their attacks on them. They called instead for more loan finance, so that the foreign capitalists would stay at arm's length from the Third World societies and allow them greater autonomy. But in the 1980's, as the loans to the Third World increased dramatically, and many of the poor countries were trapped behind debt repayment obligations that were impossible to meet, there were reverse pleas for greater equity financing, calls for foreigners to take a greater stake in the fortunes of the Third World.

As history unfolded after the Second World War, the Marshall Plan, under which the United States had financed European recovery, proved not to be a good model for providing capital to the Third World. Governments of the rich countries sent foreign aid to the poor, but on the whole they have not been generous, and the United States and Britain in particular have reduced their commitment to aid, expressed as a percentage of their GNPs. The distribution of American aid has been remarkably skewed, being heavily directed to countries that have strategic and military importance to the United States, rather than to countries where the need is greatest. The multilateral agencies such as the World Bank have done better, but they are constantly strapped for funds. In the private sector, banks and corporations have provided quite a lot of capital to Third World countries, but the process has been continually surrounded by controversy and bad will, whether because of the domination of local economies by multinational corporations or because of impossible debt burdens. One by one, Third World countries have discovered that foreign capital is not the answer to their problems and that they must look internally for most of their capital investment.

To understand the process of internal capital formation, it is useful to think of a country's output, or production, as being divided between two uses. It can be devoted to present uses, that is, to consumption, to provide for current needs. Or it can be devoted to future uses, meaning that it can be used for investment in capital. These two uses compete with each other. Resources that are directed towards capital investment cannot also be used to meet today's pressing needs. Put differently, any decision to invest in future productivity implies a sacrifice, a reduction in the resources available today. This is the case whether the decision is made by individuals, by companies or by governments—and whether it is made under a capitalist system or a socialist one. A family can decide to invest in a home workshop—provided that they reduce their expenditures on food and clothing to come up with the funds. They have a chance of greater prosperity in the future, but today there is hardship. A company may decide to use its profits to expand its factory, and to do so it increases its profits by reducing its wage costs. In the long run the society will have a bigger factory with more employees; in the short run the current employees suffer. A socialist country like the Soviet Union increases its investment in capital goods by reducing the consumer goods that its factories produce, and as a consequence its people suffer shortages. It is one of the truths of economics that cannot be avoided: resources devoted to capital investment must be taken away from current consumption (unless borrowed from abroad).

Investment that uses domestic resources therefore requires sacrifices that are particularly difficult for a poor country to bear. But until the mid 1960's, economists were convinced that an increase in savings, and the capital investment that went with it, were absolutely essential to economic development. Since it was increased capital that produced increased output, there was no substitute for the raising of investment and savings. Nobel Prize winner Sir W. Arthur Lewis of Jamaica, the Third World's most influential economist, wrote:

> The central problem in the theory of economic development is to understand the process by which a community which was previously saving and investing 4 or 5 per cent of its national income or less, converts itself into an economy where voluntary saving is running at about 12 to 15 per cent of national income or more. This is the central problem because the central fact of economic development is rapid capital accumulation (including knowledge and skills with capital.)[3]

The famous "Lewis model" put savings and capital formation on center stage. And not just the Lewis model, but practically every serious attempt to understand the process of economic growth postulated capital formation as the main issue.

The actual experience of Third World countries turned out to be much more complicated than these economic models suggested, however. It is no longer completely obvious that the central issue in economic development is how a country changes from a 5 percent saver to a 12 percent saver. Some countries with relatively high rates of saving and capital formation have had low rates of economic growth, and vice versa. Furthermore, the growth of production has not always brought with it significant improvements in the quality of life of ordinary people.

The fact that investment in capital is not the principal determinant of economic growth was first discovered in the developed countries. Economic historians, attempting to apply the abstract models of the economic growth theorists, came up with a startling result. They tried to estimate the proportion of the United States' economic growth that could be ascribed to the increase in its capital stock, and the proportion that could be ascribed to the growth of the labor force, fully expecting the two together to sum to about 100 percent. They were mistaken. Try as they might, and using different methodologies, they were always left with at least half of the growth unexplained. The term they coined for the unexplained portion of the growth was the "residual." Since the residual was so large, it followed that a great deal of U.S. economic growth was the result of some unknown and unmeasured factors, not capital or labor. Candidates for these factors included technology, education, entrepreneurship, managerial capacity, even spiritual energy and enthusiasm. All of a sudden attention was shifted from exclusive concern with capital formation to these rather more nebulous but perhaps more important factors.

This more complex view of economic growth did not push capital formation out of the picture altogether. The importance of capital was rescued by another Nobel Prize winner, Robert Solow of the Massachusetts Institute of Technology, who pointed out that while technology or new ideas were no doubt critical, they had to be "embedded" in new capital projects, in plant and equipment, before they could increase output. So new capital was still thought to be important, but it was important principally because it worked together with new technological developments.

The message arrived quickly in the Third World—that technological advancement was important. But that led immediately to a quandary: what technology? The great research and development efforts were in the developed countries, not in the Third World. Should the Third World devote itself to copying the advanced countries' technology—to reading their journals, copying their blueprints, importing their machines and courting their multinational corporations? That was certainly a cheaper and more feasible course of action than attempting to do all the research and development work themselves. But the suspicion arose that the technology of the developed countries might be inappropriate for the Third World. The developed countries faced high wages and labor shortages, and therefore a great deal of their industrial research went into labor-saving technology—automation, robotics, computerization and the like. But in the Third World, the economic problems were entirely different. Most countries of the Third World had lots of workers, many of them underemployed, most of them living on very low incomes. The technology they needed was labor-using technology, not labor-saving. Another sort of problem arose in agriculture. The developed countries had made extraordinary advances in agricultural technology—improving yields, inventing new crops, increasing weights of livestock, developing more potent fertilizers, and so on. But much of this technology was inapplicable to the Third World, with its very different climates, soils and vegetation.

So technology transfer from the rich countries to the poor is part of the answer, but only part. The new emphasis on technological development as a central component of economic change implies that the Third World has to do its own research, has to devote its own resources to developing better methods of production. Research and development is both expensive and risky: there are no guarantees that money invested will yield useful results. There is a guarantee, however, that an absence of investment in research and development will yield no useful results—and so Third World countries are increasingly facing up to the need for technical education and for applied research.

There have been some signal successes in the development of new technology appropriate to Third World conditions. Most notable have been the agricultural discoveries that have constituted the basis for the "green revolution": the new high-yield varieties of rice and wheat that have raised agricultural production in many areas of Latin America and Asia.

This new understanding of the process of economic development has been salutary. From a misplaced emphasis on foreign aid, savings, investment and capital formation, economists have arrived at a more balanced assessment in which it is the interaction between technical change and new investment that is important. But at the same time, the old certainties are gone; no longer can one predict exactly how much capital is needed to produce a certain growth rate. The precision of the earlier planning models has been lost. The simple answer—that more saving and investment will necessarily raise standards of living—has been shown to be wrong.

Investment in Human Capital

At the same time as the role of capital formation was being questioned, new attention was being paid in the Third World to the importance of the human beings whose life task it was to labor and produce.

The early models of development had been constructed by economists in the modernization school around the simple but bizarre assumption that labor was somehow a homogeneous commodity, just a series of interchangeable hands, one much the same as the next, and that therefore the only way to improve the productivity of labor was to provide workers with more and better machines. But this is nonsense. Some workers are healthier and stronger than others, and some are better educated and more skilled. Some are better motivated. The quality of the labor force has a great deal to do with its economic productivity.

The idea of "investment in human capital" gained currency in the 1960's and 1970's. A new group of economic theorists proposed that just as a country could invest in its stock of physical capital, its machinery and its factories, so too could it invest in its human capital by increasing the skills and capacities of its workers. In what seemed like a moment, health, nutrition, literacy and technical training became issues that transcended relief and welfare; they appeared to be the key to economic development.

Third World leaders came to understand that while wages were low in their countries, labor was not cheap. Labor was actually expensive, because it lacked education, training and energy, and it was therefore relatively unproductive. In fact, a considerable amount of good work has been done to improve labor quality in many Third World countries, although the initial flash of excitement, that somehow this was the answer, has faded as the problems of widespread poverty have proven intractable even to this strategy.

The new approach to human capital made it clear that improvements in health care were not only a matter of providing for the welfare of the sick and disabled, although that was important. Recent planning documents in many Third World countries have insisted that expenditures on health care should be thought of as an investment in the future of the country, an investment that will pay off in a stronger and more capable working population.

As noted in Chapter 2, some countries have made significant progress in the period since independence in extending public health, sanitation, mosquito eradication and paramedical care. The achievements of China are remarkable, and so too are those of India. But in other areas health care is still very primitive. In most African countries there are very few doctors, and even those tend to live in the cities and cater to a middle-class clientele, often being quite ignorant of the sorts of tropical diseases that afflict the majority of the people.

For poor countries, fancy high-technology western medicine cannot be the answer, since there is no way that such expensive care can be made available to most of the people. The Chinese have shown that well-organized teams of public health workers can make a remarkable difference to the health of a population and to its longevity—and that as these improve, the economic productivity of the workers improves as well.

Basic to the health of a Third World population is its food and nutrition. Although most Third World countries are predominantly agricultural, with most people living on the land, nutritional standards are often inadequate. In fact, food deficiencies are more prevalent in rural areas than in urban, because rural people are on the average poorer.

There are two separate aspects of nutritional deficiencies: caloric shortfalls and lack of specific nutrients. Calories in food are converted by the body into energy, and nutritionists have established levels of calorie intake that appear to be necessary for people involved in daily physical work. In many areas of the Third World these standards are not met even on average, and since the distribution of food is unequal, a high proportion of the population lacks sufficient food to work a fully productive day. Muscle strength is reduced, as are coordination, speed and attention span.

Deficiencies of specific nutrients are various and are responsible for widespread diseases in the Third World, including kwashiorkor (resulting from insufficient B vitamins), which produces characteristic bloated bellies, and anemia (resulting from a lack of iron). The most harmful deficiency in much of the Third World is in protein intake, a particularly serious problem in fetal development and infancy, when brain cells and intellectual capacity are being developed. Malnutrition at this stage of human growth probably leaves physical and mental deficiencies that cannot be reversed at later ages, even if nutrition is improved. Of course, malnutrition is generally not reversed at older ages. The nutrition of children, for example, once they are weaned from their mothers' milk, is frequently much worse than the nutrition of infants.

Improvements in nutrition are therefore urgently needed, not just for the welfare of people living in the Third World, but for their future prospects. The elimination of hunger could increase tremendously the capacity of the population for productive labor.

Human capital means education, in all its dimensions—from basic literacy through technical training and on-the-job skill enhancement to higher education. Yet, Third World educational systems have frequently failed the people, because they have been too meager and because they have often been badly conceived.

Investment in human capital is not the only purpose of education—people often value school quite apart from the job benefits it will generate in the future—but it is an important one. Just like the decision to invest in physical capital, the decision to invest in human capital involves a present sacrifice, in favor of anticipated future gains. Education requires an out-of-pocket expense, and since it keeps the students out of the labor force it also lowers their current earnings. The trade-off is a particularly difficult one for poor people living in Third World countries: a family often sacrifices a great deal by keeping a son or daughter in school.

The most important educational issue in most Third World countries is basic literacy. Close to a billion people in the Third World cannot read or write. This is a tremendous personal handicap, as it restricts them from interaction with much of the rest of the world. From the point of view of the country's economic development, it is a formidable barrier. People who cannot read cannot follow written instructions; in villages they are condemned to subsistence methods, unable to understand new technologies. Several years of primary education are frequently not sufficient to ensure basic literacy. Most children do learn to read after a few years of school, but once they leave school two things happen. The most ambitious leave their rural communities, unsatisfied with the prospect of the poor subsistence life they see around them and hoping for greater prospects in the cities. Many of those who stay behind lose their reading skills in a few years, because they have no opportunity to continue reading. As a consequence, it is common to find villages whose inhabitants are for the most part illiterate, although they have been to school.

One of the most creative responses to the problem of literacy has been pioneered in Latin America by Paulo Freire, who has taught reading skills to adults using materials that give them power and have a practical effect on their lives. The point of literacy, in Freire's philosophy, is to allow poor people to take control of their lives and to confront the power structures that are oppressing them. So instead of getting "Dick and Jane" readers, the peasants themselves decide what works they need to learn to read. They learn to read legal contracts, they learn the language of organizing and they develop a political analysis through talking about their lives, an analysis that leads them toward social action. This approach to adult literacy has been highly effective in countries like Cuba and Nicaragua, although other countries have found it too politically threatening to adopt.

In many respects the secondary and higher educational systems in Third World countries have represented a waste of resources. The systems are often inappropriate to the pressing economic needs of the country. Educational philosophies that were adapted from the colonialists are in some cases the last great vestige of colonialism. The most glaring colonialist legacies have, for the most part, been eliminated: French-speaking African schoolchildren no longer memorize facts about "our ancestors, the Gauls." But the overall approach to education remains.

In much of the former British Empire, schools still use the same grading and examination systems left to them by their masters, as a way of keeping standards high. But the imprint of colonial education is a curious one. During the colonial period, the top British military and civilian administrators were graduates of exclusive schools and of Oxford and Cambridge, where they were educated in history, literature, philosophy and classical languages. Such a course of study was thought to be the best background for the generalists whose responsibility it was to govern a far-flung empire—and it may well have been. It is not, however, the best curriculum for the majority of students in the Third World today. But the conviction frequently remains that the best education is a general one, an education that deals with great ideas and significant literature, not one that immerses students in technical detail. As a consequence, higher educational systems in the Third World very often turn out a surplus of teachers and, worst of all, lawyers—but leave their countries with a significant shortage of techni-

cally trained people: engineers, scientists, economists. In many parts of
Africa and the Indian subcontinent, there is the startling phenomenon
of significant unemployment among the highly educated—people
whose training and aspirations are inappropriate for the urgent needs
of their countries, and who are not able to make a contribution to
their societies even after years of education.

The insight that human capital is critical is correct; skilled, capable,
energetic people are absolutely central to economic development, certainly as important as physical capital. But human capital is not a magic
key. Countries that have made significant progress in health, nutrition
and education have benefited, but they have not automatically made
the transition to prosperity. Most alarmingly, the levels of investment in
human beings are still extremely low in most of the Third World. Many
governments that were struggling with huge debt burdens actually
reduced spending on health and education. Health and education may
be important determinants of economic development, but they are
equally consequences of development. A desperately poor society simply cannot afford to invest the resources that are needed in its own
people. If it could, it would not be desperately poor. Many Third
World countries have made significant improvements in health and literacy in the last several decades, but these improvements do not come
cheaply or easily, as even the richest countries are learning. So the discovery of the concept of human capital did not lead to a transformation of the human condition.

Industrialization and Agriculture

Economic policy in the Third World is overwhelmingly biased in favor
of industrialization and urbanization, and against agriculture. This bias
has had very negative consequences.

The origins of the bias are understandable, since, after all, the economic development of the rich countries entailed urbanization. Two
hundred years ago, most of the people in Britain, France, Russia and
the United States worked the land, providing for their own families'
needs and perhaps producing a little surplus. As those countries
became richer, people left the land and entered the cities to find
employment in factories and urban services. The migration out of agriculture continues to this day; less than 2 percent of the U.S. population
now works the land.

This shift from rural to urban, from agriculture to industry and services, has been so universal as almost to constitute the definition of
economic development. Third World countries have attempted to follow this pattern, but for the most part they have failed.

The hidden secret behind the urbanization of the now rich countries was that it depended upon almost miraculous improvements in

productivity on the farms. It was this part of the process that the Third World missed. In the United States, for example, technological progress in agriculture has actually outstripped progress in factory production. In the middle of the nineteenth century in the United States, one farm family produced enough food to support itself and one other family. In the late-twentieth century, one farm family produces enough food to support itself and fifty others. As a result, hardly anyone is needed any longer in farming, and more are leaving every day. The fact that the U.S. population has moved out of farming is a testament, strangely, to the unprecedented success of the farming sector—a success that is due not only to innovative individual farmers, but also to the strong participation of the government in agricultural research.

Among the world's richer countries, only the Soviet Union neglected agricultural productivity, and this neglect is responsible, in large measure, for the low standard of living of most people in that country today.

Typically, Third World countries have followed the Soviet example rather than the western European and North American. They have tried to industrialize without developing a productive agricultural base, and the result has been a perpetuation of poverty, both rural and urban.

An example indicates the difference in approach, and the consequences. In North America and western Europe, farming communities have more than their share of political power and as a result are able to secure price supports, subsidies and all sorts of other benefits from their governments (that is, from the nonfarmers). Government regulations keep the price of food relatively high, and the high prices provide an incentive to farmers to produce more food than is actually needed. Except in occasional periods of drought, the farm problem in those areas is one of surplus—too much food for too few customers.

In contrast, in many countries of the Third World, governments respond to the evident distress of poor urban people by enacting legislation to keep the price of food artificially low. In some cases, the political future of the government depends on continuing these price ceilings on food: without them the urban poor might overthrow the government. But by keeping food prices low, the governments are in effect confiscating farmers' incomes. Rural people frequently find that it is not worth their while to invest in agricultural improvements, since the low price of the food that they sell will not cover the cost of those improvements. As a result, food production stagnates. The typical farm problem in the Third World is shortages—insufficient food to go around. These shortages are not God-given; in many cases they are the logical consequence of well-meaning but wrongheaded government policy.

This is only one example among many. What it reflects is a stronger political influence from the cities and a relative powerlessness of the countryside—not in every Third World country, but in many. Nothing has been more harmful to the Third World than the neglect of its agricultural sector. Country after country that was once self-sufficient in food or even a food exporter is now a food importer—Mexico, for example, can no longer feed itself. The world's breadbasket is not the Third World but the great plains of North America.

The agricultural problems of the Third World are very different from those of the developed countries, because the Third World is for the most part tropical.[4] While there are different types of tropical ecosystems, they all lack a winter season that in the temperate climates stops growth. The continuous, year-round heat in the tropics results in continuous biological growth and reproduction and therefore tremendous competition among species for survival. Any new plant or animal introduced into the ecosystem by human beings is immediately attacked by biological predators, and its chances of survival in a healthy state are low. Again and again, attempts to innovate with new agricultural crops in the Third World have failed because of the unrelentingly hostile climates.

There is, therefore, an overwhelming need for agricultural research in the Third World, to develop species that will improve farm productivity and be able to survive. There have already been some successes. With the help of the Rockefeller Foundation, research stations have invented high-yielding types of wheat in Mexico and rice in the Philippines—and these new seeds have had considerable success in other parts of the Third World, particularly in south Asia. This "green revolution" brought with it its own problems, however. The need for increased irrigation, increased fertilizer and much more precise timing of the cultivation sometimes resulted in the displacement of small peasant farmers by large landowners who had better access to loans and other resources.

New agricultural research stations are slowly being established throughout the Third World, but a great deal more must be done. The agricultural discoveries that have been made so far are only a small fraction of what is needed. New attention also has to be paid to packaging green revolution technology in such a way that it can support rather than displace poor people.

Economic development certainly does imply industrialization and urbanization, but pursued by themselves they are dead ends. The major cities of the Third World are being stifled by migrants forced out of the countryside. In the early 1990's, Mexico City had 18 million people, São Paulo 14 million and Calcutta 11 million, most of them poor. Everywhere in the Third World the cities are growing faster than the national population, but they are not providing decent jobs and housing. Urbanization can proceed successfully only if it follows upon agricultural progress so that the people can be fed. This is a lesson that has cost the Third World dearly to learn, and that has still not been effectively learned in many countries.

Population Control

Perhaps the most controversial subject related to the economic development of the Third World has been the control of population growth.

The basic facts of population growth are overwhelming. Between 1960 and 1993 the world's population grew from 3 billion to over 5.5 billion, and projections show that it is almost sure to grow to 8 billion by the year 2020. The growth rate of population in the Third World has fallen since 1960, but only from about 2.3 percent a year to about 2.0 percent a year. United Nations projections show that the Third World's share of world population will rise from 77 percent in 1990 to 84 percent in 2025.[5]

The controversy has centered on the question of whether this rapid population growth represents a major obstacle to development. The lowering of population growth rates in the Third World has been seen by some as the single most important task, the necessary condition for economic progress; without a reduction in population growth, many people have argued, the Third World cannot avoid a future of deprivation and starvation. From the opposing side, concern with population growth has been seen as irrelevant and as serving the ideological function of "blaming the victim." Large families serve the interest of poor people in the Third World, say some, and increasing numbers of people mean increasing numbers of hands and minds to tackle the pressing social problems.

It is hard to untangle the truth from all of this controversy, but the most telling piece of evidence is that throughout their recent history, in both their leftward movements like the Cultural Revolution and in their more pragmatic phases, the Chinese have put great emphasis on reducing family size. They have been remarkably successful, cutting their population growth rate in half, from 2 to 1 percent a year, between the 1960's and the 1990's.

Population growth rates are determined almost precisely by the gap between birth rates and death rates (migration can make a difference, but usually not much). A population with a birth rate of 35 per thousand and a death rate of 15 per thousand has a growth rate of 20 per thousand, or 2 percent a year; that is to say, it is doubling every 35 years.[6] If the birth rate is 45 per thousand and the death rate 10 per thousand, as is the case in some Third World countries, the annual growth rate is 3.5 percent, leading to a doubling in 20 years. If, on the other hand, the birth rate can be reduced to 20 per thousand, a death rate of 10 per thousand will yield a 1 percent growth rate and a 70-year doubling time.

The level of childbearing determines not only the growth rate of a population; it also determines the shape of its age pyramid. The higher the birth rate, the younger is the population; this relationship holds almost independently of the level of the death rate.[7]

These two effects of the birth rate—on the population growth rate and on the age distribution—have important implications for economic development. If fertility falls and the growth rate is reduced, whatever economic growth a Third World country achieves can be directed toward improving standards of living rather than simply providing for an increased number of people at the same standard of living. If fertility falls and as a consequence the age distribution of the population grows older, the "burden of dependency" is reduced. That is to say, each adult of working age has fewer dependents to provide for and therefore more choices—to provide more amply for the young people who remain dependent, to increase his or her own consumption standards and/or to increase savings and thus provide for greater increases in future income.[8]

There are other implications of lowering birth rates and population growth. Fertility reduction leads in the long run to a smaller ultimate population size, with less pressure on limited land and natural resources and less crowding in cities. It has proven very difficult for demographers to estimate an optimal population size for a given country—still there is no doubt that there is some size that is "too large," some size that puts undue pressure on limited natural resources and causes incomes to fall. Whether or not Third World countries are close to these sizes now, they will certainly approach and exceed them if population growth continues, with repeated doublings in size.

Economic calculations are almost invariably made over a short term—a small number of years, a presidential term, a generation—we seldom think much beyond a generation. In the case of population growth, however, it is important to think about the long run, say several hundreds of years. In the long run, the growth rate of population (indeed the growth rate of almost anything) must average out to zero. If a population growth rate is less than zero, if it is negative, if deaths exceed births, then the population will decline and eventually disappear. If the growth rate is greater than zero, the population will expand beyond any fixed limit. A growing population will eventually mean standing room only, then layers of people standing on top of each other, an obvious impossibility. Therefore, in the long run, the only sustainable population growth rate is zero.

The only way to achieve zero population growth is to have death rates equal birth rates. This can happen at any level of birth and death rates: both can be high, say 40 or 50 per thousand as in prehistoric societies, or both can be low, say around 10 per thousand. Therefore, if the world is to enjoy the fruits of economic development, if people are to live comfortable lives in good health with a full lifespan of years to look forward to—that is, if they are to enjoy low death rates—then birth rates in the world must fall to low levels.

There is plenty of dissent to the view that a lowering of birth rates will make an important contribution to economic development in low-income countries. Some observers point to a positive correlation between population growth and economic growth in the Third World, arguing that an increasing population provides for its own needs without lowering average living standards. Some argue that the burden of dependency is a myth, that families in the Third World have large families because they want them, and in particular because large families provide status and income for the parents in the present and security for them in their old age, that a large family is a blessing, not a burden. Some argue that while large populations put pressure on fixed resources, this is a global problem that originates in the rich countries, not in the poor countries, since rich people use on average much more of the earth's scarce resources than do the poor.

Most countries of the Third World have embarked upon some sorts of programs to reduce childbearing, believing that rapid population growth makes development more difficult. In some cases, public policy consists of making birth control information and technology available to families, so that they can make informed choices about the number of children they will have, and so that women who so desire can be spared the physical strain of constant pregnancies. Other countries go further—India, for example, has a very extensive public relations campaign urging families to opt for a smaller number of children. And a few have gone still further, such as China, which instituted policies insisting that families have just a single child, and which for a period enforced this policy broadly. In some areas of China, the government has detailed information about the fertility history of the women, even about their menstrual cycles and their birth control methods. Families that choose to have a second child rather than an abortion can be fined large sums of money and even demoted or fired from jobs.[9] The Chinese authorities are absolutely convinced that their economic development efforts will be crippled if rapid population growth resumes. While scattered evidence indicates that they may have withdrawn somewhat from their most severe fertility restrictions in the late 1980's, they are still strongly committed to a continued reduction in birth rates.

The 1960's and the early 1970's were the high point of concern about population growth as a factor in economic development. There was almost a crusade for a worldwide lowering of birth rates and a faith that successful birth control programs would lead to early improvements in living standards. And, in fact, quite a lot was achieved: although populations are still growing quickly, the rates of growth throughout most of Asia and Latin America (not Africa) have fallen considerably.

But the enthusiasm has declined. Population control is seldom cited any more as the single factor that will make the difference. In fact, economic demographers now confess to considerable difficulty in actually finding a relationship between population growth and economic development in their data.[10] Just as in the case of human capital, many observers are inclined to believe now that falling birth rates may be a result of economic development, more than a cause. It may be impossible to convince poor rural people, living constantly on the brink of economic disaster, that their ultimate welfare does not depend upon their having a large family. Perhaps a prosperous society, with resources to spend on social security, unemployment insurance, medical care and pensions is needed before families will relinquish the idea that their security depends upon their children.

At the same time, U.S. policy has become more negative in the area of birth control. The United States was once at the lead of those urging family planning programs and birth control—indeed those policies were heavily criticized by people on the left in both the United States and the Third World who saw American policy as racist. No more. Under pressure from the domestic right, the Republican administrations refused funding to any international program that countenanced abortion (as most did) and withdrew all American initiative in the area of population control. It was an easy bone to throw to conservative critics.

Basic Human Needs

Until the 1970's, few economists or politicians, in either the rich countries or the poor, gave much systematic thought to the basic meaning and goals of economic development in the Third World. The problem seemed if anything too clear: a low standard of living. The solution seemed clear as well: raise production.

The initial thinking about the definition of economic development was that it could be measured, simply and precisely, as gross national product per person. Gross national product is the money value of all final goods and services produced in a country during a year. By definition, according to national income accounting conventions, this measure of a country's production is equal to the income earned by the population. Therefore GNP per capita is a measure of the average income in a country—and economic development was thought to be measured simply by an increase in this average figure. The differences in these average figures among countries are very large—as the data in Chapter 2 showed—from U.S.$150 in the lowest-income countries to over $20,000 in the highest. It was well understood that GNP per capita was just a shorthand representation of economic development, but it was thought to be a meaningful one. Sir W. Arthur Lewis, the Jamaican economist, argued that economic growth was desirable not because it increased people's happiness (it probably did not) but because it increased the range of human choice. In a poor society, people (particularly women) are captives of their poverty, chained to a life of subsistence, drudgery and insecurity; with increased wealth they have opportunities to choose different occupations, different homes, different consumer goods, different amounts of leisure. It was the freedom of choice that came with economic growth that justified the attention paid to it.

The 1970's saw a reaction against the view that increases in gross national product necessarily led to an improvement in living conditions. If the purpose of economic development was to improve the lot of the majority of the people in a country, then it became increasingly obvious that such improvement might not be associated at all with increases in GNP. It all depended on what sorts of goods and services were produced, and who got them. Furthermore, a misplaced fixation on GNP led to the erroneous conclusion that the countries with high GNP, in Europe and North America, represented models to which the Third World could and should aspire. Such a view of development, it was argued, was both impossible and harmful. It was impossible for the entire Third World to have per capita GNPs the level of that of the United States, because the earth's natural resources were too limited and its ecology too fragile, to permit it. It was harmful because it deflected attention away from improvements in living standards that were both urgently needed and attainable.

At the World Bank, Robert S. McNamara and his associates from both the Third World and the developed countries began to direct attention to the critical needs of the most destitute, the "absolute poor" as he called them. At the Institute for Development Studies in Sussex, England, Dudley Seers and his colleagues called for an economic development strategy that focused on "basic needs." According to this new way of conceiving of development, the size of the gross national product became less important than its composition and its distribution.

The new "basic needs" approach to development in the 1970's took poverty, rather than low GNP, as its target. The basic needs of each person were thought to include sufficient nutritious food, adequate shelter from the elements, decent clothing, protection from disease, and elementary education. These basic necessities were unavailable to hundreds of millions, perhaps billions, of people in the Third World. The test of economic development, in the eyes of this new school, became whether these basic needs were being met, not whether average GNP was growing.

The basic needs approach makes a considerable difference in one's assessment of economic development. That is to say, if one takes as the criterion for economic development the success of a country in meeting the basic needs of its population, rather than the growth rate of its GNP, then some countries that once seemed to be failures now seem successes, and vice versa. Cuba, for example, is a failure under the GNP test, but a success under the basic needs test; Brazil the opposite. The growth of Cuba's GNP has been slow since its revolution, as it has staggered between conflicting strategies—to stop depending only on sugar or to increase sugar production, to be more self-sufficient or to be more dependent upon the Soviet Union. At the same time, however, it has provided basic literacy and health care to a population that had lacked them, and has improved nutritional standards among the poor. Brazil during the two decades from the mid-1950's to the mid-1970's was the miracle of the Third World, with a rapidly advancing industrial sector, growing productivity and a soaring GNP. But the right-wing military regimes of Brazil built this miracle on the backs of destitute peasants and urban slum dwellers, people like Carolina María de Jesús.

Academics were enthusiastic in the 1970's that the basic needs approach could transform the understanding of economic development and cause resources to be redirected toward the most urgent uses. That hope has been lost. Third World governments found their attention drawn to what seemed to be more pressing international issues—in the 1970's the proposals for a New International Economic Order, and in the 1980's the debt crisis. They had little interest or energy left over for basic needs. But the problem with a basic needs approach to development went deeper than that.

Basic needs was for the most part a concern of outsiders, of academics (from the Third World as well as from developed countries) and of international agencies like the World Bank and some of the United Nations affiliates.[11] It was never embraced by the majority of Third World governments and bureaucrats, and for very good reason. A real regard for basic needs would have represented a threat to their own positions of power, and to the positions of influential groups of people upon whom they depended.

Poor people lack power—they lack economic power, of course, and in most societies they also lack political and even moral power. They have little influence over national policies, and they are frequently regarded by those who do have power as being responsible for their own poverty. What the basic human needs strategy really implied, therefore, was that people with power would voluntarily relinquish some portion of their power and transfer it to people whom they thought of as both undeserving and threatening.

Little wonder, then, that many Third World governments regarded the basic needs approach to economic development as an unwarranted intrusion into their own internal affairs. They were generally happy to receive outside assistance to promote overall economic growth. For the most part, however, they recoiled at the suggestion that outsiders had any business telling them how to organize their own societies. Some countries, of course, were moving aggressively on their own to address basic needs—countries like Cuba, China, Sri Lanka and Korea. But in the great majority of cases, the propaganda for basic needs fell on deaf ears. While the ideas are still held in high regard among intellectuals and some spokespeople for the poor, they have largely died, or at least gone into a quiescent phase, in the corridors of power.

The failure of the basic human needs approach revealed the weakness of the modernization theory of social change. The proponents of basic human needs assumed, incorrectly, that governments would act in a disinterested fashion to attack the most serious problems faced by their people. They failed to understand what the Marxists and dependency theorists understood well, that most Third World governments represented the powerful interests of their countries. The very existence of poverty is a consequence of unequal power. The basic human needs doctrine was naive and unsuccessful, because it was posited upon a voluntary transfer of power.

OPEC and the Increase in Oil Prices

In the decade from 1973 to 1983, the most promising development for the Third World seemed to be the increase in oil prices masterminded by the international cartel called OPEC, the Organization of Petroleum Exporting Countries. The price increases completely transformed the economic prospects of the oil exporters. It was welcomed by the oil-importing Third World countries as well, because although it caused immediate hardships for them, it seemed to promise a transformation of the entire international economic system that could benefit them in the long run. The Third World united around the hope that the OPEC price increase could be the precursor to a New International Economic Order, or NIEO (discussed in the next section). As events unfolded, however, the price increase proved to be only a temporary advantage to the oil exporters, and the NIEO proposals collapsed in the 1980's, a victim of the debt crisis.

Petroleum is the biggest single commodity in world trade. Reserves are found in many parts of the world, but the largest fields are in North Africa and the Middle East. Until the early 1970's, the great multinational oil companies, based in the United States and western Europe, produced most of the Middle Eastern oil. They paid royalties to the host countries, sold the oil for an average price of about U.S.$3 a barrel and made substantial profits. The oil-producing countries, joined together in the OPEC organization, were powerless to get a better deal from the oil companies.

In the 1970's this situation changed dramatically. Initially, Libya nationalized a few of the smaller oil companies operating in that country. But the cataclysmic change occurred in 1973 when the Saudis and the other major OPEC countries decided to use oil as a political weapon. Determined to punish the United States for its support of Israel in the October war, the OPEC countries reduced overall production and then instituted a total boycott of oil exports to the United States and some (not all) of its western allies. This was only a short-run strategy: the OPEC countries soon discovered a tool much more advantageous than the boycott. They took control of oil pricing away from the oil companies and within a few months quadrupled the price of oil, to about $13 a barrel. By March 1974, the U.S. boycott was suspended, OPEC having found that it was much more effective to have the Americans buy oil at this high price than make them go without it. Over the next few years, the OPEC countries went further and actually nationalized the oil production facilities that were held by the companies.

This price increase was easily the biggest shock the international economy had sustained since the Second World War. Oil is, after all, the world's most important commodity, the basis for almost all of world industry and much of its agriculture. The shock was repeated in 1979, when OPEC raised the price once again, this time to over $30 a barrel. This action had a tremendous impact on all of the world's countries, both rich and poor. Some of the most important effects are still being played out in the 1990's. Many of the long-run results were unforeseen and actually harmful to the oil exporters. But in the immediate wake of the OPEC action in the mid-1970's, there was jubilation. A group of Third World countries had finally succeeded in turning the tables on the rich countries. Rather than see their own countries sucked dry by low-priced exports that went to fuel western industrialization, the OPEC countries were now bleeding the developed countries, showing that their former masters were vulnerable, that their prosperity depended upon the resources and the cooperation of the oil exporters.

The price increases led to inflation, recession and unemployment in the United States and the other developed countries, and at the same time to an extraordinary accumulation of wealth by the oil-exporting countries. The OPEC countries used their new wealth to import consumer goods to raise living standards among their populations and to embark upon ambitious programs of industrialization, bringing in foreign plant and equipment as well as technicians and laborers.

By a decade after the first price increase, however, the OPEC strategy had failed, a victim of its own short-run success. OPEC had initially been able raise oil prices because it controlled so much of the world supply and could cut back on that supply, thereby creating shortages. The industrialized countries were so addicted that they could not reduce their use of oil significantly, and they were therefore vulnerable. By the mid-1980's, however, when the world had gotten used to 10 years of high oil prices, the easy advantage of the oil exporters disappeared. OPEC could no longer restrict the supply of oil. The OPEC member countries actually cheated on their agreed quotas, seduced by the high prices into producing more and more oil. Only Saudi Arabia was willing to restrict its exports significantly, and eventually even it refused to play the patsy. Outside OPEC, the high world prices made it profitable for other countries and companies to explore for oil in risky circumstances and to produce it even when the costs were very high. Tremendous new resources were exploited—for example, on the north slope of Alaska and in the North Sea between Scotland and Norway

At the same time as supply was expanding, demand was being reduced. Over a period of years, the oil-consuming countries learned how to conserve, how to be energy efficient, how to produce more output with less oil. The result of the declining demand and the expanding supply of oil—both caused by the high price—was a worldwide glut, and as a consequence the price fell precipitously. From highs of just under $40 a barrel, the price fell to $9 in 1986, then rebounded by the early 1990's to about $20. This might seem to be still a fairly high price compared to the period before 1973 but for one thing. From 1973 to the early 1990's there had been significant worldwide inflation of all prices—brought about, ironically, by the oil price increases in the first place. Prices had risen on average about four times. In real terms, therefore, in terms of the amount of other goods and services that a barrel of oil could be exchanged for, the price of oil in the early 1990's was just slightly above what it had been before 1973. The oil market had come full circle. The revenues of OPEC were $287 billion in 1980, and just $84 billion in 1988. The oil exporters had lost their entire advantage.

The lesson was long and painful and may be repeated. In 1990, in the midst of the Persian Gulf crisis, the price of oil more than doubled, to about $40 a barrel, then fluctuated wildly in the succeeding months. The prospects for future oil prices are, of course, uncertain, but consistently high prices could well lead again to temporary wealth among the oil exporters and to both recession and inflation in the rest of the world. The industrialized countries are vulnerable in the 1990's because the relatively low prices of the 1980's lulled them into abandoning their energy-conservation policies. There may be cycles of conservation and profligacy if oil prices move up and down in cycles. But it is now obvious that it is impossible for a group of Third World countries, even a group as powerful as OPEC, to manipulate world prices to solve their economic problems on a permanent basis. That hope has disintegrated.

The New International Economic Order

Inspired by the apparent success of the OPEC cartel, the Third World countries united in the 1970's around a series of proposals, dubbed the New International Economic Order, for the fundamental restructuring of the international system. At the United Nations, and in a long series of conferences, they argued that the current system was unjust and that a comprehensive set of changes was needed.

Many Third World countries were heavily dependent upon the export of a small number of primary commodities to the developed countries—cocoa from Ghana, ground nuts from Senegal, rubber and tin from Malaysia, coffee and sugar from Brazil, fruits from Central America and so on. They believed that the prices for these commodity exports were unduly low, were unstable and were falling over time. Consequently, they placed at the center of their demand for a New International Economic Order the issue of commodity price agreements.

What they wanted was an overall agreement, between Third World exporters and developed country importers, that the prices of commodity exports would be kept both stable and high. The two features were equally important. Stability was needed so that the Third World countries could make realistic long-run plans, knowing just what their export earnings would be. High prices were needed to give the exporters an economic advantage, a lever to improve their economic growth. The model was the OPEC price increase that had been imposed unilaterally by the oil exporters. The other Third World exporters knew they were not strong enough, and their commodities not critical enough, for them to be able to get away with imposing unilateral price increases—hence the demand that the rich countries join with them collectively in this restructuring of international prices. They called for a "Common Fund," to be created by the rich countries and used to buy up commodities whose world prices were low.

Although commodity prices were at the heart of the NIEO, there were a number of other components. Calling themselves the Group of Seventy-Seven, the Third World countries pressed a series of demands. These included a restructuring of the international monetary system, so that new purchasing power, or "international money," would be placed in the hands of the poor countries. They called for controls over the investments of multinational corporations; while they welcomed the participation of foreign companies in their countries, they wanted to ensure that the companies came in under terms that were acceptable and beneficial to the host countries. They called for increased foreign aid, but this was not at the center of the proposals, because aid was thought to create a relationship of dependency. Their slogan was "trade not aid." In the realm of international trade, in addition to commodity price agreements, the NIEO called for preferential tariffs on manufactured exports—that is, the developed countries would continue their tariff barriers on manufactured goods against each other but would eliminate them against imports into their markets from the Third World.

There were a number of objections to the various planks of the NIEO, made for the most part by academic economists and by spokespeople for the developed countries. Basically, the objections came down to skepticism that an international economy managed by governments would serve the long-run interests of the poor countries better than a free market. While the developed countries were willing to talk about a new international order, there was no indication in the 1970's that they were willing to acquiesce in one.

By the 1980's, however, the NIEO had almost dropped from sight as a serious set of negotiating proposals. It was killed partly by the objections of the developed countries, but more by the course of world events. The collapse of OPEC was fundamental. If a monopolistic oil cartel could not succeed in the long run, what hope was there for cartels in other primary commodities produced by the Third World? As the OPEC boom turned into a bust, Third World enthusiasm for the NIEO subsided. Adding to the decline of the NIEO was the extraordinary debt crisis that emerged as the most serious economic problem of the 1980's. The search for an answer to the debt swept away consideration of any other issues. While the demands for a New International Economic Order were still trotted out regularly at conferences, no one had much hope for them, and the developed countries stopped taking the debate seriously. Graduate students no longer wrote dissertations on them.

Development Waylaid by the Debt Crisis

The experience of the previous decades has swept away the old orthodoxies, the old certainties about economic development, leaving very little in their place. In almost every country, poverty is just as pervasive in the Third World as it was in the past, but the commitment to a basic needs strategy of development is almost everywhere abandoned; most countries no longer give even lip service to a structure of economic change that will address the overwhelming needs of the very poorest. The keys of savings and investment, human capital, and family planning have all proven to be useful, but far from the single solution that some once thought them to be. On the international front, the oil cartel has collapsed, and with it the coalition of Third World countries demanding a New International Economic Order. Most amazing of all, the idea of the big push, with the corresponding requirement of government planning, ownership and control, is in retreat. There is a new respect for capitalism and the discipline of the market, but still skepticism that they can provide the total answer. Very little, it is now clear, is actually understood about economic development.

Dominating the discussion of economic development has been a wholly new problem, the debt burden. The origin of the debt crisis lies with the OPEC price increases of the 1970's. The price increases produced a tidal wave of change in international monetary relations. Billions upon billions of new funds flowed into the coffers of the oil exporting countries. The oil exporters used some of these funds to increase their imports of goods and services from abroad, but their imports could not absorb all of their new oil earnings. They were left over with a huge volume of liquid cash. What to do with this cash became known as the "recycling" problem.

Much of the surplus cash was invested by the OPEC countries in the great banks of the United States and the other developed countries. The banks in turn, awash in funds and looking for opportunities to lend those funds at a profit, discovered eager borrowers among the governments of the oil-importing Third World countries. These oil-importing countries were in ideological solidarity with OPEC, but at the same time they were stretched to the limit by the high prices. Unlike the developed countries, they could not reduce their consumer use of oil—for private automobiles, home heating and the like—because very little of their oil went to consumer uses. Almost all of the oil in the Third World importing countries was used to support industry—so any attempt to cope with the crisis by reducing oil use would have crippled their manufacturing sectors, the very sectors they saw as the leading edge of their economic development programs. Third World governments undertook to borrow money from the great banks, therefore, largely to cover the cost of the imported oil. They also borrowed to pay the bills on imported consumer goods for their new middle classes. Most amazingly, once the oil boom was in full swing, some of the oil *exporters*, like Mexico, began to borrow large amounts to cover their growing consumption.

Foreign borrowing by a developing country is not always a bad idea. In the nineteenth century the United States built its railways with funds borrowed from the British, and certainly benefited from the transactions. But to be beneficial, the loans must be invested in productive new projects. To take an example, a Third World country may borrow money from abroad to construct a new irrigation network. If the project is successful, it will generate new jobs and higher incomes. A portion of the new income is used to pay back the loan plus the interest on the loan, and there is still income left over from the project to improve the living standards of the local people. If, on the other hand, the loan is used simply to pay for the purchase of consumer goods or other goods that are already being imported from abroad, then no new productive activity is begun and no new revenue is generated. The repayment of the debt then becomes a burden: the borrowers have to lower their living standards in order to come up with the funds to pay the loans back.

This is the story of the Third World debt crisis. Both the borrowers and the lenders conspired to make some of the worst loans in the history of international finance. The borrowers were desperate for the funds because of their high oil bills. The lenders were desperate to make the loans, because they owed interest payments to the OPEC countries and needed to be earning interest on the funds in order to be able to make those payments. So neither side had an incentive to look at all closely at the true picture, which was that very few of these loans were actually going into the financing of new, productive, financially sound projects in the Third World.

In the late 1970's and early 1980's the crisis hit. Country after country—particularly but not exclusively in Latin America—found itself completely over-committed to debt repayment schedules that it could not possibly meet. In 1980, Mexico's debt repayments amounted to 50 percent of the value of its exports, Brazil's 63 percent, Argentina's 37 percent, Peru's 47 percent and Chile's 43 percent—they and many other Third World countries were completely over their heads. The crisis was exacerbated by rising world interest rates and by declining prices for Third World exports. If the loans were to be repaid, the people's standards of living would collapse.

The search for a solution to the debt crisis dominated thinking and negotiations about economic development in the 1980's. It was a crisis that at times threatened not only the economies of the Third World, but the stability and prosperity of the entire international economic system. Worst case scenarios were not hard to imagine. For a few years, the Third World debts were actually greater than the net worth of the lending banks. In other words, if the debtor countries had refused to honor their debts, the banks would have collapsed as business entities. The specter of the collapse of the world banking system is frightening, calling up memories of another world depression, perhaps worse than the 1930's. By the mid 1980's, however, this danger receded as most of the banks succeeded in accumulating enough reserves to buffer themselves against the danger of Third World loan defaults. For the nine largest American banks, the ratio of Third World loans to net worth fell from 280 percent in 1982 to just 100 percent in 1989.[12]

For the developed countries the debt crisis was only a potential danger, but for the Third World it was a monumental present disaster. In 1981, there was a net positive flow of funds from the rich countries to the Third World of $42.6 billion; by 1988 there was a net reverse flow, from the poor countries to the rich, of $32.5 billion, most of the shift occurring because of debt servicing.[13]

Third World countries simply could not afford to pay off their debts. To see the problem, one must understand that to pay off debts to the United States, Mexicans must have U.S. dollars. U.S. banks will not accept Mexican pesos; if they would, the debt crisis would be easily solved, because the Mexicans would just print more pesos—but the banks won't. Where can the Mexicans get dollars? They cannot just buy dollars with their pesos, because if they tried to do this the value of the peso would collapse: foreigners do not want to hold pesos. So the Mexicans must export more goods to the United States and other countries (thus earning dollars) than they import from those countries (spending dollars); they must run an export surplus.

But this is easier said than done. It is not simple for Mexico to increase its exports, since Mexican industries find it difficult to compete in international markets, and since the rich countries protect their own industries against the threat of foreign imports. So because the Mexicans must run an export surplus in order to make payments on their debt, they are forced to reduce their imports. There are many complex ways of doing this, but what they all amount to in the end is reducing the incomes of the Mexican people, so that they will be unable to buy so many goods from abroad.

In other words, the debt crisis has led directly to a staggering drop in the standard of living of Mexicans and of other Third World peoples facing the debt burden. In the six year presidency of Miguel de la Madrid in Mexico, from 1982 to 1988, real wages (that is to say, money wages corrected for changes in the cost of living) fell by 40 percent. Poverty increased extensively, and whole sections of the middle class were wiped out. In just 2 years, from 1985 to 1987, Nigeria's per capita income fell by more than half, from $800 to $380. No wonder that economic development in the Third World seemed to have taken a back seat in the 1980's. The struggle was no longer for economic development in many countries; it was to resist massive deterioration in living standards.

The prospects for a resolution of the debt crisis in the 1990's are uneven. Sovereign governments of Third World countries can of course suspend or reduce payments, and some have. There is no international policeman who will slap them in a debtor's jail; the British Royal Navy has not performed this function for a hundred years. But there are constraints to the renunciation of debts. Countries that do not meet their debt obligations live in fear that the international banking community will refuse them further financing in the future, because they have demonstrated that they are a bad credit risk. Peru was refused any consideration at all from the great banks when it unilaterally reduced its debt payments. There have been a few attempts in the Third World to develop a common strategy among the debtors. Fidel Castro of Cuba, for example, urged all the Latin American countries to unite in repudiating their debt, reasoning that while the banks might single out one or two countries for retaliation, they could not act against all of them. The debtor countries have been unwilling, however, to take this risk.

Some progress has been made in reducing the debt burdens. Complex agreements have been reached in some countries between the local government, the United States government, foreign banks and the International Monetary Fund to reduce the obligations, spread them over a longer period and swap some of the fixed debt instruments for equity. Consequently, the overall ratio of debt service repayments to GNP has fallen somewhat in Latin America. In some countries, most importantly in Mexico and Brazil, the agreements have had a major impact, freeing those countries to resume their path of economic growth. The agreements are not universal, however, and many countries are still laboring under a severe burden.

The problem of the debt crisis has not been simply that the debts have been high. It has been that the debt crisis has overridden consideration of most of the other initiatives that might lead to genuine economic development. Indicative of the change of perspective was the reorientation of the World Bank. The World Bank was established after the Second World War to direct capital to the war-ravaged countries of Europe, and then towards the developing countries. For its first two decades it was a fairly conservative institution, funding only relatively secure projects and taking few risks. Beginning in the late 1960's, under the leadership of former U.S. Defense Secretary Robert S. McNamara, it took a much more adventurous stance. It was at the forefront of concern for basic needs, for attacking absolute poverty and for addressing the inequitable distribution of income. It took a number of important initiatives in health care, family planning, literacy and education. It developed programs to help poor peasants keep a stake on the land, and not be displaced by commercial agriculture. In the late 1960's and the 1970's, the World Bank was still subject to criticism, some of it quite valid, by people who claimed it did not go far enough, that it still represented the interests of the rich countries and was unwilling really to act to empower the poor. Nevertheless it had moved an enormous distance in a progressive direction, towards the meeting of genuine human needs. Almost all of this initiative was lost after 1980. Under the direction of Presidents Robert Clausen, Barber Conable and Lewis Preston, the World Bank was consumed with the debt problem, with trying to devise solutions to keep the deterioration of Third World economies within manageable proportions. This is a constructive role for an international institution to play in a period of crisis—but it is a long way from the commitment to real economic and human development that it once was proud to embody. In this respect the World Bank mirrors the face of policy makers throughout the world.

A few countries in the Third World are going through a spectacular spurt of economic change, while the majority are creeping along slowly, stagnating, or actually deteriorating under the burden of foreign debts. The material promise of the nationalist independence movements has not been fulfilled. The majority of people on the planet are still poor and ill fed.

There is some hope. Perhaps the successful Third World economies will provide lessons that can be adopted by other countries. Perhaps the majority of the Third World countries will discover that while there is no single magic key to economic development, still, slow progress can be made by working steadily on a number of fronts. Perhaps communities of poor people will find ways to join together and reclaim some of the power that has been stripped from them.

The task ahead is very difficult, however, and the prospects of success hardly rosy. Those prospects would be immeasurably improved if the Third World could count on the partnership of the rich countries. As Chapter 7 shows, it cannot.

Suggestions for Further Reading

Arndt, H. W. *Economic Development: The History of an Idea.* Chicago: University of Chicago Press, 1987.

Freire, Paulo. *Pedagogy of the Oppressed.* Translated by Myra Bergman Ramos. New York: Herder and Herder, 1970.

Gillis, Malcolm, Dwight H. Perkins, Michael Roemer, and Donald R. Snodgrass. *Economics of Development.* 2d ed. New York: W. W. Norton and Company, 1987.

Haq, Mahbub ul. *The Poverty Curtain: Choices for the Third World.* New York: Columbia University Press, 1976.

Kamarck, Andrew M. *The Tropics and Economic Development: A Provocative Inquiry into the Poverty of Nations.* Baltimore: The Johns Hopkins University Press, 1973.

Lipton, Michael. *Why Poor People Stay Poor: Urban Bias in World Development.* Cambridge: Harvard University Press, 1977.

South Commission, *The Challenge to the South.* New York: Oxford University Press, 1990.

Streeten, Paul. *First Things First: Meeting Basic Human Needs in Developing Countries.* New York: Oxford University Press, 1981.

Notes

1. Quoted in Timothy M. Shaw, "The Non-Aligned Movement and the New International Division of Labor," in Kofi Buenor Hadjor, ed., *New Perspectives in*

North-South Dialogue: Essays in Honour of Olof Palme (London: I. B. Tauris, 1988), 185.

2. Hong Kong is not an independent country but a British colony, due to be ceded to China.

3. W. Arthur Lewis, "Economic Development with Unlimited Supplies of Labor," *The Manchester School of Economic and Social Studies* 22 (1954), 139–91.

4. For an excellent discussion of this neglected aspect of economic development, see Andrew M. Kamarck, *The Tropics and Economic Development: A Provocative Inquiry into the Poverty of Nations* (Baltimore: The Johns Hopkins University Press, 1973).

5. United Nations Development Program, *Human Development Report 1990* (New York: Oxford University Press, 1990).

6. As noted in Chapter 4, the number of years to double is found by dividing the annual percentage growth rate into 70.

7. The reason is that when mortality improves, it generally does so both at young ages (infant mortality) and at old ages, and it therefore leaves the overall age distribution of the population more or less unchanged. But when fertility falls, this reduces only the number of babies, no one else. Therefore, the lower fertility, the smaller the proportion of young people in a population.

8. This way of looking at the economic consequences of population growth was proposed in Ansley J. Coale and Edgar M. Hoover, *Population Growth and Economic Development in Low-Income Countries: A Case Study of India's Prospects* (Princeton: Princeton University Press, 1958).

9. In 1988, in a publicized case, the United States gave political asylum to six Chinese fleeing from their country's birth control policy, people who already had a child and did not want an abortion. The Chinese government, naturally, protested.

10. For a good summary of the empirical problems that the demographers have run into, see National Research Council, *Population Growth and Economic Development: Policy Questions* (Washington, D.C.: National Academy Press, 1986).

11. For a recent, comprehensive UN report in the basic needs tradition, see *Human Development Report 1990* (New York: Oxford University Press, 1990).

12. John Ravenhill, "The North-South Balance of Power," *International Affairs* 66 (October 1990), 731–48.

13. United Nations Development Program, *Human Development Report 1990* (New York: Oxford University Press, 1990), 5.

CHAPTER SEVEN

North-South Relations

There is no longer a clear division between what is foreign and what is domestic. The world economy, the world environment, the world AIDS crisis, the world arms race—they affect us all.
— President Bill Clinton
Inaugural Address, January 20, 1993

As the Cold War fades away, we face not a "new world order" but a troubled and fractured planet.
— Paul Kennedy[1]

We need bread for the hungry rather than weapons in space.
— Willy Brandt[2]

ON THE WHOLE, the rich countries have not been helpful to the world's poor people. The existence of widespread world poverty is not solely their fault, of course; it is a much bigger problem. But the countries of the north, absorbed by their own problems of security and economy, have turned their backs on one of the great moral challenges to face the globe, and in countless ways, big and small, have acted to make the problem of poverty worse, not better.

The End of the Cold War

For four and a half decades after the Second World War, international relations were dominated by the cold war, the confrontation between the United States and its allies on the one hand and the Soviet Union and its allies on the other.

The cold war colored almost every aspect of public life. In the United States, generations of politicians were judged by their anticommunist credentials and their commitment to stand up against the Soviet threat. In the Soviet Union, the foreign threat was used as a justification for dictatorship. An arms race squandered untold sums of money that might otherwise have been used to improve the human condition. For the most part, the rich countries treated their relationships with the poor countries as an extension of the cold war, seeking allies in the Third World and seeking to counter what they regarded as the expansionist aims of their enemies.

Then in a few short months around 1990, the cold war ended. It ended for the most unexpected and dramatic of reasons, the complete collapse of the Soviet Union as a political entity. Of the former cold war rivals, only one remained.

By the 1980's, the Soviets had become fatally overextended abroad, at the same time that their domestic economy was deteriorating. Premier Gorbachev took a series of what in retrospect appear to be desperate, futile efforts to salvage the Soviet state. He pulled back radically from foreign involvement. The Soviets withdrew from the war in Afghanistan in 1988, and drastically cut economic aid to Cuba and other dependent countries. They permitted the client states of their eastern European empire—Poland, East Germany, Czechoslovakia, Hungary, Bulgaria and Romania—to break away from their control in 1989. They stood by powerless as Germany was reunited in 1990. At home, Gorbachev's regime permitted much freer political expression and attempted to restructure the failing economy. But it was all in vain. The end of the Soviet Union came in 1991 when, following an abortive coup by communist hardliners, Gorbachev was forced to accept the independence of all of the Soviet republics and the repudiation of communism.

The successor state in Russia, led by the democratically elected Boris Yeltsin, faced enormous domestic problems. The economy deteriorated rapidly, as central planning was abandoned but free-enterprise capitalism had yet to take hold. Politically, the adherents of the old guard fought Yeltsin for power at every turn, trying to turn the country back from radical economic and social reform. Regional, ethnic and national conflict spread. Trying to retain control of the country, Yeltsin turned to western Europe and North America for aid. The former enemy of the west had been transformed into something between an ally and a client. The bipolar conflict that had lasted for almost half a century disappeared.

Its disappearance left the world with an enormous, unanswered question. What was to replace the cold war as the organizing principle of international relations? At the time of the Persian Gulf war in 1991, President Bush called for a "new world order," by which he apparently meant a world in which the most powerful countries would cooperate with rather than oppose each other, and would join forces to counter aggression. Once the war was over, however, he did little to advance this idea. His successor, President Clinton, has been even less successful in forging a new world order. Bush at least was able to persuade the western powers to join in support of a common policy in the Persian Gulf war; Clinton could not build an international consensus in response to the war in the former Yugoslavia.

In terms of relationships between the north and the south, the question of what will replace the cold war is critical. The end of the cold war might free the countries of the north to cooperate with the south in genuinely helpful ways. Or it might lead the north to neglect the south completely, since it no longer needs the countries of the Third World as cold war allies.

On the positive side, it may be possible to reduce world military spending substantially, and declare a "peace dividend." Hundreds of billions of dollars could be made available for other urgent needs: to reduce government deficits, to fund important domestic programs and to support economic development in the Third World. Freed from the constraint of viewing foreign policy in an anti-Soviet context, western policymakers may be able to focus for the first time upon the real needs of the countries of the Third World, and the ways in which they could join in a partnership with those countries.

This is just a hope. There is certainly the danger that as the Soviet threat passes, and Third World countries no longer need to be seen as pawns in the cold war chess match, the United States and the other rich countries will lose interest in them altogether. One ominous sign at the beginning of the 1990's was that the European Community, which had developed close aid and trading relationships with the former colonies in sub-Saharan Africa, as well as in the Caribbean and the Pacific, seemed to be turning its back on Africa as it pursued a new interest in supporting the emergent democracies in eastern Europe.

The Illusion of the North-South Dialogue

As the former colonies became independent, they tried to challenge the idea that the dominant issue in world affairs was the east-west conflict of the cold war. They tried to shift the axis ninety degrees, proposing that the most important international issues were north-south ones, the relationships between the rich and the poor countries. The Third World countries of the south confronted the industrialized countries of the north. In international organizations, and at a series of conferences lasting over decades, they tried to negotiate with the industrialized world, to reshape the international order and secure some economic advantages for the poor.

The north-south axis traces its origins to the April 1955 meeting of the leaders of twenty-nine independent African and Asian countries at Bandung, Indonesia, in the First Conference of Afro-Asian Solidarity. The leaders considered their countries to be "nonaligned," and they used the term *Third World* in that sense, as meaning that they were allied with neither the eastern nor the western blocs in the cold war. At a later meeting in 1961, with more participants, they adopted the name Non-Aligned

Movement (NAM). The NAM supported decolonization and noninter-ference by the former colonizers in the affairs of the Third World.

The first impulse of the new Third World countries was to declare their neutrality in the great east-west power struggle. Very soon, however, neutrality ebbed as an organizing principle, and they turned to partisanship in their own behalf, the cause of the south. For many years, they confronted the governments of the developed countries in what became known as the north-south dialogue, demanding fundamental changes in world economic and political relationships.

The cause was pressed in many arenas. As each colony became independent it joined the United Nations, and by the 1960's that organization was dominated by Third World countries. They were able to control the UN General Assembly, where each country has one vote, as well as the affiliated UN organizations that are created by the General Assembly. The Third World countries made development, decolonization and north-south relations the principal agenda of the United Nations.

In 1964, the United Nations sponsored the first UN Conference on Trade and Development (UNCTAD) in Geneva. UNCTAD became an institution, with its own secretariat, and thereafter sponsored international conferences every several years, conferences at which the south pressed its case for concessions from the north and the restructuring of international economic relationships. Its first secretary-general was the Argentinean economist Raúl Prebisch, and its ideology was that of the dependency theorists.

The north-south dialogue reached its height in the 1970's, with the comprehensive proposals from the Third World for a New International Economic Order, or NIEO (see Chapter 6 for a summary of the proposals). In 1973, the fourth NAM summit, in Algiers, created the Group of Seventy-Seven and announced the program for the NIEO. Then, in December 1974, the UN General Assembly adopted the Charter of Economic Rights and Duties of States, a document incorporating most of the NIEO platform. The vote adopting the charter was lopsided, with only six nays and ten abstentions. Significantly, however, the nays included the big three of the north: the United States, Britain and West Germany. Following the adoption of the charter, a whole series of new negotiations was undertaken.

A United Nations commission, chaired by Willy Brandt, the former chancellor of West Germany, and composed of representatives from all parts of the world, was established in 1978 to "suggest ways of promoting adequate solutions to the problems involved in development and in attacking absolute poverty." It reported in 1980, endorsing most of the proposals for the NIEO.

Throughout the 1970's, the governments of the major northern powers were willing to engage in discussions about the issues raised by the south. For the most part, they were not willing to endorse the southern platform, but they studied it and proposed alternatives. Some of the governments of the smaller northern countries—for example, the Scandinavians—were enthusiastic in their endorsement of the NIEO. There was reason to think that good-faith negotiations were under way. If a full NIEO were not to be adopted, there might still be some movement in the direction proposed by the south.

These hopes came to naught in the 1980's. One reason was the victory of Ronald Reagan and the Republican party in the 1980 general election in the United States. Far more than his predecessor, Jimmy Carter, Reagan espoused a free-market, private-sector solution to economic problems, one that was quite incompatible with the NIEO proposals of the south. This became crystal clear at the Cancún, Mexico, meeting of twenty-two representative heads of state in 1981, called to consider the proposals of the Brandt Commission. Reagan and the Americans listened politely to the Third World platform but made no commitments whatsoever, and as a result the conference came to no conclusions.

After Cancún, very little more was heard of the NIEO. As explained in Chapter 6, the collapse of the OPEC oil cartel and the worsening debt burdens of the 1980's led Third World countries to concentrate on their own crises at home and to lose much hope for a restructuring of the international economy.

With the collapse of the south's agenda, it became obvious that the Third World had little bargaining power in international politics, that almost all the power resided in the north. For a few years in the 1970's, it had seemed that north-south issues might compete with the east-west confrontation for the honor of the principal theme in international politics, but that turned out to be an illusion. By the 1980's and 1990's, it was clear that the policies of the rich countries toward the poor would be determined principally by their perceptions of their own self-interest, not by the demands of the poor.

To understand the relationships between the north and the south, therefore, one must turn to the north, to its changing power centers and conflicts.

The Decline in U.S. Hegemony

Two major structural changes are reshaping international relations in the 1990's. In some respects they appear to be contradictory. On the one hand, the end of the cold war leaves the United States as the world's strongest country. On the other hand, however, the United States itself appears to be declining in relative power. The United States' relative economic strength has ebbed since its high watermark in the 1960's, particularly in comparison to Japan and Europe. It was defeated in a major war in Vietnam. There is uncertainty, therefore, about whether the United

States is still the star of the show or is becoming a has-been in world affairs.

Bewilderment about the role of the United States is hardly new; throughout most of the twentieth century, the American position in the world order has shifted frequently, leaving perceptions and realities wide distances apart.

Just prior to the First World War, the countries of western Europe appeared to be stronger than the United States. Americans had little sense of being a world power, and they saw no need to enter into a European conflict that seemed not to concern them. However, once they did enter the war in 1917, it was American strength that ensured victory for their allies. In the interwar period there was no doubt that the United States was a great power, but Americans were uncomfortable with this fact and to a large extent conducted their foreign affairs as if theirs were an isolated country. Global leadership stayed in Europe, as the United States rejected membership in the League of Nations. Once again, the United States did not enter into the world war when it was declared in 1939, preferring a policy of neutrality. Again, however, it was the American entry in 1942, after the Japanese attack at Pearl Harbor, that eventually brought victory to the democracies. At the end of the Second World War, the Europeans' strength was spent and the United States emerged unambiguously as the major world economic and military power. This time there was no thought of isolationism, as the United States confronted a hostile Soviet Union across an "iron curtain." Most Americans who are now adults grew to think of their country in this latter way, as the world's most powerful country, or at least one of the two most powerful—the leader of the "free world" engaged in a monumental struggle against the forces of communism led by the Soviet Union. Most western Europeans came to think of themselves as uneasily allied with the United States, but caught geographically in a potential conflict zone between the two great superpowers.

The picture of the United States as the noncommunist world's strongest country was fairly accurate in the 1950's and the 1960's, but it became less accurate after that time. U.S. hegemony slipped. Little by little, but inexorably, the United States has been losing its position of dominance in the world. The evidence for this is manifold.

Part of the evidence is economic. Although U.S. production of goods and services has increased since the Second World War, other countries' production has increased faster, and therefore the relative position of the United States has slipped. In 1950, the United States produced almost 40 percent of the world's output, but in 1990 about 24 percent. The United States produced 45 percent of the world's manufactured goods in the 1950's, and just about 25 percent in the 1980's. After the Second World War the United States was dominant in the world economy, but since that time the Europeans and the Japanese have caught up and in some respects surpassed the United States. Productivity growth—the rate of growth of output per worker—was much slower in the United States in the 1970's and 1980's than in the rest of the developed world: other countries were winning the technological race. The United States may have recovered its rate of productivity growth in manufacturing towards the end of the 1980's and the beginning of the 1990's, but whether this represents a permanent reversal of declining fortunes remains to be seen.

The decline in the United States' dominance has been accompanied by basic structural shifts in the world economy. Prior to 1971, the world currency was for all intents and purposes the U.S. dollar; the value of each other currency was fixed to the dollar and to gold, and almost all countries made payments to each other in dollars. The position of the dollar was one that befitted the dominant world economy. After 1971, as the American economy weakened relative to other economies, the dollar no longer had the strength to retain the position of unquestioned world currency. Other currencies fluctuated in value with each other and with the dollar in a system called "floating exchange rates." The unthroning of the U.S. dollar is the clearest indicator that the age of unchallenged American economic control is gone.

In the field of foreign investment, too, the world has gone topsy-turvy. The United States used to send enormous sums abroad, with its multinational corporations expanding throughout almost every other country. After the 1970's, it became a major importer of investment funds, with Japanese, Middle Eastern, European and Canadian funds—and even money from the Third World—invading every sector of its economy. From being the world's greatest creditor nation, it became the greatest debtor.

Even more dramatic than the economic decline was the military debacle in Vietnam. The United States entered the Vietnam War gradually in the late 1950's and early 1960's, without any understanding that it was descending into a quagmire that would bring into question its military dominance.

The cause of the American loss was political, both in Vietnam and in the United States. In Vietnam, the United States and its South Vietnamese allies never succeeded in winning the allegiance of the Vietnamese peasants. The south's Viet Cong guerrillas and the army of North Vietnam both promised land reform and freedom from oppression to the peasants, and as a consequence the Americans never enjoyed the complete support of the people for whom they were ostensibly fighting. In the United States, dissension and opposition to the war reached levels never before seen. University campuses were in almost open rebellion against the war policy of the government. Many Americans could see no purpose in the sacrifice of their young people's lives to support an unpopular autocratic regime. In the end, the United States found that it could not win the war militarily, short of nuclear escalation (and President Nixon had the sense not to go this far), and that it lacked the political support at home to continue battling. The United States withdrew its troops in 1973, hoping that the South Vietnamese army could prevail on its own. But that was a forlorn hope; in less than 2 years, the North Vietnamese had taken over and unified the country.

U.S. bombers had destroyed bridges and installations, while U.S. ground forces had won battles and razed villages—but in spite of their use of history's most technologically advanced weaponry, the enemy was not defeated. By the 1970's it appeared that the U.S. military was no longer omnipotent. The United States went into Vietnam as the world's strongest military and political force; it emerged greatly weakened, with serious questions about its ability to exert its authority on a world scale.

Military conflicts in the 1980's appeared to confirm this verdict. America was successful only against the small country of Panama and the even smaller, defenseless Caribbean island republic of Grenada. In Lebanon, the United States committed Marines for a brief period, but was unable to influence the course of the conflict in that country and was unable even to protect its own barracks against attack. In Nicaragua and Angola, the United States was unwilling to deploy its own troops, and its surrogates, the rebel armies fighting against the governments of those two countries, were not successful in spite of extensive U.S. military aid.

In the early 1990's, however, the United States seemed in many eyes to have regained its preeminent position in the world, as Soviet power collapsed and as Americans led a victorious military coalition in the Persian Gulf. Certainly the end of the cold war was real, and the demonstration of military prowess in the desert sands was overpowering. Nevertheless, there is reason to think that this opinion—that American power has been restored—is illusory.

In his provocative book, *The Rise and Fall of the Great Powers*, historian Paul Kennedy argues that empires are established by countries as a consequence of their economic superiority. As they dominate more areas of the world, they are increasingly called upon to impose "law and order" in the world, to put down local rebellions and international conflicts. The demands on their military resources increase without limit, and the military spending detracts from their ability to invest, develop new technology and advance economically at home. Meanwhile, other countries that are protected by the umbrella of the imperialist's military forces are spared the necessity of extensive military expenditures and are free to direct their resources toward the growth of their own economies. A contradiction inevitably arises for the imperial power: its military responsibilities grow but its economy lags, while its competitors threaten and then overtake it in terms of productivity and technology. Eventually the imperial country is so weakened by its military expenditures that it has to cede its dominant position to its upstart competitors and retreat to a more circumscribed niche in the corridors of world power.

Kennedy's scheme nicely describes the rise and fall of the British Empire, and it is hard to see why it does not describe the trajectory of American power in the second half of the twentieth century as well. America's world dominance was the consequence of its economic superiority after the Second World War. The country's military expenditures grew enormously. The United States developed a staggering nuclear arsenal to counter the perceived Soviet threat. It also spent huge sums on what are now called "conventional" weapons, and the troops that go with them, to fight wars and counter rebellions in the Third World. As a result, U.S. investment in the economy declined and productivity stagnated. The Japanese caught up with the Americans economically, and so did the Europeans, led by the Germans.

Seen in this perspective, the American role in the Persian Gulf war may be an indicator not of renewed American dominance, but of an even more quickly deteriorating position. Once again, the United States took the military lead, as it has throughout the second half of the twentieth century. It spent not only billions of dollars but made its most major commitment of military personnel since the Vietnam conflict. This time, however, it was clear from the start that the United States could not afford the expenditure. It went hat in hand to its allies, asking for financial and military assistance, admitting that it could not bear the burden of the military action alone. For the most part, its allies were forthcoming, but not to such an extent that they were seriously encumbered financially. In fact, they were playing out Professor Kennedy's scenario. They were willing to be protected by the United States' military forces, make modest contributions and be left free to pursue their economic goals.

President Bush declared that the Gulf war had finally put to rest the Vietnam syndrome, but it may turn out to have been a dramatic indicator of the contradiction between the United States' aspirations and its capabilities, a further marker on the road away from world dominance. While the war seemed at the time to be a remarkable military victory, it appears less impressive in hindsight. The military action and the associated economic embargo did not remove the Iraqi president, Saddam Hussein, and his regime from power, and they did not stop that regime's continued suppression of Shiites and Kurds within Iraq. The victorious allies have not cooperated effectively in dealing with other cases of military aggression, most notably in the former Yugoslavia. It is not at all clear, therefore, that a new world order with the United States at its center has replaced the world of the cold war.

What is the new structure of the post-cold war world likely to be? Predictions are notorious for their inaccuracy, but nevertheless one makes them. The United States may remain one of the world's strong countries, but it will probably not be dominant. There will likely be several poles of power. One pole will certainly be Japan, a country whose economic growth since the Second World War has been phenomenal, and which is not burdened by military expenditures.[3] The western Europeans have also recovered fully from the Second World War, and will play an increasingly important role in international affairs. Germany will be the strongest European country, and its importance will be enhanced by cooperation with its neighbors in politics, the economy and the military. There are therefore at least three power centers in the emerging world.

International power will be more complex than this, however, because for some purposes other countries will be able to exert authority. For 10 years the OPEC oil producers pulled the strings in the world economy. The Chinese are still a very poor people, but their economic growth together with their large population size give them a potential place among the great powers. The newly industrializing countries of Asia are still too small to constitute a center of world power, but that may change if their economic growth continues unabated. The peoples of the former Soviet bloc are likely to be consumed for a generation by their own problems—their competing nationalisms and the need to restructure their economies—but in time they may reemerge as world powers.

Foreign Policy During the Cold War: The Globalist Perspective

During the period of the cold war, the countries of North America and western Europe formed a political, military and economic alliance for the purpose of protecting their security and confronting the Soviets. The United States took the leadership position in this western alliance and in comparison to its allies adopted the strongest and most rigid anticommunist positions. The Canadians and the Europeans remained under the protection of U.S. might and for the most part supported U.S. positions, although they frequently toyed with somewhat more liberal or conciliatory policies with respect to the Soviets. Throughout this period, however, it was the foreign policy of the United States, not of its allies, that was predominant.

The United States built an enormous nuclear and conventional military arsenal to counter the Soviet threat. Its geopolitical policy was one of "containment," that is to say, keeping the Soviets and their allies penned up to the maximum extent possible.

Both the United States and the Soviet Union extended the cold war struggle to the Third World. Each viewed its interest as being to secure the allegiance of Third World governments and to prevent its foe from extending its influence.

During most of the cold war period, U.S. foreign policymakers viewed the Third World from what is sometimes called a globalist rather than a regionalist perspective. A regionalist perspective would have taken the local conflicts seriously; it would have seen the Nicaraguan revolution as the struggle of an oppressed peasantry against a dictatorial military regime and the South African conflict as a movement for racial justice. The globalist perspective was to see almost all of the Third World societies as pawns in an enormously complex chess game being fought by two master players—the Soviet Union and the United States—the stakes being the freedom of the people in the western alliance. In the globalist perspective, the regional issues were for the most part secondary and unimportant. The globalists had no difficulty in embracing authoritarian dictators if they took the right stand against the Soviets: "He may be a son of a bitch," the saying went, "but he's our son of a bitch."

The contrary policy, regionalism, was actually attempted for four years in the late 1970's, during the much-maligned presidency of Jimmy Carter. The Carter administration put human rights, rather than anticommunism, in the place of honor in its Third World policy, the consequence being that the United States offended a number of its erstwhile allies. The Carter policy was less than completely successful. While it gave hope to the victims and the oppressed in the Third World, it did not produce many concrete changes. The administration underestimated the military determination of the Soviets in Afghanistan, and it was drawn into a humiliating hostage crisis in Iran. Carter's critics on the right were extremely sharp, arguing that he was giving up the historic American role of opposing Soviet expansionism. And in the end it was Carter's ineffectiveness in foreign policy, more than anything, that led to his electoral defeat after one term.

With Ronald Reagan's victory in the 1980 presidential election, the philosophy of globalism returned. Reagan came to office with an explicit mandate to restore U.S. power, to recover from the decline the country was seen to have suffered. Reagan and the majority of the people who elected him saw the world in bipolar terms, with the United States leading the free world against the "evil empire" of godless Soviet communism. As Reagan saw it, the principal threat to American well-being was Soviet expansionism. The central thrust of foreign affairs in the 1980's was therefore to reassert U.S. power throughout the world and to confront the Soviets at every turn. In Central America, in the Middle East, in southern Africa, in the Pacific—in fact, throughout the Third World—U.S. policy became to support those who opposed the communists. Other considerations mattered little.

The U.S. government under President Reagan downplayed the issue of human rights in the Third World, for example, making it clear that the main criterion for U.S. friendship was that Third World regimes be anticommunist, not that they treat their own citizens decently. The United States consequently supported a series of military regimes in Latin America, even against the centrist democratic governments that eventually replaced them. In South Africa, the U.S. policy of "constructive engagement" was perhaps intended to pressure the white ruling regime to renounce apartheid, but was perceived as a pro-apartheid policy working against the freedom of the black majority, all in the name of anticommunism. In El Salvador the United States supported a right-wing government against what it saw as a Marxist rebel movement, and in Nicaragua it supported the rebels against what it saw as a Soviet-dominated revolutionary government, in each case the purpose being to deny the Soviets a foothold in Central America. In the Philippines, up until the very last moment, the United States supported the dictator Ferdinand Marcos because he was a bulwark against communist rebels.

The tragedy in this policy was that in country after country it put the Americans squarely against the aspirations of poor people. Furthermore, it was not a necessary policy, since the great majority of Third World peoples and their governments had only a marginal interest in the great cold war power struggle. In fact, in country after country, one can see in hindsight that the Americans actually created geopolitical problems for themselves where none needed to exist. In Vietnam, Ho Chi Minh explicitly sought American friendship at the end of the Second World War, long before he looked to the Soviets for help. In southern Africa, black resistance movements tolerated communist influence only because they saw the Americans in support of the white minorities. In Central America, peasants would have preferred to live in peace and friendship with the United States; their leaders turned to the Soviets for help only because the Americans supported the landowning factions.

The regionalist perspective was kept alive principally in the foreign policy of some of the United States' allies. Once the British were reconciled to their withdrawal from empire, they generally supported the U.S. position, at least under their Conservative governments. Other allies, however, dissented somewhat. The Canadians and the Scandinavians tried to establish relationships with Third World countries that promoted economic development. The French maintained unique connections to their former colonies, particularly in Africa, while the Germans and the Japanese cautiously began to create new bridges to Third World countries. But the impact of all of these slightly different policies was much weaker than that of the Americans.

The U.S. government, as the leader of the western coalition, has confronted the Third World in a number of ways in the recent past. Militarily, the United States generally intervened in the armed conflicts of the Third World on the side of the privileged, against the poor. While it did not have many clear military successes for itself and its allies, it was frequently able to prevent or delay victories for its opponents. The enormous expenditures of the rich countries on armaments represented tragically lost opportunities, decisions to opt for wasteful destruction rather than positive social change. In the area of human rights, U.S. policy vacillated, but throughout most of the period since 1980 the U.S. government abandoned Third World victims of state-sponsored violence—unless those victims happened to be subjects of an unfriendly government. In its foreign economic policies, the United States deemphasized foreign aid and allowed a debilitating debt crisis to stifle the hope of development in many countries. Through its irresponsible federal budget policy it stacked the deck against the world's poor.

Military Policy

The military policy of the United States has been directed toward several different purposes. The centerpiece has been nuclear deterrence, and throughout the cold war period it is fair to say that deterrence was effective. After the Second World War there were no direct armed conflicts among the United States, the western Europeans and the Soviet Union. The developed countries were deterred from war, partly by their memories of the awful carnage of the two global conflicts of the first half of the century, and even more by the mutual terror engendered by their enormous nuclear arsenals. Ruth Leger Sivard calculates that the world's stockpile of nuclear weapons contains over 1,000 times the TNT equivalent of the explosive energy used in all wars since gunpowder was invented about 600 years ago.[4] Since there is no sure defense against a nuclear attack, peace depends upon the fear that any attack would be followed by calamitous retaliation. Deterrence is uncertain, however, since fear may not always be sufficient to prevent the use of nuclear weapons. Nuclear arsenals have long been sufficient to destroy the world many times over. While the tensions among previous cold war enemies have now dissipated, the danger of the proliferation of nuclear arms and their use by other powers still persists.

While the world has been saved, so far, from nuclear annihilation, it has suffered enormous losses in terms of expenditures on the military. With the end of the cold war and a reduction in the number of shooting wars in the Third World, global military expenditures fell somewhat in the early 1990's. Nevertheless, in 1990, the equivalent of U.S. $880 billion was spent worldwide on armaments, a sum equal to 4.9 percent of global production. Military expenditures in the world proceeded at a rate of $1.7 million a minute. Global military expenditures were equal to the total income of more than half of the world's people, living in the forty-four poorest countries. In constant dollars, military expenditures in 1990 were 2.2 times the level they were in 1960. In the 30 years since 1960, total world expenditures on arms, calculated in 1986 U.S. dollars, was $17 trillion, or $17,000,000,000,000,000.

Even for the world's richest countries, this is an enormous financial burden, producing no net positive result but instead leading humankind closer to annihilation. If these same resources were devoted to eliminating poverty on a world scale, the human race could be well on its way to both justice and comfort.

No serious wars have broken out among the industrialized countries since 1945, with the exception of the conflict among the republics of the former Yugoslavia. In the Third World, however, warfare has been continual.

Since 1945, the United States has participated directly in three wars in the Third World: in Korea, in Vietnam and in the Persian Gulf region. It has participated indirectly in many more, generally supporting the "anticommunist" side. According to one estimate, the United States has intervened militarily in the Third World over 110 times since 1945.[5] A doctrine called low-intensity conflict was developed in the Pentagon in support of these sorts of conflicts. In the phrase of Michael T. Klare and Peter Kornbluh, low-intensity conflict refers to "guerrilla wars and other limited conflicts fought with irregular units,"[6] while mid-intensity conflicts are regional wars such as that between Iran and Iraq fought with modern weapons, and high-intensity conflicts are global or nuclear wars.

Low-intensity conflict became the modern way of fighting anticommunist wars in the Third World by proxy, without actually engaging U.S. troops. After Vietnam and until the Persian Gulf crisis, the Congress would not allow the overseas commitment of large numbers of U.S. troops. Under the doctrine of low-intensity conflict, the United States participated in wars without actually committing troops. Foreign military officers were trained in the United States, often in guerrilla and anti-guerrilla tactics. U.S. advisers were stationed in foreign countries. U.S. weaponry was made available to foreign forces, and funding was provided. Not the least valuable of these contributions, U.S. government public relations networks sold the message of the foreign armed force that was being supported. Low-intensity conflict measures were used sometimes in support of a government that was facing an insurgency, as in El Salvador and the Philippines, and sometimes in support of an insurgent movement, as in Nicaragua, Angola or Afghanistan.

Sivard estimates that since 1945 more than 20 million people have died in wars, almost all in the Third World. Of these, a significant majority were civilians, not military personnel.

Not all of the Third World's wars involved the United States or the Soviet Union, but many of the major ones did. A brief review of some of the recent wars is revealing.[7]

In Latin America, Colombia has experienced civil war since 1948, with right-wing death squads, left-wing guerrillas, cocaine traffickers and the army confronting each other in shifting sequences of allegiances that have caused about 1,000 deaths each year. The United States provides military support to the government.

In Peru, two insurgent movements, the Shining Path (a Maoist movement supported mostly by Indians in the mountains) and the Tupac Amaru Revolutionary Movement, are arrayed against the government. U.S. support for the government has been sporadic.

In Central America there have been many conflicts. In El Salvador, the Farabundo Marti—the National Liberation Front (FMLN)—engaged in guerrilla actions against the government, while right-wing death squads as well as the army carried out terrorist actions against the revolutionaries and their supporters. At the beginning of the 1990's, a peace agreement appeared to be holding. The Guatemalan National Revolutionary Unity is the guerrilla movement representing Indians fighting against the government. The armies of both El Salvador and Guatemala have been supported by the United States. In Nicaragua, the contra rebellion was supported by the United States until the electoral defeat of the Sandinista government. In Panama, the United States staged an invasion in 1989 to arrest the country's dictator Manuel Noriega and to obstruct the flow of illegal drugs.

The deaths in the Latin American conflicts have reached over 600,000, almost half of them in Colombia. The issues are somewhat different in each country, but there is a common theme. In most cases, the insurgents have been peasants fighting for access to land, and they have been opposed by forces allied to landowners (except in Nicaragua where it was the insurgents who were allied with the landowners). This is by far the most important source of the Latin American conflicts—the inequitable distribution of land and the poverty that results from the denial of basic economic rights to Indians and peasants.

There is also an ideological overlay to the conflicts. Some of the peasant movements adopted Marxist language and ideas, and some received aid from the Soviets or the Cubans. The ideologies were important, but they did not imply that the peasant movements were simply passive agents responding to the stimuli of their Soviet masters. The United States, however, frequently treated them this way.

Africa has suffered from the highest level of warfare relative to its population size, with over 5.5 million deaths since 1945. In the southern part of the continent, most of the military conflicts have been related to the anomalous role of the white-supremacist Republic of South Africa. In South Africa itself, continuing violence has taken hundreds of lives on a regular basis. Some of the violence has been between rival groups of Africans in the townships, and some has been the result of guerrilla actions by revolutionary groups against the government and of the repressive response by the government. The peace talks in the early 1990's held the promise of a transition to a democratic, majority-ruled state by 1994, but the talks did not end the violence. The American contributions to a resolution of the South African crisis have been ambiguous. On the one hand, the Reagan administration's policy of "constructive engagement"—that is to say low-key, unthreatening negoti-ations—seemed actually to reinforce apartheid because it was such a weak response. On the other hand, the economic sanctions enacted by the United States and other western governments may have served to push the white South Africans away from their rigid policy of apartheid and toward negotiations.

Again in South Africa, anticommunism was for a long time at the root of American diplomacy. The United States supported the South African government as a stronghold against communism, purporting to see the revolutionary African National Congress as a Soviet front whose victory would threaten U.S. geopolitical interests.

Outside the Republic of South Africa, there have been two more major wars in the southern region of the continent. In Mozambique, the Renamo resistance movement, supported by South Africa, has been engaged in a civil war against the Marxist state that gained independence from Portugal in 1975. Casualties are estimated at about a half million, with atrocities legion. On the west coast of southern Africa a war raged in the former Portuguese territory of Angola from the date of its indepen-dence in 1975. The Angolan government was supported by the Soviet Union and by up to 50,000 Cuban troops. In opposition to it was the UNITA movement, strongest in the southern part of the country, led by Jonas Savimbi and supported by both South Africa and the United States. Free elections in 1992, supervised by United Nations teams, were intended to bring an end to the Angolan warfare, but after a hiatus the fighting continued. The Angolan conflict was connected to the one in Namibia, or South West Africa, occupied against international law by South Africa until its independence in 1990.

Throughout southern Africa, therefore, the United States allied itself with the white supremacists and their clients, claiming to do so because of the necessity of combating Soviet expansionism. It was not a claim that carried much weight with black Africans. If the United States had chosen to support the aspirations of the majorities, the Africans in turn would have had no need to seek the help of the Soviets, who in any case proved to be undependable allies. The withdrawal of active Soviet support, fol-lowed by the collapse of the Soviet state, improved the prospects for an end to hostilities.

There have been numerous other recent wars in Africa, most of them caused by ethnic conflicts within countries whose boundaries had been established artificially by the European colonialists, and by resistance to dictators. They occurred against the background of appalling poverty and in some cases famine. The wars in the Sudan and in Somalia brought widespread starvation. If it is possible to make distinctions, they were the most tragic of the Third World's wars, occurring among people who were so destitute as to be just on the edge of survival itself, wasting what few resources they had on destroying each other.

The catastrophe in Somalia was marked by the starvation of thousands each day, while international relief efforts were stymied by battles of rival warlords. As a consequence, an international military force, led by the United States, intervened at the end of 1992 in order to establish peace and to allow the relief efforts to proceed in relative safety. The mission seemed successful in the short run, and this raised the question of whether Somalia might be the model for future American military interventions in the Third World. The thought of the United States assuming once more the role of global policeman seemed rather more than the country could even bear to think about, however. No proposals were seriously considered, for example, for intervention in nearby Sudan, where local warfare and starvation were just as serious as in Somalia. Moreover, once the Americans handed over peacekeeping duties to a smaller, multinational UN force in early 1993, civil strife resumed. This time, UN troops were among the dead.

In Asia, the destructive struggle in Afghanistan entered a new stage in 1988 with the withdrawal of the Soviet forces. Contrary to most predictions, the Soviet withdrawal did not produce a rebel victory, and the war continued. The guerrillas, who throughout the decade controlled most of the countryside, received extensive U.S. assistance, probably at least 1 billion dollars. The guerrillas claim that a million Afghans have been killed. Sivard estimates more than 700,000, the great majority of them civilians.

The Philippines insurgency, dating from at least 1969, is led by two groups: the communist New People's Army and a Moslem group, the Moro National Liberation Front. There was some hope of national reconciliation when the government of Corazón Aquino took over from deposed dictator Ferdinand Marcos, but the fighting continued throughout her term of office and beyond. The United States gave strong support to Marcos against the rebels and has continued that support to his successors. Over 80,000 lives have been lost.

The warfare in Cambodia has been catastrophic. Destabilized by the neighboring Vietnam War and the attendant secret bombing in much of its countryside, Cambodia fell victim to the Khmer Rouge rebels from 1975 to 1978. The Khmer Rouge revenge against their own countrymen in "the killing fields" was so severe as to be genocidal, one of the most piteous slaughters the world has had the misfortune to experience. The Khmer Rouge were overthrown by Vietnam in 1979, and a puppet regime was installed. Armed conflict continued thereafter between the government and a shifting coalition of rebel groups, including the Khmer Rouge. Meanwhile, the refugee camps in Thailand bulged with people who had fled Cambodia and who lived largely without hope, either of returning to their country or of being absorbed into another. Vietnam withdrew its occupying forces in 1989, and internationally supervised peace talks began. The result of the peace talks was a coalition government representing all of the political factions in the country.

Peace was threatened, however, both by the failure of the Khmer Rouge to abide completely by the terms of the agreements, and by the failure of the government to accept its defeat in free elections in 1993. Cambodia remained dangerously close to explosion.

In the Middle East, Lebanon has been a battlefield since 1975, with conflicts between Christian and Moslem factions, abetted from the outside by Palestinian, Syrian and Israeli forces. As an administrative entity, Lebanon has been destroyed; there is no authority capable at present of governing it.

The Palestinian uprising in the occupied territories of Israel cannot be listed as a substantial war, since deaths numbered in the hundreds, but it had importance beyond its casualty level. The revolt of the Palestinians indicated that after four decades the Israelis were still far from having found a way to live in peace in the Middle East, coexisting with their Arab neighbors. The early 1990's showed some hopeful signs, however. The Israelis and the Palestinians agreed to negotiate with each other in a process sponsored jointly by the Soviet Union and the United States; with the breakup of the Soviet Union, the United States took over sole responsibility. In 1992, the Israeli government of the hard-line Likud party was defeated, in large measure because the Israeli people believed that the Labor party had a more flexible approach to the peace process. In the negotiations, the new Israeli government gave some indications that it might be willing to accept a form of Palestinian self-rule. While a durable peace in the region was still a long way off, hope was kindled that it might one day be achieved.

U.S. policy in the Arab-Israeli conflict was not driven by an anticommunist reflex as clearly as it was in much of the rest of the Third World, at least after 1972 when the Egyptians cut their ties with the Soviet Union. The Soviet Union retained some interests in the Middle East, particularly in Syria, but they were not strong enough to present an immediate challenge to the United States. The pressing dilemma for the United States was that it was drawn on the one hand to the Arabs out of regard for their petroleum reserves, and on the other hand to the Israelis because of cultural identity. The United States is absolutely committed to the survival of Israel as a Jewish state; no U.S. national political leader could remain in office without professing that faith. At the same time the economic health of the industrialized world depends upon maintaining an even flow of oil from the Middle East and the Persian Gulf. As a result, the United States supports both Israel and the moderate and right-wing Arab regimes.

Iran and Iraq have been the scene of almost continuous military turmoil since the Iranian revolution in 1979. Iraq invaded Iran in 1980, and the war continued for 8 long years with about 1 million casualties. It was essentially a struggle for regional dominance between two bitterly opposed Moslem regimes; in the end no territory changed hands and nothing was settled. The Iranians were particularly profligate in the wasting of boy-soldier's lives, and the Iraqis scorned world opinion by repeated use of poison gas, sometimes against their own population. Although the United States was not a participant in the war, it "tilted" toward Iraq, hoping to constrain what it regarded as the virulent anti-American policies of Iran. Iraq also received assistance during the war from a number of other countries, among them Britain, France, Germany, Saudi Arabia and Kuwait.

Iraq's dictator, Saddam Hussein, built up one of the Third World's largest arsenals of military hardware and maintained an army of about 1 million soldiers. By the end of the Iran-Iraq war, he had accumulated a series of complaints against his allies, Kuwait and Saudi Arabia. Because of his extraordinary military expenditures, he had a pressing need for cash; he therefore opposed his neighbors' policy of selling large quantities of oil, increasing world supplies and thereby lowering the world price of oil. He argued that Kuwait should cancel the debts that Iraq owed it, incurred during the war with Iran. Furthermore, Iraq had long considered that Kuwait was legitimately one of its provinces.[8] On August 2, 1990, the armed forces of Iraq invaded and occupied Kuwait, claiming it as Iraq's nineteenth province.

Thus was set in place the events that led to the most significant military commitment by the United States and its western allies since the Vietnam War. President Bush immediately organized a world coalition against the Iraqi invasion and secured twelve resolutions from the United Nations Security Council. Troops were sent to Saudi Arabia to prevent an incursion into that country. In October 1990, the United States announced a policy of putting enough troops (its own and its allies') into the region to permit an offensive campaign against Iraq to drive it out of Kuwait. At the end of November, the Security Council voted to permit the use of force if the Iraqis did not withdraw from Kuwait by January 15, 1991. They did not withdraw, and President Bush ordered a military attack to begin on January 16. A month of air strikes was followed by 4 days of ground incursions, which produced an Iraqi withdrawal from Kuwait.

As with most wars, the causes were complex and open to dispute. The Iraqis apparently believed that they could annex Kuwait with impunity. One of the reasons for this belief was that the United States gave at best mixed signals about how an invasion would be regarded by the outside world. The Americans and their coalition partners decided to draw a line in the sand, however, and went to war, partly to secure a free flow of oil from the region, partly to reverse unjustified aggression, and partly to neutralize what they regarded as a major force for instability in the world. While the coalition forces met their narrow goal of driving Iraq from Kuwait, they did not succeed in deposing Saddam Hussein or in completely neutralizing his military capability.

The political problems of the region are unlikely to be solved by war-

fare. They include the Israeli-Palestinian conflict, the legitimacy of unde-
mocratic leadership in the Middle East, conflict between the poor and
the rich and the relationship of Islam to the state. Egypt in particular is
under threat from Islamic fundamentalists, who would like to see a revolution there similar to the one in Iran. All these issues await resolution.

The wars of the Third World have been terribly costly to the participants in financial as well as human terms. Measured in constant 1986
dollars, Third World countries spent $28 billion, or 3.9 percent of their
total gross national products, on the military in 1960. In 1987, they spent
more than five times as much, $144 billion or 5.2 percent of their overall
production. This is an amount almost as great as the investment in plant
and equipment in the world's poor countries. It exceeds the amount
spent on health and education. The Third World can hardly afford to
squander on destruction resources that might be available for development—but that is what many of its countries are doing.

They are abetted by the outside world. In 1960, arms imports into the
Third World from the rich countries were negligible; in the mid 1980's
they amounted to over $30 billion a year. Since that time they appear to
have fallen somewhat, but they remain substantial.

The United States' record in the wars of the Third World is not
encouraging. In some instances it has played a peacekeeping role. Examples include the Camp David Accords that President Carter engineered
between Israel and Egypt and the U.S. cosponsorship (with the then-
Soviet Union) of the more recent peace talks between Israel and the
Palestinians, the incursion into Somalia and the unsuccessful attempt to
persuade its allies to impose a peace in Bosnia. With the threat of a
Soviet veto in the Security Council gone, the United States has turned
increasingly to the United Nations as a forum for the resolution of conflicts. In many cases, however, the United States either declined to intervene when it might have played a peace-keeping role, or supported one
side in the conflict based upon its perception of that side's position in
the cold war. Determining its allegiances principally upon geopolitical,
anticommunist criteria, the United States has usually taken the side of
the rich against the poor. By adopting this position, it has actually
neglected its own long-term interests. In extreme cases like Nicaragua,
the war was for all intents and purposes a creation of U.S. foreign policy,
since the rebel Contra movement would not have persisted, perhaps
would not even have existed in the first place, without U.S. support.

Human Rights Policy

The concern with anticommunism skewed many aspects of the United
States' relationships with the Third World, not just military affairs. In the
area of human rights, for example, American initiatives were distorted
and nullified by an anticommunist bias.[9] A vignette will illustrate. On

Human Rights Day, December 10, 1984, President Reagan welcomed to the White House twelve foreign victims of human rights abuses, but not one came from a country friendly to the United States. They came from the Soviet Union, Poland, Iran, Cuba, Nicaragua, Afghanistan and Cambodia, but there was no citizen of South Korea, Iraq, the Philippines, South Africa, Argentina, El Salvador or Guatemala.

Beginning with the United Nations Charter adopted in 1945, a series of treaties has established international law on human rights. The principal precedent for these agreements is the Nuremburg trials after the Second World War in which Nazi leaders were convicted of war crimes and crimes against humanity. The Universal Declaration of Human Rights was adopted in 1948. Pacts now ban war crimes, racism, torture, genocide, political prisoners and religious and gender discrimination. This is a startling and potentially transforming development, for the signatories to these agreements are proclaiming that there is an international law that stands above national policy. That is, a government may be found guilty of human rights violations in terms of international law, even though it acted legally in terms of its own laws. The International Court of Justice, as well as regional human rights courts in Europe, Latin America and Africa, hear cases and render judgments. The execution of the judgments is still dependent upon the voluntary compliance of the country found guilty, but in some cases this compliance has been forthcoming. The United States, however, protecting its own national autonomy, has refused to sign most of the human rights treaties and has thereby weakened its moral authority as a voice for decency in the world.

Human rights violations throughout the Third World are massive. The Nobel Prize–winning organization Amnesty International documents the status of political prisoners around the world and organizes campaigns for their release. Restricting itself to prisoners who do not espouse violence, it estimates numbers in the hundreds of thousands. Communist countries and others aligned with the former Soviet Union have perpetrated atrocities, and so have right-wing governments and countries aligned with the United States. Military regimes in the Third World, whether of the left or of the right, are much more apt to violate human rights than are civilian and democratically elected governments.

The imprisonment and torture of political prisoners was extensive during the years of military government in Argentina; the number of the "disappeared" in that country is estimated at 15,000. So also in Chile, under the military dictatorship of General Augusto Pinochet, critics of the regime and supporters of former communist premier Salvador Allende were tortured and killed, probably in the number of 20,000. In Guatemala, Honduras, El Salvador, Peru, Paraguay, Haiti and Colombia there has been state-sponsored violence against citizens and also in some cases pillage against innocents perpetrated by insurgent groups. The victims include old women, pregnant women and young people. In Cuba as well, an unknown number of political prisoners are held in wretched conditions.

In Latin America, one of the most heartrending consequences of state-sponsored violence has been that family members cannot bury their loved ones. Relatives of the murdered fear to identify them, lest they too be subjected to violence.

Human rights violations are not confined to Latin America. In Africa, the majority of the countries are controlled by the military. Most, from South Africa to Ethiopia, are guilty of at least some violations, and there are cases in which the atrocities are enormous. In Asia and the Middle East too there are widespread practices that constitute infractions of the human rights treaties—in China, Pakistan, North and South Korea, Afghanistan, Bangladesh, Burma, Indonesia, the Philippines, Iran, Iraq, Syria, Libya, Israel and other countries. The majority of the world's people are not secure from state retaliation in the expression of their political (and sometimes religious) beliefs.

One might expect that the United States, with its Bill of Rights embodying the protection of speech, religion, the press and political dissent, would proclaim human rights throughout the world as the foundation of its foreign policy. It could, and there was a brief moment when it did. The Carter presidency (1977-1981) represented the high point of U.S. commitment to human rights. Carter came into office announcing that human rights would be the centerpiece of U.S. foreign policy: that he would recommend that the United States ratify the human rights treaties, that the United States would investigate and publicize human rights violations throughout the world and that it would divert foreign aid and trade concessions away from countries that were in serious violation. The commitment to human rights as a central component of foreign policy struck a responsive chord with Americans. Even Henry Kissinger, President Nixon's secretary of state who had not placed human rights very high on his own agenda, applauded the new policy:

> The aim of the Carter administration had been to give the American people, after the traumas of Vietnam and Watergate, a renewed sense of the basic decency of this country, so that they may continue to have the pride and self-confidence to remain actively involved in the world.[10]

President Carter and his secretary of state, Cyrus Vance, understood that instituting an effective international human rights policy was no simple matter. The policy would come into conflict with international relationships that were important to the United States for a variety of strategic and commercial reasons. On the other hand, if the United States regularly compromised its stance with countries that were important strategically or economically, then it would end up with a human rights policy that applied only to poor, weak countries—not a tenable position. Because the contradictions were never fully worked out, Carter's human rights policy remained somewhat incoherent during his 4 years in office.

Whatever its failings, it was a serious attempt to insert some morality into international affairs, and it stands in revealing contrast to the rather cynical policy of the Reagan and Bush administrations that followed. In Reagan's view, and those of his principal foreign policy advisers, the Carter human rights policy had been a disastrous episode for the United States. Jeane Kirkpatrick, a professor from Georgetown University who became Reagan's U.N. ambassador, wrote in *Commentary* magazine that Carter's policy had led to "the alienation of major nations, the growth of neutralism, the destabilization of friendly governments, the spread of Cuban influence, and the decline of U.S. power" in Latin America.[11] She drew a distinction between "authoritarian" regimes, with which the United States should have friendly relations, and more extreme "totalitarian" regimes that it should shun. By not unexpected coincidence, the authoritarian regimes were all on the U.S. side of the cold war curtain, the totalitarian regimes on the other.

As Reagan came into office, his principal goals in foreign policy were to contain Soviet influence and to reassert American strength. These priorities implied that if human rights violations were committed by governments friendly to the United States, they would be ignored; if committed by unfriendly governments, they would be publicized for propaganda purposes. In country after country, Reagan's state department hastily removed whatever constraints had been imposed by Carter's state department because of human rights violations. In South Africa, the anti-apartheid policy of Carter and his U.N. ambassador, Andrew Young, was replaced by the policy of constructive engagement, which in effect implied approval of apartheid. In the Philippines the Marcos government was given a blank check in its fight against insurgents. In El Salvador U.S. arms exports found their way into the hands of the right-wing death squads. In Argentina the United States resumed cordial relationships with the dictatorial military government. In Guatemala Reagan's state department lifted the embargo on arms sales that had been imposed by Carter because of human rights violations. In international development banks the Carter administration had opposed loans to over twenty countries because of their disregard for human rights; the Reagan administration opposed almost none for this reason, only those to communist countries.

For the most part, the Republican administration abandoned the victims of human rights abuses. It was tone-deaf to the issue. Reagan's bewilderment at the public outcry when he chose to visit the Nazi SS graveyard in Bitburg, Germany, in 1986 symbolized the betrayal of values that many Americans had thought were at the heart of their country.

In Reagan's second term, political pressures in the United States along with changing events in the Third World forced the government to make some concessions in the area of human rights. Confronted with the obvious failure of constructive engagement to lead to anything constructive in South Africa, the government imposed economic sanctions. It facilitated the flights of dictators Duvalier from Haiti and Marcos from the Philippines, hoping to open those countries up to more democratic governments. But these actions were rather minimal. The United States had next to nothing to do with the overthrow of oppressive military regimes in Latin America—in Brazil, Argentina, Uruguay, Peru and Ecuador—and their replacement by democratic, elected governments. The credit for the dramatic turn to democracy in Latin America is due not to the United States but to the Latin Americans, helped to some extent by European countries.

The Bush administration, 1989–93, was no more sensitive to human rights. It resisted attempts by the Congress to impose sanctions of any kind against China for its use of force against its own people demonstrating for democracy in Tiananmen Square in 1989. It refused to criticize Iraq for the use of chemical weapons against its own Kurdish population; only after the invasion of Kuwait did Iraqi human rights violations become an important issue for the U.S. government.

President Clinton's campaign for office in 1992 included several speeches discussing human rights as a factor, but only one factor among many, in the formulation of U.S. foreign policy. Some hope existed, consequently, that the U.S. government might assume a more active role on behalf of people victimized by their own governments. Early signs were not reassuring, however. Clinton broke a campaign pledge by continuing Bush's policy of excluding Haitians from the country, denying them an opportunity to show that they were political refugees, and the Supreme Court upheld the legality of this policy. By mid-1993, he was unable to draw U.S. allies together to put an end to the "ethnic cleansing" in the former Yugoslavian republic of Bosnia. And in his first half-year in office, he declined to impose any economic sanctions against China in response to its human rights abuses.

Foreign Economic Policy

In their economic policies as well, the United States and many of its allies have largely rejected the idea of partnership with the world's poor. In 1968, World Bank president Robert S. McNamara appointed a distinguished international panel with former Canadian prime minister and Nobel Peace Prize winner Lester B. Pearson as chair, to make recommendations about international cooperation for development. The Pearson report was entitled *Partners in Development*, and it made a strong plea for extensive participation by the rich countries in the solution of the development problems of the poor. Perhaps the report was naive, but it was not laughable in 1968 to expect the developed countries to devote a significant fraction of their national income to foreign aid, and to do so in sensitive and intelligent ways that would promote the advancement of the world's poor. But with the Vietnam War, the OPEC crisis and the widespread world recession of the 1970's, aid was cut back, and what survived was used mostly for political purposes and not to alleviate poverty.

A decade later a second international commission, this one under the leadership of another Nobel Peace Prize winner, Willy Brandt, was appointed by the United Nations to report on the state of international development. The Brandt report, entitled *North–South: A Program for Survival*, paid little attention to foreign aid, tacitly acknowledging that aid had failed to contribute much to development. Brandt called instead for cooperation in trade, investment, industrial policy and monetary relations, an overall package similar to the New International Economic Order. The Brandt Commission was probably naive also, but there was some cause for optimism at the end of the 1970's that the world was ready for some major structural economic changes that would promote development.

These hopes have come to little. The United States cut back its aid in the 1970's, and it took no steps to reform the international economy in ways that would make development easier in the 1980's. The record of some of the other western developed countries is marginally better, but with the United States in full retreat from a sense of responsibility for world poverty, the actions of these other countries were not enough to make the difference.

In recent years, U.S. economic policy toward the Third World consisted principally of two components. The first was to assert that the rich countries could help the poor best by growing fast themselves. This is not in itself a nonsensical proposition. The faster incomes in the north grow, the greater will be the imports from the south, and the greater stimulus to growth this will provide in the poor countries. A prosperous north will be less likely to impose restrictions on Third World imports in order to preserve jobs for its own workers, and it will be more likely to generate funds for investment in other countries. But it is a peculiarly self-serving doctrine. One can make it with a straight face only if one denies that there are any limits to the total production that the earth can support. Otherwise, if one recognizes limits, one immediately realizes that sacrifices, not self-indulgence, will be required from the rich in order to redistribute goods and services to the poor in a more equitable world.

The second component of U.S. economic policy has been to insist that Third World countries adopt free-market systems, that they restrict the role of government, central planning and public ownership. It is, of course, true that a number of Third World countries went overboard in the past, attempting too much government control, and that many of them have decided to make more use of the decentralized free market. By and large, however, these are policy decisions that the Third World countries are coming to on their own, without the dubious benefit of U.S. propaganda.

Foreign Aid

U.S. foreign aid has declined so much in both quantity and quality as to be almost irrelevant to the economic development of the Third World. The Pearson Commission in 1968 called for the rich countries to devote 0.7 percent of their national incomes ($7 out of every $1,000) to development aid. At the time, the United States was contributing almost 0.4 percent, and some of the other developed countries were contributing more, although none was at the 0.7 percent level. In 1970, the United Nations adopted the 0.7 percent target in its Strategy for the Second Development Decade. In the intervening decades, however, the aid proportion has actually fallen. In the United States the figure for 1990 was 0.21 percent. The United States gives the largest absolute amount of aid of any country, but its economy is relatively large, so its ratio of aid to GNP is the lowest of any of the western, developed countries, save Ireland. Some donor countries have reached or exceeded 0.7 percent: the World Bank reports that in 1990 Norway contributed 1.17 percent of its GNP in foreign aid, the Netherlands 0.94 percent, Denmark 0.93 percent, Sweden 0.90 percent and France 0.79 percent. On average, however, the 18 richer countries of western Europe, North America and Japan have reached only half of the goal, just 0.36 percent of GNP. Some of the other countries that have fallen short are Britain (0.27 percent), Germany (0.42 percent), Japan (0.31 percent) and Switzerland (0.31 percent). Two middle eastern oil-exporting countries make substantial contributions to foreign aid, mostly to other Arab countries: Saudi Arabia, 3.90 percent of GNP in 1990, and the United Arab Emirates, 2.65 percent.

Quantity is only one of the problems of foreign aid, however. Aid amounting to 0.21 percent of the United States' national income could make a significant impact on Third World development if it were skillfully directed where it is most needed. The real scandal is that U.S. foreign aid has little to do with economic development. One obvious indicator of this is that it does not go to the countries that most need it. At the end of the 1980's, for example, sub-Saharan Africa received only 6 percent of the aid budget, as compared to 9 percent a decade earlier. Frances Moore Lappé and her colleagues have calculated the distribution of U.S. bilateral aid (that is to say, aid given directly to foreign countries and not sent through international agencies) from 1981 through 1986. The total amount in this 6-year period was $76.9 billion. Of this, 18.3 percent, or $14.1 billion, was used for development assistance, 12.2 percent was used for food aid, 1.2 percent was used for the Peace Corps and narcotics interdiction, and fully 68.3 percent, more than two thirds, was used for what is called "security assistance." Security assistance was divided into two categories, 27.8 percent of the total for economic support, and 40.5 percent for military aid.[12]

The largest amount of U.S. foreign aid is designated for military use and is not intended to alleviate poverty. The recipient of the largest amount of funds is a small, fairly high-income country, Israel. Other major recipients include countries with severe human rights problems, including Turkey, South Korea and El Salvador.

Next in size to military assistance is the Economic Support Fund, the fastest-growing component of the aid budget in the 1980's. These funds are used for economic projects, but the purpose is not to help poor people; it is to shore up the strength of U.S. allies. According to one State Department explanation, "These funds provide the resources needed . . . to stem the spread of economic and political disruption and help allies in dealing with threats to their security and independence."[13] Again, the single largest allocation goes to Israel, with Egypt a close second, the aim being maintaining stability and U.S. influence in the region.

More than 10 percent of U.S. foreign aid is in the form of food, and some of this is very valuable. Some is allocated to famine relief and in fact saves lives. It is revealing, however, to understand the motivation for most of the U.S. food aid. It is not to save lives, but to support the market price for American farmers. The government buys surplus grains and other food products from its farmers, helping in small measure to reduce the excesses that threaten ruin in the U.S. farm states. More than one half of the food shipped overseas is sent under the aegis of Public Law 480, under which the food is sold to Third World governments and paid for in their currency. The funds generated are normally used by the United States to contribute to the country's development effort and this is sometimes helpful. But since the recipient government has bought the food, it turns around and sells it rather than gives it away. That is to say, the people who get the food are people with the money to buy it, not the truly poor. The program does affect the rural poor in one way, however. Since it adds to the supply of food in the country, it contributes to a lowering of the overall price of food and therefore reduces the income of poor farmers.

One understands immediately that to save lives the world's rich should contribute to famine relief when droughts strike. Beyond that, however, it is hard to construct a good argument for continuing food aid. Food aid in normal (that is, not crisis) times may seem to be an expression of generosity, but it really perpetuates dependency. Third World countries should be able to feed themselves. If they cannot, they may need assistance in producing food. Foreign aid should be directed toward improvements in agricultural technology. It should also be directed toward helping the poorest farmers to keep their land and to get access to the other resources they need to be productive. That is how foreigners can help alleviate hunger in the Third World, not by providing handouts. Food aid is a band-aid approach, covering up festering wounds.

Just 18 percent of U.S. foreign aid is used for "development assistance," a very small portion. The two largest recipients are India and Bangladesh, two countries with very high poverty levels that do make good use of most of the funds. Objections are often raised by critics of both the left and the right to the use of even this category of funds, and some of the objections are justified. Development assistance monies sometimes go into the hands of the rich, or are used in ways that rigidify the social structure and serve ultimately to bar the poor from access to the resources that they need. But while abuses exist, the principal objection is that such a tiny portion of what the United States calls foreign aid is even intended to alleviate poverty.

There is a curious consensus today in the United States and in the Third World against foreign aid; aid has almost no supporters. Critics on the right in the United States see no reason why their country should give away its hard-earned resources, except for strategic purposes. American critics on the left have no faith in foreign aid, since they see it being used primarily for ideological and geopolitical purposes rather than to bring about fundamental changes to improve the lot of the world's poorest. In international meetings, Third World governments deemphasize aid, since it seems to place them in a subservient position. There are lobbies for particular aid programs—aid to Israel, aid to the Philippines, for example—and liberals have some residual faith in aid channeled through multilateral organizations such as the United Nations, the World Bank and the regional development banks. But the contrast with the opinion of the 1960's is striking. The Pearson Commission report in 1969 saw foreign aid as the essence of the relationship between the rich countries and the poor, and it argued in the strongest terms for more of it. Today, foreign aid for economic development is an afterthought.

The Debt Crisis

More harmful than the cutback in development aid was the Third World debt crisis, a crisis that was centered in Latin America but that spread throughout the world, in Africa and Asia as well (see Chapter 6). The situation is comparable to (although larger than) the European debts owed to the United States after the First World War; American insistence that those debts be repaid led to political instability in Europe and was probably one of the important causes of the Second World War. The failure to solve the current debt crisis may have similar results if it leads to the destabilization of governments.

The United States and the other developed countries operating through the International Monetary Fund and the World Bank have developed policies relating to the debt crisis, but they are policies that impose a terrible price on Third World people. New loans are sometimes arranged to the debtor countries to help them meet their immediate payments; these loans come in some cases from public agencies and in others from the banks, and they are sometimes made at interest rates that are lower than the current commercial levels. In some cases, arrangements have been made to cancel some of the debts, or reduce their size, or to transform them into forms that are easier for the debtor countries to pay off. But there is a quid pro quo for this that goes by the bureaucratic but dreaded term *conditionality*. There are conditions to be met. Before the International Monetary Fund will provide substantial help to a debtor country, the country must agree to economic reforms that will enable it to pay more of its debts on its own in the future. Usually these involve changes like reducing domestic government expenditures, cutting urban wages, reducing food subsidies, eliminating controls on the private market and increasing exports. It is possible that in the long run these reforms may lead to strengthened, more competitive Third World economies that will be able to avoid future debt traps. But in the short run they create havoc; what they really amount to is reducing the standard of living of the local people, so that the government can pay the interest on its debts to the great banks.

For the ordinary people of the Third World, then, the debt crisis is inescapable. Either the country must struggle completely on its own to make the payments, or it must take active additional steps to reduce the standard of living of its people in return for getting only very partial assistance in making the payments. The consequences have been catastrophic. Throughout Latin America and Africa, economies stagnated and even regressed in the 1980's. Incomes fell, poverty increased and whole segments of the middle class were wiped out.

With the economic dislocation has come political instability. In country after country, local governments have been unable to deal with the debt crisis in such a way as to protect their own people. They have lost their ability to govern. In some countries this instability has been strangely constructive, at least in the short run. Their inability to handle the debt crisis was one of the important reasons for the collapse of military governments in Brazil, Argentina, Uruguay, Peru and Ecuador, and their replacement by democratic governments. In Mexico, the election of 1988 showed that many of the people were alienated from the PRI government that had ruled the country as a one-party state since the revolution. The ruling party was held responsible for the drastic fall in living standards that had occurred as Mexico struggled unsuccessfully with its debts. The PRI retained power only very narrowly and perhaps through vote fraud, but the opposition parties were firmly in place and the era of one-party rule in Mexico was likely over. In the short run, therefore, it seems that the debt crisis has helped to dislocate some dictatorial regimes.

But this is only the short run. It is not certain that democratic regimes will be able to deal with the debts any better than the dictators could.

Most debtor countries face tremendous popular pressure to renounce their debts unilaterally, and some of the democratic governments may do this. Whether they can escape international financial retaliation is doubtful, however. Brazil suspended payments on most of its $113 billion foreign debt in February 1987, but a year later, in February 1988, it resumed them. Brazil had thought that it would have enough bargaining power to force the banks and international agencies to renegotiate the debts, but it discovered that it had very little. The flow of new credit to Brazil collapsed when the payments were suspended, and the economy was in immediate danger. In 1985, Peru unilaterally restricted its debt repayments to 10 percent of its export earnings; it has not gone back on this policy, but it has paid the price of being completely shunned by international financial institutions.

So the prospects for the major debtors renouncing their debts are bleak. But if they try to remain in good international standing by making their payments, they will have to continue to impose penalties on their own people, and if they do this for long, it is possible that the new governments will not be able to survive. If they cannot survive, there will be a swing back to authoritarian governments, of the right or of the left, and the precious moment of democratic opportunity will have been lost.

This is what is at stake in the debt crisis—the economic well-being of millions of people and the future of democratic government. Little in the creditors' response to the crisis has given much indication of a realistic understanding of this. The Bush government's "Brady Plan" was too small in scope to resolve the crisis. The Americans have been concerned mostly with the solvency of their own banks, fearing that if the debts were renounced, the banks' future would be perilous. This is a legitimate worry, but it is a problem that is receding and that the United States government has the resources to handle. As a problem it shrinks in comparison to the damage that is being caused by the debt crisis in Latin America and elsewhere in the Third World.

The United States should be taking the lead, along with other developed countries, international organizations and the banks themselves, to take care of the debt problem once and for all. There should be an international agreement to cancel much of the debt until the portion that remains is small enough to be handled by the debtor countries while still allowing them to grow. There should be a ceiling on interest rates. If necessary, the United States should be prepared to use public funds to compensate its own banks for some portion of their losses (not all of the losses, since the banks are heavily at fault in the debt crisis for having made ill-advised loans in the first place). Few policymakers have shown an interest in such a comprehensive solution, however.

Fiscal Policy, Trade and Foreign Investment

U.S. economic policy has damaged the Third World in important additional ways. Under Presidents Reagan and Bush, the United States ran up extraordinary government deficits—tax receipts falling far below the level of government expenditures. One way to understand the size of these deficits is to focus on the national debt. When the government runs a deficit it borrows money; it follows that the national debt is equal to the sum of all of the deficits ever incurred, since the presidency of George Washington, minus the (rare) government surpluses. When Reagan entered office in 1981, the national debt stood at less than 1 trillion dollars; Bush left in 1993 with a debt of over 4 trillion. In 12 short years, a fiscally "conservative" regime incurred deficits over three times the value of all the deficits in previous U.S. history and therefore almost quadrupled the national debt. The deficits were the result of an unprecedented peacetime increase in military expenditures, coupled with a large cut in tax rates.

To Americans, the consequences of these deficits were obscure, although it is likely that the damage will last in various ways for generations. It took the rather bizarre presidential candidacy of Ross Perot in 1992 to bring the implications of the deficit squarely to the American people. In the Third World, however, the effects were felt immediately.

It is useful to divide the effects of the deficit into the period of the 1980's when the U.S. economy was growing, on the one hand, and the early 1990's when the economy was in recession, on the other. In the 1980's, when the U.S. government entered credit markets to borrow enormous sums of money, it forced interest rates to rise.[14] These high interest rates immediately had the consequence of raising the interest payments that Third World countries had to pay on their debt. So even without borrowing additional funds, Third World countries found that they had to make larger payments on their loans, because the government of the world's richest country was unable to pay its own bills.

The government deficit and the high interest rates of the 1980's had another effect. Funds from around the world began pouring into U.S. banks and other financial institutions to take advantage of the high interest rates. The intricacies of international finance are complicated, but in the end it amounted to foreigners lending the United States a great deal of the money to cover its government's deficit. This was a very peculiar and ultimately harmful phenomenon. From the American side, it meant that the United States went in 8 years from being the world's largest creditor country to being the world's largest debtor. The loans to foreigners will have to be paid off in the future, or else interest payments to them will go on indefinitely and the American people will find their incomes lower because of it. That is to say, the United States created a future debt problem for itself very much like the current Third World debt problem, although, of course, it will have more resources with which to cope with it.

From the side of the Third World, this development meant that private U.S. investment resources dried up. To understand this, it is helpful to remember the controversy about the multinational corporations. In the 1960's and the 1970's, there was a great deal of concern in the Third World about the harmful power of the multinational corporations that in some respects dominated their economies and societies. Despite all the concerns about the multinationals, however, very few people in the Third World actually wanted them to leave. What they wanted was to be able to control the multinationals better so that they would act in the interests of the local people. They wanted the multinationals to hire more local workers, to provide better training, to mitigate harmful environmental impacts, to reinvest their profits rather than repatriate them back to their home countries and to respect local laws and customs. But they wanted to attract and retain the companies, with their large investment resources, their modern technology and their ability to create jobs and tax revenues.

In the 1980's, however, as a consequence of the U.S. government deficit and the high interest rates, capital investment no longer flowed in large amounts from the United States to the Third World. It flowed in the other direction, from foreign countries, including the Third World, to the United States. These sorts of capital flows were unprecedented. The last time capital resources were imported in large amounts into the United States was when the United States was itself a developing country, in the late nineteenth century, when British funds came in to build the railroads. After the United States became a dominant world power, however, it always provided capital to the rest of the world.

In the 1980's, therefore, the United States with the world's largest economy became an international Robin-Hood-in-reverse. It took from the poor in order to indulge itself. Of course, most of the capital flowing into the United States came from Japan, Europe and some of the richer oil exporters. Some of it, though, came from the Third World. People with investment resources in Mexico, fearing the collapse of the Mexican economy and political instability, transferred their funds to U.S. stocks and bonds. A decade before, they would have invested in a Mexican company, creating wealth and jobs at home. Meanwhile, very little new investment was going from the United States into the multinational corporations abroad. The United States was draining the Third World. Whatever the problems created in the past by the expansion of the multinational corporations, they paled in comparison to this systematic draining of Third World resources.

This draining of investment resources occurred in addition to the interest payments made by Third World governments on their debts.

Together, the two amounted to extraordinary, insupportable burdens on many Third World countries.

There was a further very harmful consequence of the U.S. budget deficit. They led to large capital inflows, as just explained, and this in turn led to an increase in the exchange rate of the U.S. dollar. Foreigners wanted dollars so badly in order to invest in the United States that they were willing to pay a premium price for them. But foreigners importing U.S.-produced exports then found that they also had to pay extra to buy the dollars they needed in order to buy those goods.[15] The result was that U.S. net exports fell. The United States was pricing itself out of international markets and was finding it much more difficult to sell its exports abroad.

So the government deficit and the resulting high value of the dollar were the principal causes of the trade deficit that became so well known in the United States, the large excess of imports over exports. American politicians took dubious pleasure in blaming the Japanese for their trade deficit, claiming that the Japanese refused to play fair with American exports. But the Japanese really had very little to do with it, certainly far less than the U.S. government's budget deficit. As long as the federal government was unable to live within its means, the United States would find itself flooded with foreign goods and unable to sell abroad.

The response of the American people and their politicians to the trade deficit has been counterproductive. Rather than address the real cause by reducing the government deficit, they have tried to place the blame on foreigners, and have created a strong protectionist movement in the United States. While successive governments have worked to establish a North American Free Trade Area, they have had difficulty countering the widespread pressure to reduce imports from other parts of the world. The argument goes that other countries are harming the United States by refusing to buy its exports; therefore, the United States should retaliate by refusing to buy theirs. This trend runs completely counter to decades of U.S. trade policy, which has been to argue for more open, freer, less controlled international trade. In the long run, protectionism will hurt Americans; it will raise the cost of the goods they buy and it will utterly fail to address the real problem of the trade deficit.

In the immediate short run, however, protectionism harms the Third World. Third World countries desperately need to increase their export sales to the United States. They need to earn dollars so that they can make their debt payments and so that they can import capital goods for development as well as consumer goods. They have to gain access to the markets of the world's rich countries if they are to have the resources to grow. As the United States throws up protectionist barriers around its markets, Third World exports languish. Recent U.S. restrictions on the import of textiles, for example, have been exceptionally harmful to many

Third World producers.

This is an essential issue. Even people on the liberal left in the United States frequently come out against increased imports from Third World countries. They see factories shutting down in the United States in sectors such as textiles, steel and electronics, then reemerging in the Third World and selling their goods in the American market. They complain that the businesses are motivated by greed and that Third World exports can compete against American products only because of "cheap wages." The truth, however, is that wages are "cheap" in the Third World because people there are poor, and because the productivity of labor is low. If we are ever to have a more equitable world, in which labor is not cheap, it will occur in part because manufacturing is distributed more evenly over the globe's surface and not just in the rich countries. For that to happen, industries must move from the rich countries to the Third World, and the Third World must have markets in the rich countries.

So the consequences of the United States' budget deficit in the 1980's were indirect but nevertheless harmful to the Third World—by raising the interest payments on Third World debts, drying up the flow of new capital investment into the Third World and creating a protectionist movement in the United States that attempted to reduce imports from the Third World. Perhaps the harm caused by U.S. fiscal policy was unintended, but it was destructive nonetheless.

In the early 1990's, the impact of U.S. economic policies changed somewhat. The U.S. economy, along with much of the developed world, slipped into a sustained recession, with rising unemployment and stagnant production. In an attempt to stimulate the growth of the economy, the Federal Reserve System acted to lower interest rates to levels not seen since the great depression of the 1930's. As a consequence, U.S. assets were no longer so attractive to foreigners, capital flows into the United States declined greatly and the value of the dollar in foreign exchange fell. None of this provided much stimulation to economic growth in the Third World, however, since the recession led to a contraction of American markets for foreign goods, and since funds that might have been used for foreign investment were being gobbled up by the government deficit.

European economic policies have been little more helpful than the American. The biggest culprit in Europe has been its "common agricultural policy." The Europeans have long been committed to massive price supports for food, intended to buoy up farmers' incomes. These artificially high prices would normally attract large imports from other countries, particularly Third World countries, which would take away markets from the European farmers. So, as a consequence of the price supports, the Europeans are forced to erect high barriers against agricultural imports from the Third World. Years of negotiations have not succeeded in persuading the Europeans to reduce their agricultural price supports and welcome imports from the Third World. The consequence is that the poor countries suffer from being excluded from European markets.

A Problem of Democracy

In sum, the foreign political and military policies of the United States and its allies were dominated until recently by a globalist, anticommunist, geopolitical perspective that blinded the country to the real aspirations of the world's majority. Of course, the United States existed in a dangerous world: there was conflict with the Soviet Union and geopolitical concerns were relevant. But they did not need to be predominant in the Third World. When Third World peoples were insurgent, and when they expressed anger toward the United States, it was not fundamentally because they were allied with the Soviet Union. It was because they were crying out against the injustice of their poverty and exclusion. The rich countries could have joined with them in their struggles, but for the most part they turned a blind eye.

With the end of the cold war, and the emergence of a new world order, whatever it turns out to be, there is a chance that the policy of the rich countries could change in a productive direction, but there are few concrete indications that this is happening.

For the rich to stand so rigidly against the advancement of the world's poor is dangerous for their own future health, wealth and safety. Just in terms of their own economic well-being, the rich would be more secure if there were greater wealth in the rest of the world, so that they would have more prosperous foreign markets in which to sell their goods. But more important than that, if the world continues to be radically divided between rich and poor, the rich will never be secure against attack from the poor. Nuclear technology will surely become more widely scattered around the globe and the poor countries will have more opportunities to threaten the rich. So why do the prosperous countries generally ignore the problems of the world's poor?

Fundamentally it is a problem of democracy. The rich countries' political systems work well in many respects because they are democracies and some of their failings exist because they are not democratic enough. The rights of working people were enacted into legislation because working people fought for them, and because there are a lot of working people who vote. When racial minorities and women in the United States were excluded from the vote they had few rights; their power has grown as they have asserted the vote and held politicians accountable for their rights. Welfare programs and safety nets for the poor exist in large measure because the poor have a political impact—although it is not as great an impact as it would be if the voter turnout among the poor were higher. Of course, money influences government policy too and the middle classes get more from politics than do the poor because they pay for it. But democracy is one of the great accomplishments of the developed countries. The people who vote can influence public policy in their interest.

The foreign policy of the rich toward the Third World is unhelpful because the Third World has no vote in their elections. It is a curious matter. The rich countries have global impacts and global responsibilities—but their political system, democracy, leads them to see those responsibilities in a narrow way.

It is a cliché that politicians are only interested in the next election, and they are therefore unwilling to tackle long-run problems. But the cliché simply pushes the issue back one step, off the politicians' shoulders and onto the people's who elect them.

Some Americans who have come to understand that their country is no friend of the poor have substituted another myth. It is that "the people" of the United States would like to be in alliance with the world's least fortunate, but that their good intentions are disregarded by the country's political, military and business leaders. The leaders' self-interest carries them in a malevolent direction, contrary to the wishes of the majority of the people. This is a comfortable myth, one that fits in well with the populist ideologies of many on the left, but there is little evidence for it. In fact, average working people in the United States show no more sympathy for the Third World than do their leaders. They are just as apt to see Third World struggles through globalist, strategic lenses as are their leaders and many believe themselves threatened by Third World economic growth that may lead to plant closings. Many people in the United States certainly favor a more equitable world, but at election times, no political party calls for a better deal for the world's poor countries. The conclusion is inescapable that the United States as a country—not everyone in it, but a national consensus—stands against the sorts of changes in the world that would lead to dignity and progress for the great majority.

The political situation is somewhat more positive in western Europe, where the social democratic parties and others on the left—including some of the governments of the smaller countries—promote a policy of partnership with the world's poor.

Why do so many people in the rich countries not understand the acute danger that confronts them from the persistence of world poverty over generations, and elect more politicians who will take some positive action? The answer, it seems, is that events in the future usually seem vague, uncertain and not very pressing. Perhaps the people voting today will not even be alive if and when the possible disaster hits. Most people have perhaps some concern for the world their children will inhabit, but it is not an urgent matter to them and their unborn descendants are hardly thought of.

This is the problem confronting people who are committed to a sensible environmental policy, and it is the problem confronting those who favor foreign policy directed against world hunger and poverty. There are few votes in it. We are using up the globe's scarce resources today, resources that will not be available to future generations, but future generations have no vote, no power to force us to conserve. We are rejecting the world's poor, but the Third World has no vote in the elections of the north, nor does it have much bargaining power. Least of all do future generations of the world's poor, generations that may actually threaten world security, have any influence over elections and policy in the north.

Is there a way out? By far the best answer would be for the United States and the other rich countries to awaken to their global responsibilities and redirect their foreign policies to bring them into alignment and partnership with the aspirations of the poor. It is not impossible that this could happen. In the recent past, some leaders in the rich countries have made attempts—people like Willy Brandt, Jimmy Carter, Robert McNamara, Olof Palme, Lester Pearson and Andrew Young. The decade of the 1990's is a time when this spirit could be rekindled. As the cold war fades in memory, and as the power ranking of the rich countries is adjusted, the industrialized world could reduce its military budget and direct some of the savings toward aid. Freed of the need to see every struggle in the world in geopolitical terms, it could offer a hand of friendship to the poor.

Suggestions for Further Reading

Barnet, Richard J. *Intervention and Revolution*. New York: World Publishing, 1968.

Brandt, Willy, et al. *North–South: A Program for Survival*. Report of the Independent Commission on International Development Issues. Cambridge: The MIT Press, 1980.

Drinan, Robert F. *Cry of the Oppressed: The History and Hope of the Human Rights Revolution*. San Francisco: Harper and Row, 1987.

Kennedy, Paul. *The Rise and Fall of the Great Powers: Economic and Military Conflict from 1500 to 2000*. New York: Random House, 1987.

Kennedy, Paul. *Preparing for the Twenty-First Century*. New York: Random House, 1993.

Lappé, Frances Moore, Rachel Schurman, and Kevin Danaher. *Betraying the National Interest*. New York: Grove Press, 1987.

Spero, Joan Edelman. *The Politics of International Economic Relations*, 2d ed. New York: St. Martin's Press, 1981.

Notes

1. Paul Kennedy, *Preparing for the Twenty-First Century* (New York: Random House, 1993), 349.

2. Willy Brandt, "North-South: The Task Ahead," in Kofi Buenor Hadjor, ed., *New Perspectives in North-South Dialogue: Essays in Honour of Olof Palme* (London: I. B. Tauris, 1988), 35.

3. The peace treaties at the end of the Second World War, and the Japanese constitution, severely restrict the size of that country's military sector.

4. These and later figures in this chapter on military expenditures and warfare are taken from Ruth Leger Sivard's marvelously comprehensive *World Military and Social Expenditures* (Washington, D.C.: World Priorities, annual).

5. Frank Furedi, "Superpower Rivalries in the Third World," in Kofi Buenor Hadjor, ed., *New Perspectives in North-South Dialogue: Essays in Honour of Olof Palme* (London: I. B. Tauris, 1988), 125.

6. Michael T. Klare and Peter Kornbluh, eds., *Low Intensity Warfare* (New York: Pantheon Books, 1988), 6.

7. Some of the following information about the wars of the Third World comes from *The Economist*, March 12–18, 1988.

8. For a good historical background to the Persian Gulf war, see Joe Stork and Ann M. Lesch, "Why War? Background to the Crisis," *Middle East Report* (November–December 1990), 11–18.

9. For a good introduction to U.S. human rights policy, see Robert F. Drinan, *Cry of the Oppressed: The History and Hope of the Human Rights Revolution* (San Francisco: Harper and Row, 1987).

10. Quoted in Drinan, 86–87.

11. Jeane Kirkpatrick, "Dictatorships and Double Standards," *Commentary* 68, no. 5 (November 1979), 34–35.

12. Frances Moore Lappé, Rachel Schurman and Kevin Danaher, *Betraying the National Interest* (New York: Grove Press, 1987), 9.

13. Quoted in Lappé et al., 15.

14. The interest rate is simply the price of money. When the government attempts to borrow huge amounts, it creates a shortage of money and consequently forces the price of money, that is, the interest rate, to rise—just as the price of lettuce rises when there is a shortage of lettuce.

15. Foreigners buying U.S. exports cannot pay in their own currency, since U.S. producers want to be paid in dollars. They must exchange their own currency for dollars, then use the dollars to buy the U.S. goods. With the rising exchange rate of the dollar, foreigners found that they had to exchange more of their own currencies in order to buy U.S. exports, even if the price of those exports stayed constant in terms of the dollar. In other words, the rising exchange rate made U.S. exports more expensive to foreigners, and as a result they reduced their purchases of those exports.

CHAPTER EIGHT

Into the Future

I believe the time has come for higher expectations,
for common goals pursued together, for an increased
political will to address our common future.
—Gro Harlem Brundtland,
Our Common Future

What we need is an enthusiastic but calm state of
mind and intense but orderly work.
—Mao Tse-tung

THE PROMISE OF the independence movements has largely been lost. The optimism the Indians felt as the British flag was lowered, the enthusiasm of the Ghanaians as they became the first of the newly autonomous African countries, the cheering of the Viet Cong as they entered Saigon in triumph and renamed it Ho Chi Minh City, the earnest determination of Salvador Allende's followers as they took over the reigns of government in Chile—these hopes and countless others throughout the Third World have crumbled. No doubt it was inevitable that the euphoria of the moment would be short-lived; the expectations were infinite and could not possibly be fulfilled. But over the last several decades so little has changed. While there have been pockets of success, there have also been vast areas of deterioration. Populations have continued to grow, and today there are more people living in poverty in the Third World than in the period just after the Second World War.

The hopes for alleviating poverty and for asserting human dignity have been unfulfilled. Both had been battered in the age of imperialism. Third World economies had been exploited for the benefit of the colonialists, and Third World peoples had been treated as inferiors. It was the task of the independent countries to reverse this, to bring material welfare as well as hope and pride to the majority from whom it had been denied. For the most part, however, they have failed, and they have been abetted in this failure by the rich countries.

Development in a World of Limits

Not least among the failures has been the paucity of thinking about the kind of world that today's people would wish for their descendants. We

216

do not think a great deal about our descendants. Because the current problems facing the Third World are both overwhelming and obvious, most of the ongoing debate has to do with how those problems arose, and how to deal with them. For example, the three theoretical schools outlined in Chapter 3 all have prescriptions for dealing with poverty. The modernizationists focus on government economic policy together with the accumulation of capital and technology. The dependency school calls for cutting off ties with the capitalist world system, and the Marxists put their faith in the creation of either a dynamic capitalist class or a socialist revolution.

These are different strategies for change, but they are not well-worked-out visions of what a desirable world might look like in the future. A careful observer can perhaps discern long-run visions that may be inherent in the strategies, but they are hidden. One expects that the modernizationists would hope for a world in which freedom of individual choice is enhanced, the dependency school for a world in which power is equalized and the Marxists for a world in which class conflict and alienation disappear. But none of these hopes is spelled out carefully enough to inform the strategies of today. Most people in authority are reluctant to think very seriously about the future, lest they be labeled visionaries or devotees of science fiction. Yet, without a reasonably coherent idea about where we should be going, we are in danger of taking wrong turns that may permanently preclude our descendants from a decent life.

Curiously, almost everyone seems to agree upon one aspect of the future, and that is that the Third World should be striving for "development." The term *development*—with or without its common modifiers, as in economic, political or social development—is used almost universally to name the task facing the Third World. It is, however, a problematic term, masking more than it reveals. As political scientist Douglas Lummis has pointed out, Europeans of previous eras coined common adjectives for people who were different from them—words like *barbarian, savage* or *backward.* Today these terms are in disuse, for obvious reasons, but they have been replaced by a term that has the same function, *underdeveloped.* The rich countries are seen as developed, and the poor as underdeveloped, or in some cases less developed or even developing. Their goal is development.

Underdeveloped is a more benign label than *savage,* but the message it connotes may be misleading. For if what *development* means is something like the society of the United States or of western Europe, then it may be both inappropriate and unattainable. *Development* is a word much like *modernization;* it seems to imply that there is a single path, and that the rich countries offer to the poor countries an image of what they can be if they are successful. But in truth there are many possible paths, many ways in which poverty can be replaced. *Development* does not have a single meaning.

Furthermore, the standard of living now enjoyed by the inhabitants of the richest countries may very well not be available in the future to the world's poor, because such high consumption levels would stretch the earth's resources to the point of breaking.

No one knows with certainty just what the limits of the earth's nonrenewable resources are. One can find in print enormously varied estimates. Some claim that the earth's crust will be depleted of life-sustaining resources within the lifetimes of people now alive, while at the other extreme some think that with improved exploration, technology, energy use and recycling, the supplies are virtually limitless. In the face of this uncertainty, we should take seriously the possibility that the globe does not have enough exploitable mineral resources to support a western European or North American standard of living for its current 5 billion people. If this seems unduly pessimistic, one need only reflect briefly upon the momentum of the population explosion. Even if birth rates around the world fall fairly quickly, the population will continue to grow for several more generations. Demographers estimate that there is almost no chance that the world's population will level off before reaching 8 billion people, and that there is a good chance it will reach 15 billion within the next century. So even if the earth's resources are thought to be sufficient to provide amply for the world's current population, we need to consider whether they can provide for three times the current population. Simply to assume, as some do, that human ingenuity will overcome all limits seems foolhardy, to say the least.

Even if nonrenewable natural resources were not the limiting factor, the ecological capacity of the earth would exert binding constraints. The "greenhouse effect," created by the emission of carbon dioxide from fossil fuels, may already be causing droughts and temperature increases. If the greenhouse effect has not done so yet, it certainly will alter the world's ecology in the future if average fossil fuel consumption approaches North American standards, while the world's forests (which absorb carbon dioxide) are being cut down. The greenhouse effect could be mitigated by a reduction in the use of fossil fuels and greater dependence on nuclear energy, but nuclear energy has its own serious safety problems. In any case, all energy use produces heat pollution as a by-product, and so as the use of energy increases, as it must if global living standards are to rise significantly, the earth's temperature will likely rise. Even a small increase in temperature would imply a massive change in the world's ecology and a significant reduction in food crops. One cannot be certain, but there probably are limits to the amount of production the world can sustain, limits that will impinge upon humankind within the next several generations, if they have not done so already.

The World Commission on Environment and Development, under the leadership of Norway's prime minister, Gro Harlem Brundtland, called in its 1987 report for new thinking about a kind of development that was sustainable, that could be maintained indefinitely.

Neither the developed countries nor the Third World are prepared, however, to deal with the limits to growth. In almost every country, rich or poor, the predominant ethic is growth, not limits. The entire subject of natural limits to growth is one that interests some academics and some environmental activists, but that has hardly been acknowledged by "practical" people of affairs, neither politicians nor business people. At the present time, it is the rich countries that are using up the world's scarce supplies of mineral resources, that are polluting the atmosphere and using energy in such a way as possibly to raise the earth's temperature. Yet, hardly a voice in the rich countries suggests slowing their rate of economic growth in order to preserve an ability to maintain even the current standard of living for a longer time into the future. There is, to be sure, an important environmental movement in the rich countries, many of whose recommendations have been adopted as public policy by governments. These policies are directed mostly, however, at reducing air and water pollution and preserving wilderness areas. No public policy is designed to slow economic growth; quite the contrary, policy is directed consistently at increasing growth, at increasing the production of goods and services.

Spokespeople of the Third World initially reacted angrily to suggestions that there were natural environmental limits to growth that would restrict their advancement. In the 1970's, when the environmental movement was at its peak in the rich countries, and the discussion of limits to growth was fashionable at least in academic circles, Third World representatives denounced the whole argument as a new form of imperialism. Mahbub ul Haq's influential book *The Poverty Curtain* devoted a third of its pages to denouncing and refuting the environmentalists' call for an end to economic growth. The environmentalists' fears were greatly overstated, he argued. And furthermore, if there was a problem at all, it was a problem of the developed countries, not of the Third World, since the Third World with its low levels of production was hardly depleting the earth's scarce resources at all, nor polluting the atmosphere. At the United Nations Stockholm conference on the environment in 1973, Third World speakers sought to turn the environmental conversation on its head, arguing that poverty was the world's greatest pollutant, and that until the problem of poverty was addressed it was fatuous to worry about other forms of pollution.

By the 1990's, the tone of the conversation had changed considerably. The theme of the UN's Earth Summit in Rio de Janeiro in 1992 was the compatibility of economic development with environmental protection.

Whatever the changing responses to environmental issues, the strong possibility exists that there are constraining limits to growth. The world's resources and ecology may be insufficient to support a high standard of living for a rapidly growing population.

In a world of limits, development probably cannot mean that everyone will have a personal automobile, an air conditioner and a food freezer. It will not be the usual experience of most people to take long jet flights and vacation in secluded seaside resorts. Some people in the Third World may aspire to goals like these, but not everyone will be able to achieve them. It is perhaps unjust that this sort of lifestyle may be unavailable to the majority, but unjust or not, it may well be a fact.

It will probably not be possible for the world's poor to follow the economic trajectory of the world's currently rich. If the word *development* implies a common pathway to be followed by all, then it is misleading. Development can still be a useful term, but it needs to be given empirical content that has some realistic meaning.

The first priority for development simply has to be the meeting of basic human needs. No matter that the term fell from fashion in the 1980's, it is still the main imperative. The world's poor are still desperate for decent shelter and clothing, for sufficient nutritious food, for public health and medical care and for elementary education. That has not changed. Economic growth in the Third World that fails to address those needs can hardly be called development. In addition, development should mean the creation of a society in which people have choices that can be made with some degree of personal autonomy. Development should mean the securing of freedom from the violation of basic human rights, the respect for ethnic and religious differences and the existence of political forms that allow people to express their conflicts.

It may be possible for everyone in the world to have a bicycle and access to a cheap, efficient public transit system. Perhaps there can be shared food-processing facilities for small communities rather than a fully equipped, American-style, all-electric kitchen. Perhaps industries will place emphasis on the provision of decent jobs rather than on labor-saving technology. Perhaps leisure activities will be centered on books, exercise, conversation and walking. Perhaps political systems will be developed that nurture dissent and that provide for the peaceful transition of power from one group to another. Perhaps prisons will be reserved for the humane rehabilitation of criminals. These are some of the elements of a true, attainable development.

To pose the issue this way is immediately to raise the question of the redistribution of the world's income. For if the entire world population can sustain only a moderate level of affluence without taxing the carrying capacity of the globe, is it plausible to expect that that level will be the result of averaging very high living standards in some countries with relatively low standards in others? No, it is not plausible, unless the huge gap between the rich and the poor is maintained through coercion. If our descendants are to enjoy relatively peaceful lives in a world of limits, they will have to find a way of eliminating the extremes of both wealth and poverty, a way of allowing the majority of people to live in a comfortable but modest style.

At present we are moving in the opposite direction: the gap between the rich and the poor is growing. Even when growth rates are relatively comparable in the different parts of the world, the gap increases. For example, when average incomes are $15,000 a year in a rich country, growth of 2 percent means an increase of $300—but when the starting base is just $300, growth of 2 percent means an increment of $6. In this quite typical case, the gap between the rich and the poor grows by $294 a year.

This cannot continue for a long time. The argument is sometimes made that growth in the rich countries is good for the prospects of the poor countries, because growth means expanding markets for the Third World, an increasing demand for their exports. This has some validity in the world as it is currently structured. But if further increases in global production become impossible at some time, because of the earth's limits, the poor countries will not acquiesce in the incredibly skewed distribution of world income. They will demand redistribution, from the rich to the poor.

The rich countries would not dream of acquiescing in redistribution at the present time. For them, an unchanging standard of living is deemed a failure; their entire social system is predicated upon increases. A decline in living standards is unthinkable. Nevertheless, it is quite possible that the time will come when the rich are forced to cut back, as the price for avoiding nuclear global conflict.

It is strongly in the interests of the currently rich to do everything possible to improve the prospects of the Third World, to join with them in a partnership to lift the burden of their poverty. The more hopeful the prospects are for a decent life in the Third World, the longer the demand for redistribution will be delayed. Even if the rich are not motivated by a spirit of fraternity, they should be motivated by an instinct for self-preservation.

A Hope for Partnership

I take it as a matter of faith that the rich could join in a partnership with the poor, that they could adopt the struggle against world poverty as a common endeavor. The betrayal documented in these chapters is a tragedy precisely because it is not inevitable. This is a controversial view, one on which the schools outlined in Chapter 3 take different positions.

Most dependency theorists have no hope that there is anything the rich countries are likely to do to help the poor in their development. They have created a long literature criticizing foreign aid, the World Bank, foreign investment, technology transfer, trade patterns, military actions and the many other ways in which the rich countries interact with the Third World. Through the prism of dependency theory, all of these connections between the north and the south are seen as ways of exploiting the world's poor and crippling them, not as ways of helping them. People in the dependency school often argue that the Third World has had most success at times when and in places where it has been left on its own, having little contact with the wider world system.

The Marxists tend to agree with the dependency theorists, that the rich countries are unlikely to be helpful to the poor. Their disagreement lies in the fact that the Marxists do not see the external connections of the Third World as being so important and focus instead on the internal class structure.

Only the modernizationists believe that policies undertaken by the rich countries can make a real contribution to the development of the Third World. This is the heart of the modernization approach, and it is seen as naive by the other two schools. The dependency theorists and the Marxists generally believe that most government policy is illusory, that the forces of capitalism are too strong to permit mere policy to change outcomes. They criticize the modernizationists for not understanding the *interests* of the rich countries and the fact that these interests constrain their policies. It would be irrelevant, and hopelessly sentimental, they believe, for people of good will and representatives of the poor to try to persuade the governments of the rich to behave differently.

They may be right, but I do not believe it. The people in the prosperous countries are not of a single mind; they engage in debate and political competition, and they argue over policy. It is possible for them to behave responsibly. The fact is that the rich countries engage in policies that affect the poor. They have enormously powerful tools: their military policy, their trade policy, their diplomatic policy, their financial policy and more. There is no question but that these tools will be used; the question is whether they will be used helpfully or harmfully. People in the rich countries who are concerned about world poverty have a responsibility to work to see that they are used as helpfully as possible. Whatever the barriers to creating a constructive relationship between the rich and the poor, one should work for it.

This was the approach taken by the successive international commissions led by Canada's Lester Pearson and Germany's Willy Brandt. While recognizing all the obstacles to partnership, they called for a long array of policy reforms in the rich countries to advance the cause of the poor.

The Marxists and the dependency theorists may be right, that much of this policy is irrelevant. But this does not absolve one of the obligation of trying to make things better. They certainly are right that a great many of the policies that have been implemented have been harmful, or misdirected, or screens for exploitation—but to the extent that this is the case, it should direct one toward discovering better policies, not toward abandoning policy. If the relationship between the rich and the poor has been exploitative, then it is crucial to focus on the ways in which an exploitative relationship can be transformed into a productive one. In other words, it is important that people in the rich countries view themselves as active, not passive, and see themselves as being able to be of use.

From the perspective of one who thinks that helpful policies in the rich countries are at least possible, the events of recent history are cause for dismay. There is no doubt that the United States, the world's richest and most powerful country, has become less constructive in its relationship with the Third World, more exploitative, more damaging   that it is betraying the promise of social change in the Third World.

There was a moment, in the early 1960's, when the thrust of American policy seemed to be in the direction of partnership with the world's poor. Even this thrust was ambiguous, since it occurred within an anticommunist context that led Americans to make allies with many of the Third World's ruling classes. Still, there was a genuine sentiment behind it. But in the post-Vietnam period there has been almost no resurgence of this sentiment or this partnership. President Carter's call for global human rights was an important gesture, but it failed to outlast his single-term presidency. Rising oil prices and inflation in the 1970's made the United States more self-protective, not more generous. The huge Third World debt crisis of the 1980's led to American concern to protect its own financial institutions, but not to deal with the declining standards of living that the debt engendered abroad. Dominating American foreign policy in the Third World has been a concern for national security, not for human progress.

Leadership from other western capitalist countries has been somewhat more constructive, but only marginally so. And the Soviets have been worse than the Americans in terms of offering genuine assistance to the world's poor.

Why should people in the rich countries take on the responsibility of being helpful to the world's poor? The answer is that the world is completely interdependent; the rich are fundamentally affected by the Third World just as Third World people are by the rich.

In one of the great works of social science in the twentieth century, *The Great Transformation,* Karl Polanyi showed how in nineteenth-century Britain the economists' model of society—a model in which individuals are thought of as pleasure-seeking individuals with concern only for themselves and not for their neighbors—was attempted, and collapsed. The market society glorified by the economists brought riches to some but left millions destitute, and after about a generation the society discovered that it could not tolerate this. Polanyi proposed the idea of a society as a single organism, in which the individual cells are connected to each other and dependent upon each other. If one part of an organism is injured, the entire organism is threatened, and all the other parts rush to its defense. So in Britain, when millions were abandoned to poverty by the laissez-faire policies of the time, the society eventually crafted collective responses to their plight.

Can one think of the entire world as an organism in this sense, an organism in which the rich cells will come to the defense of the poor cells, for the purpose of saving the organism? It is a compelling image, since there are many ways in which the world is interconnected, in which we are dependent one upon the other.

Thinking first of economic prosperity, it is clear that the developed countries require expanding markets for exports, and that desperately poor people cannot provide those markets. This point is often not understood. People in the rich countries sometimes react with hostility as they see manufacturing jobs disappear, to reappear in Taiwan or Korea. If the Third World is to succeed in developing economically, however, there will be a major realignment of the world's production, with millions of jobs that currently exist in the north disappearing. But those jobs will be replaced by new and more productive jobs as the rich countries specialize in producing those goods and services they are best at, and selling them to the no longer quite so poor masses of the world population.

This is a lesson that northern industrialists learned at home in the Great Depression of the 1930's. A destitute work force at that time proved a handicap to industry, not a boon, because although wage costs were kept low, the poverty of the consumers meant that there was no market for the finished goods. So it turns out that the welfare state, the safety net, and Keynesian economic policies that stimulate income and employment are good for business, because they ensure strong domestic markets. Domestic policies that industrialists once denounced as "socialist" they now accept (and some even endorse explicitly) as creating the fabric within which they are able to prosper.

This lesson now needs to be learned in an international context. The most critical need companies of tomorrow will have is for expanding world markets, not for cheap labor inputs—and the way to have expanding world markets is to have growing wealth and income in the Third World.

The military security of the developed countries requires the alleviation of poverty in the Third World. In this age of nuclear and chemical weapons, the gap between the rich and the poor constitutes a frightening challenge to the future of the civilizations that the people in the privileged part of the world enjoy. It is not believable that the world's poor majority will continue to accept their fate passively and peacefully if their numbers continue to grow but their share of the world's benefits continues to fall. The disparities in wealth are growing year by year, not narrowing, and the anger of Third World spokespeople at this is all too evident. For now, their weapons are those of the weak: rhetoric in the United Nations and sporadic terrorism. But with the spread of nuclear and chemical technology, it is not hard to imagine a much more serious confrontation between the have-nots and the haves, one that could destroy a great deal of the world's accomplishments. The real military threat in the future is likely to come from the world's dispossessed, who may well turn to warfare in their struggle for a more just disposition of economic resources.

If full warfare between the poor and the rich is just a potential danger, terrorism is with us now. Terrorism is the classic weapon of the weak. While it affects only a few people directly, its random destructiveness captures imaginations and headlines throughout the world. It is inevitable that in a world marked by extraordinary inequalities, terrorism will continue.

There are many other ways in which the fate of the rich is dependent upon the progress of the poor. If Acquired Immune Deficiency Syndrome (AIDS) is not eliminated in Africa, it will continue to kill people in Europe and North America regardless of the public health measures they adopt. If the rain forests of South America and Africa are cut down, the increase in carbon dioxide in the atmosphere will lead to higher temperatures in all parts of the world, with destructive impacts on ecosystems. If employment cannot be found in the Third World, migration to the rich countries will increase regardless of police measures taken to stop it, and homelessness and poverty will spread everywhere. If wars persist between and within Third World countries, the armed forces of the north will be sucked into them.

So the people of the rich countries have strong self-interested reasons to remove their blinders and seriously address the problem of world poverty. The threats to their way of life are real. But threats are not sufficient. For the most part, threats provoke defensive, siege-like reactions, not generosity of spirit. Generosity of spirit can follow, perhaps, from a renewed understanding that we are, after all, of the same species; we share a common planet and a common future. In the end, we should address the problem of world poverty because it is intolerable for us, as human beings, to turn our backs on our sisters and brothers. The world is an organism.

But the task is not easy. Most people care deeply about their immediate family, about their spouse, their parents, their children—perhaps a few friends. Beyond that the ties are weaker. Not absent, but weaker.

One has acquaintances one knows and cares about, somewhat. Perhaps some have school spirit, or civic pride, or even a connection to the local football team. Some have an ethnic identity that is important. Patriotism for their country perhaps, for some. But identification with the poor people of the world? Farfetched. And yet, without some identification, some understanding that there is a common fate for humanity, there is not much hope.

In some respects, hope is fading. Third World governments have far too often mismanaged their affairs and thrown away the chance to address the needs of their people. The rich countries have moved backwards and closed their eyes. Narrow self-interest has been substituted for vision, partnership and commitment.

From another perspective, though, hope is growing in the 1990's. More countries in the Third World are turning toward democracy, and toward a renewed respect for human rights. As the global security concerns of the cold war recede, Americans and Europeans may be able to reduce military expenditures and redirect resources toward the Third World. Even more importantly, people in the rich countries may begin to see the needs of Third World people for what they really are. Most people in the Third World are poor and need the help of people who are better off; they are not communist insurgents seeking confrontation.

It is not beyond hope that Carolina's grandchildren will enjoy medical security, nutritious meals and a good education; that the villagers of Berat will amass enough savings to tide them comfortably through the drought years; that the Mossi will reverse the desertification of their land and make the fields green again; that the workers of Siglo XX will acquire title to their homes, safety in their mines and freedom to bargain collectively; and that the Indian cultures of Guatemala will be treated with respect. It is not beyond hope, but the achievement of these goals will require dramatic changes in behavior by the world powers—and dramatic changes in understanding and commitment by the world's peoples.

Along with preventing a nuclear holocaust, the alleviation of world poverty is the most urgent task facing humankind. We have done badly. There is a chance that we could do well in the future. The people of the rich countries could take seriously the problems that beset Third World people—they could learn from their wisdom, take pleasure in their achievements, be enriched by their cultures and join with them in their struggles.

Suggestions for Further Reading

Brown, Lester R. *In the Human Interest.* New York: W. W. Norton, 1974.

Heilbroner, Robert L. *An Inquiry into the Human Prospect.* 2d ed. New York: W. W. Norton and Company, 1980.

Schlossstein, Steven. *The End of the American Century.* New York: Congdon and Weed, 1989.

World Commission on Environment and Development. *Our Common Future* (the Brundtland Report). New York: Oxford University Press, 1987.

Select Bibliography

Achebe, Chinua. *A Man of the People.* New York: Doubleday and Company, 1967.

———. *Arrow of God.* New York: Doubleday and Company, 1969.

———. *Things Fall Apart.* New York: Astor-Honor, Inc., 1959.

Adamson, Peter. "The Rains." In James P. Grant, *The State of the World's Children, 1982–83.* New York: Oxford University Press, 1982, 45–128.

Arndt, H. W. *Economic Development: The History of an Idea.* Chicago: University of Chicago Press, 1987.

Azuela, Mariano. *The Underdogs: A Novel of the Mexican Revolution.* Translated by E. Munguia, Jr. New York: New American Library, 1962.

Bairoch, Paul. "International Industrialization Levels from 1750 to 1980." *The Journal of European Economic History* 11 (Fall 1982): 269–333.

Baran, Paul. *The Political Economy of Growth.* New York: Monthly Review Press, 1957.

Barnet, Richard J. *Intervention and Revolution.* New York: World Publishing, 1968.

Barrios de Chungara, Domitila. *Let Me Speak: Testimony of Domitila, a Woman of the Bolivian Mines.* Edited by Moema Viezzar. New York: Monthly Review Press, 1978.

Berg, Alan. *The Nutrition Factor: Its Role in National Development.* Washington: The Brookings Institution, 1973.

Berger, Peter. *Pyramids of Sacrifice.* New York: Basic Books, 1975.

Betts, Raymond F. *Europe Overseas: Phases of Imperialism.* New York: Basic Books, 1968.

Bisilliat, Jeanne, and Michèle Fieloux. *Women of the Third World: Work and Daily Life.* Translated by Enne Amann and Peter Amann. Cranbury, N.J.: Associated University Presses, 1987.

Blomstrom, Magnus, and Björn Hettne. *Development Theory in Transition: The Dependency Debate and Beyond: Third World Responses.* London: Zed Books, 1984.

Brandt, Willy, et al. *Common Crisis: North-South: Cooperation for World Recovery.* Cambridge: The MIT Press, 1983.

———. *North-South: A Program for Survival.* Report of the Independent

Commission on International Development Issues. Cambridge: The MIT Press, 1980.

Brown, Lester R. *In the Human Interest.* New York: W. W. Norton, 1974.

Cabezas, Omar. *Fire from the Mountain: The Making of a Sandinista.* Translated by Kathleen Weaver. New York: New American Library, 1985.

Cardoso, Fernando Henrique, and Enzo Faletto. *Dependency and Development in Latin America.* Translated by Marjory Mattingly Urquidi. Berkeley: University of California Press, 1979.

Chan, Anita, Richard Madsen, and Jonathan Unger. *Chen Village: The Recent History of a Peasant Community in Mao's China.* Berkeley: University of California Press, 1984.

Chilcote, Ronald H., and Joel C. Edelstein. *Latin America: Capitalist and Socialist Perspectives of Development and Underdevelopment.* Boulder, Colo.: Westview Press, 1986.

Coale, Ansley J., and Edgar M. Hoover. *Population Growth and Economic Development in Low Income Countries: A Case Study of India's Prospects.* Princeton: Princeton University Press, 1958.

Critchfield, Richard. *Shahhat, An Egyptian.* Syracuse, N.Y.: Syracuse University Press, 1978.

Cueva, Agustín. "Problems and Perspectives of Dependency Theory." Translated by José Villamil and Carlos Fortín. *Latin American Perspectives* 3 (Fall 1976): 12–17.

Davis, Peter. *Where Is Nicaragua?* New York: Simon and Schuster, 1987.

de Jesús, Carolina María. *Child of the Dark.* Translated by David St. Clair. New York: E. P. Dutton and Company, 1962.

Dos Santos, Theotonio. "The Structure of Dependency." *American Economic Review* 60 (May 1970): 231–36.

Drinan, Robert F. *Cry of the Oppressed: The History and Hope of the Human Rights Revolution.* San Francisco: Harper and Row, 1987.

Eldridge, C. C. *Victorian Imperialism.* London: Hodder and Stoughton, 1978.

Emecheta, Buchi. *The Joys of Motherhood.* New York: George Braziller, Inc., 1979.

Fanon, Frantz. *The Wretched of the Earth.* Translated by Constance Farrington. New York: Grove Press, 1968.

Fieldhouse, D. K. *Colonialism, 1870–1945: An Introduction.* London: Weidenfeld and Nicolson, 1981.

Foster-Carter, Aidan. "From Rostow to Gunder Frank: Conflicting Paradigms in the Analysis of Underdevelopment." *World Development* 4 (March 1976): 167–80.

———. "Neo-Marxist Approaches to Development and Underdevelopment." *The Journal of Contemporary Asia* 3 (1973): 7–33.

Frank, André Gunder. *Capitalism and Underdevelopment in Latin America.*

New York: Monthly Review Press, 1967.

Freire, Paulo. *Education for Critical Consciousness*. New York: Seabury Press, 1973.

————. *Pedagogy of the Oppressed.* Translated by Myra Bergman Ramos. New York: Herder and Herder, 1970.

Fuentes, Carlos. *The Death of Artemio Cruz.* Translated by Sam Hileman. New York: Farrar, Straus and Giroux, 1964.

Galbraith, John Kenneth. *The Nature of Mass Poverty*. Cambridge: Harvard University Press, 1979.

Galeano, Eduardo. *Open Veins of Latin America: Five Centuries of the Pillage of a Continent.* New York: Monthly Review Press, 1973.

Gallagher, J. A., and R. E. Robinson. "The Imperialism of Free Trade." *Economic History Review* second series 6 (1953): 1–15.

Gandhi, Mohandas K. *An Autobiography: The Story of My Experiments with Truth.* Boston: Beacon Press, 1957.

Gershenkron, Alexander. *Economic Backwardness in Historical Perspective.* Cambridge: Harvard University Press, 1962.

Gillis, Malcolm, Dwight H. Perkins, Michael Roemer, and Donald R. Snodgrass. *Economics of Development.* 2d ed. New York: W. W. Norton and Company, 1987.

Griffin, Keith. *International Inequality and National Poverty*. London: The MacMillan Press, Ltd., 1978.

Griffin, Keith, and John Gurley. "Radical Analyses of Imperialism, the Third World, and the Transition to Socialism: A Survey Article." *Journal of Economic Literature* 23 (September 1985): 1089–1143.

Hadjor, Kofi Buenor, ed. *New Perspectives in North-South Dialogue: Essays in Honour of Olof Palme.* London: I. B. Tauris and Company, 1988.

Hagen, Everett. *On the Theory of Social Change: How Economic Growth Begins.* Homewood, Ill.: Richard Dorsey, 1962.

Haq, Mahbub ul. *The Poverty Curtain: Choices for the Third World.* New York: Columbia University Press, 1976.

Harrington, Michael. *The Vast Majority: A Journey to the World's Poor.* New York: Simon and Schuster, 1977.

Harris, Nigel. *The End of the Third World.* London: I. B. Tauris, 1986.

Hartmann, Betsy, and James K. Boyce. *A Quiet Violence: View from a Bangladesh Village.* San Francisco: Institute for Food and Development Policy, 1988.

Hayter, Teresa, and Catharine Watson. *Aid, Rhetoric and Reality.* London: Pluto Press, 1985.

Heilbroner, Robert L. *An Inquiry into the Human Prospect.* 2d ed. New York: W. W. Norton and Company, 1980.

Hinton, William. *Fanshen: A Documentary of Revolution in a Chinese Village.* New York: Random House, 1966.

Hobsbawm, E. J. *The Age of Empire, 1875–1914.* London: Weidenfeld and Nicolson, 1987.

Hobson, J. A. *Imperialism: A Study.* Ann Arbor: University of Michigan Press, 1965.

Hyden, Goran. *Beyond Ujamaa in Tanzania: Underdevelopment and Uncaptured Peasantry.* London: Heinemann, 1980.

Kamarck, Andrew M. *The Tropics and Economic Development: A Provocative Inquiry into the Poverty of Nations.* Baltimore: The Johns Hopkins University Press, 1973.

Karnow, Stanley. *Vietnam: A History.* New York: The Viking Press, 1983.

Kennedy, Paul. *The Rise and Fall of the Great Powers: Economic Change and Military Conflict from 1500 to 2000.* New York: Random House, 1987.

Klare, Michael T., and Peter Kornbluh, ed. *Low Intensity Warfare.* New York: Pantheon Books, 1988.

Kohli, Atul, ed. *The State and Development in the Third World.* Princeton: Princeton University Press, 1986.

Korten, David C. *Getting to the 21st Century: Voluntary Action and the Global Agenda.* West Hartford, Conn.: Kumarian Press, 1990.

Kumar, Sehdev. "Third World Toils to Feed the West." *The Globe and Mail,* Toronto (April 15, 1988): A7.

Kurion, George Thomas. *Encyclopedia of the Third World.* 3d ed. New York: Facts on File, Inc., 1987.

Lacouture, Jean. *Ho Chi Minh: A Political Biography.* New York: Random House, 1968.

Lappé, Frances Moore, Rachel Schurman, and Kevin Danaher. *Betraying the National Interest.* New York: Grove Press, 1987.

Lenin, V. I. *Imperialism: The Highest Stage of Capitalism.* Moscow: Progress Publishers, 1975.

Lewis, Oscar. *The Children of Sanchez: Autobiography of a Mexican Family.* New York: Random House, 1961.

———. *Five Families.* New York: Basic Books, 1959.

Lewis, W. Arthur. "Economic Development with Unlimited Supplies of Labor." *The Manchester School of Economic and Social Studies* 22 (1954): 139–191.

———. *The Theory of Economic Growth.* London: Allen and Unwin, 1955.

Liang, Heng, and Judith Shapiro. *Son of the Revolution.* New York: Random House, 1984.

Lipton, Michael. *Why Poor People Stay Poor: Urban Bias in World Development.* Cambridge: Harvard University Press, 1977.

Lower, A. R. M. "Two Ways of Life: The Primary Antithesis of Canadian History." *Canadian Historical Association Report* (1943), 5–18.

Lubeck, Paul M., ed. *The African Bourgeoisie: Capitalist Development in Nigeria, Kenya and the Ivory Coast.* Boulder, Colo.: Lynne Rienner Publishers, 1987.

Lundestad, Geir. *East West North South: Major Developments in International Politics, 1945–1986.* Translated by Gail Adams Kvan. Oslo: Norwegian University Press, 1986.

Luthy, Herbert. "Colonization and the Making of Mankind." *The Journal of Economic History* 21 Supplement (December 1961): 483–95.

Maddison, Angus. "A Comparison of Levels of GDP Per Capita in Developed and Developing Countries, 1700–1980." *The Journal of Economic History* 43 (March 1983): 27–41.

Mao Tse-tung. *Quotations from Chairman Mao.* Edited by Stuart R. Schram. New York: Frederick A. Praeger, 1967.

Marx, Karl. *Capital: A Critique of Political Economy.* Vol. 1. New York: International Publishers, 1967.

Marx, Karl, and Friedrich Engels. *The Communist Manifesto.* Translated by Paul Sweezy. New York: Monthly Review Press, 1964.

McClelland, David C. *The Achieving Society.* Princeton: Van Nostrand, 1961.

McClelland, David C., and David G. Winter. *Motivating Economic Achievement.* New York: The Free Press, 1969.

McKellin, William. "Putting Down Roots: Information in the Language of Managalase Exchange." In Donald Lawrence Brenneis and Fred R. Myers, eds. *Dangerous Words: Language and Politics in the Pacific.* New York: New York University Press, 1984.

Memmi, Albert. *The Colonizer and the Colonized.* Boston: Beacon Press, 1965.

Menchu, Rigoberta. *I, Rigoberta Menchu.* Edited by Elisabeth Burgos-Debray. London: Verso Books, 1984.

Merriam, Alan P. *Congo: Background of Conflict.* Chicago: University of Chicago Press, 1960.

Mittelman, James H. *Out from Underdevelopment.* London: Macmillan Press, 1988.

Murdoch, William W. *The Poverty of Nations: The Political Economy of Hunger and Population.* Baltimore: The Johns Hopkins University Press, 1980.

Myrdal, Gunnar. *The Challenge of World Poverty: A World Anti-Poverty Program in Outline.* New York: Random House, 1970.

National Research Council. *Population Growth and Economic Development: Policy Questions.* Washington, D.C.: National Academy Press, 1986.

Nehru, Jawaharlal. *Independence and After.* New York: The John Day Company, 1950.

Nkrumah, Kwame. *The Autobiography of Kwame Nkrumah.* London: Thomas Nelson and Sons, 1957.

Oye, Kenneth A., Robert J. Lieber, and Donald Rothchild, eds. *Eagle Resurgent? The Reagan Era in American Foreign Policy.* Boston: Little Brown and Company, 1987.

Pearson, Lester B. et al. *Partners in Development.* Report of the Commission on International Development. New York: Praeger Publishers, 1969.

Polanyi, Karl. *The Great Transformation.* Boston: Beacon Press, 1944.

Pratt, Cranford. *Internationalism Under Strain: The North-South Policies of Canada, the Netherlands, Norway and Sweden.* Toronto: University of Toronto Press, 1989.

Rao, Raja. *Kanthapura.* London: George Allen and Unwin, 1938.

Ravenhill, John. "The North-South Balance of Power." *International Affairs* 66 (October 1990): 731–48.

Rheingold, Howard. *They Have a Word for It.* Los Angeles: Jeremy P. Tarcher, Inc., 1988.

Rhodes, Robert I., ed. *Imperialism and Underdevelopment: A Reader.* New York: Monthly Review Press, 1970.

Rosset, Peter, and John Vandermeer. *Nicaragua: Unfinished Revolution: The New Nicaragua Reader.* New York: Grove Press, 1986.

Rostow, Walt W. *The Stages of Economic Growth: A Non-Communist Manifesto.* 2d ed. Cambridge: Cambridge University Press, 1971.

Schlossstein, Steven. *The End of the American Century.* New York: Congdon and Weed, 1989.

Schultz, Theodore W. *Transforming Traditional Agriculture.* New Haven: Yale University Press, 1964.

Senghor, Léopold Sédar. *Chants d'ombre.* Paris: Editions du Seuil, 1956.

Sivard, Ruth Leger. *World Military and Social Expenditures.* Washington, D.C.: World Priorities, annual.

South Commission. *The Challenge to the South.* New York: Oxford University Press, 1990.

Spero, Joan Edelman. *The Politics of International Economic Relations.* 2d ed. New York: St. Martin's Press, 1981.

Stavrianos, L. S. *Global Rift: The Third World Comes of Age.* New York: William Morrow and Company, 1981.

Stockwell, Edward G., and Karen A. Laidlaw. *Third World Development: Problems and Prospects.* Chicago: Nelson-Hall, 1981.

Stork, Joe, and Ann M. Lesch. "Why War? Background to the Crisis." *Middle East Report* (November-December 1990): 11–18.

Streeten, Paul. *First Things First: Meeting Basic Human Needs in Developing Countries.* New York: Oxford University Press, 1981.

Turnbull, Colin M. *The Forest People: A Study of the Pygmies of the Congo.* New York: Simon and Schuster, 1962.

United Nations Development Program. *Human Development Report 1990.* New York: Oxford University Press, 1990.

Valenzuela, J. Samuel, and Arturo Valenzuela. "Modernization and Dependence: Alternative Perspectives in the Study of Latin American Underdevelopment." In J. J. Villamil, ed. *Transnational Capitalism and National Development.* Atlantic Highlands, N.J.: Humanities Press, 1979: 31–67.

Walker, Thomas W., ed. *Nicaragua: The First Five Years.* New York: Praeger Publishers, 1985.

Wallerstein, Immanuel. *The Modern World-System: Capitalist Agriculture and the Origins of the European World-Economy in the Sixteenth Century.* New York: Academic Press, 1974.

Waterlow, Charlotte. *Superpowers and Victims: The Outlook for World Community.* Englewood Cliffs, N.J.: Prentice-Hall, 1974.

Weaver, F. Stirton. "Positive Economics, Comparative Advantage, and Underdevelopment." *Science and Society* 35 (Summer 1971): 169–76.

Weaver, James, and Kenneth Jameson. *Economic Development: Competing Paradigms.* Washington, D.C.: University Press of America, 1981.

Wolf, Eric. R. *Peasant Wars of the Twentieth Century.* New York: Harper and Row, 1969.

Woods, Donald. *Biko.* 2d ed. New York: Henry Holt and Company, 1987.

World Bank. *World Development Report.* New York: Oxford University Press, annual.

World Commission on Environment and Development. *Our Common Future* (the Brundtland Report). New York: Oxford University Press, 1987.

"The World's Wars: Turn South for the Killing Fields." *The Economist* (March 12–18, 1988).

Worsley, Peter. *The Third World.* 2d ed. Chicago: University of Chicago Press, 1970.

Yergin, Daniel. *The Prize: The Epic Quest for Oil, Money and Power.* New York: Simon and Schuster, 1991.

Index

About the Author

JOHN ISBISTER was raised in Ottawa, Canada, and studied history as an undergraduate at Queen's University in Ontario. Experiences as a student participant in Operations Crossroads Africa in 1962, including work with Senegalese students and an hour-long private audience with President Léopold Sédar Senghor, led to a decision to pursue the study of economic development in low-income countries. He went on to receive a doctorate in economics from Princeton University in 1969, and joined the faculty of the University of California at Santa Cruz. Isbister was a founding fellow of UCSC's Merrill College, one of eight colleges at the school. Merrill College concentrates on the study of the Third World, and each year Isbister teaches a first-year core course on "Social Change in the Third World."

Kumarian Press is dedicated to bringing you quality publications on International Management and Development. Subject areas in which we publish include grassroots/community development, world hunger, women, NGOs, public administration, family planning, training, environment, and other development issues in Asia, Africa, Eastern Europe, and Latin America.

For more information or to receive a complimentary catalog, please call or write:

Kumarian Press, Inc.
630 Oakwood Avenue, Suite 119
West Hartford, CT 06110-1529
U.S.A.

Inquiries 203-953-0214 • Fax 203-953-8579
Toll-free, ordering 1-800-289-2664